The Photographers' Guide to
Great Lakes Lighthouses

Richard F. Edington

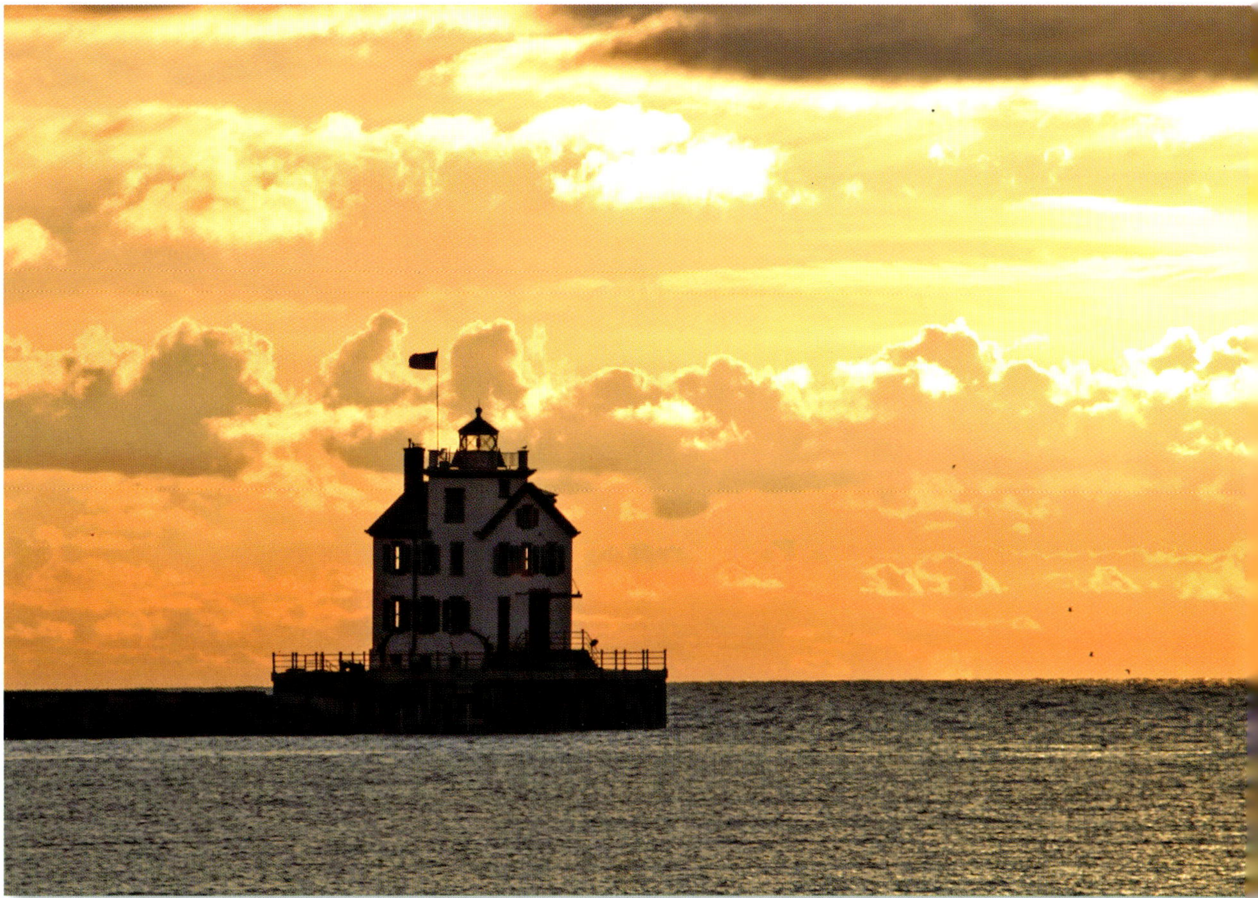

Lorain 5 *Sunset from end of pier*

DEDICATIONS

To my wife, Pat, who has waited patiently over the years "for the light to change" and supported my dream to publish this book. To my children, Jill and Mark, who have been my biggest photo fans and source of encouragement.

To the many individuals and organizations who have donated their time, work and dollars to save and preserve the historic lighthouses of the Great Lakes for all to enjoy, now and in the future.

ISBN: 978-0-615-22081-9

LCCN: 2008931781

Printed by BookMasters, Inc., Ashland, Ohio.

Front cover: Tawas Point Light—East Tawas, Michigan

Contents

Old Mackinac Point Light
Cheboygan Crib Light
Forty Mile Point Light
Presque Isle Light
Old Presque Isle
Grand Traverse
Old Mission Point
Sturgeon Point
Point Betsie
Tawas Point
Lake Michigan
Lake Huron
Big Sable
Pointe Aux
Barques Light
Little Sable
Port Sanilac
White River
Fort
Gratiot
Muskegon South Pier
Grand Haven South Pier
Holland Harbor
South Haven South Pier
Lake Erie
St. Joseph North Pier
Marblehead
Fairport West
Breakwater Light
Michigan City East Pier
Lorain West
Breakwater Light
Lighthouses of the Great Lakes

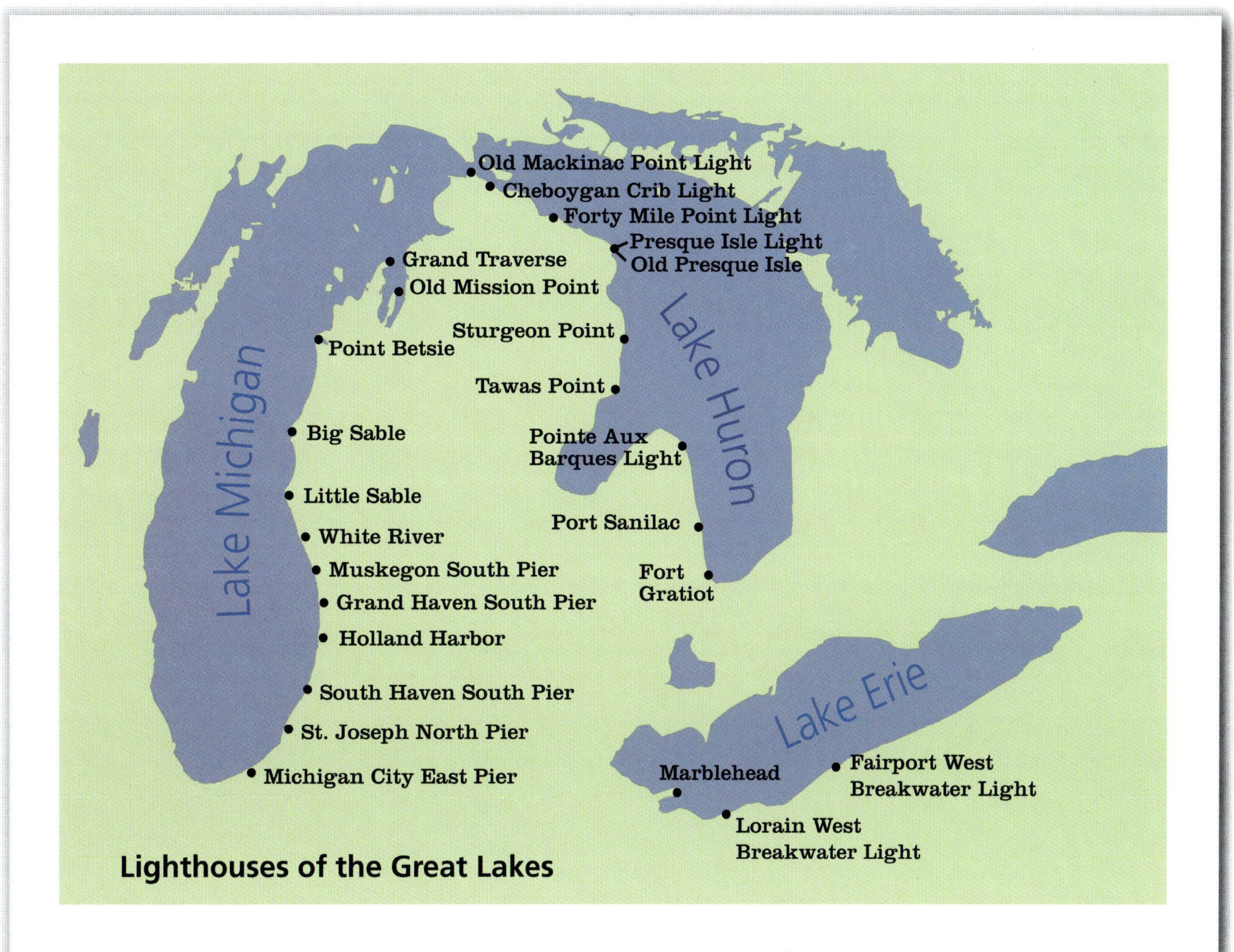

Introduction

Ever since they were built, lighthouses have intrigued those who visit them. Since cameras were invented, lighthouses have been a popular subject of photographers. Why? First of all, they are interesting from a historical standpoint, providing life saving warning signals to mariners long before modern day guidance systems. There is also the fascination with the life of the keepers and their families in these remote isolated locations. Lighthouses are generally in romantic settings: by water's edge with sandy beaches and rocky coastlines with crashing waves. And finally, they provide a strong focal point for the photographer's image. There can be no question as to the center of interest.

There are approximately 700 lighthouses still standing in the United States. Most people would be surprised to know that about 225 or one third are located on the Great Lakes. There are 90 more on the Canadian side. They come in various shapes, sizes and colors. They are located on beaches, piers, islands and bluffs. This book is devoted to twenty-five central U.S. Great Lakes lighthouses that have been chosen because of their special photogenic and scenic qualities. The other criteria for inclusion here is that they be readily accessible to photographers by land year around. They are located in Michigan, Indiana, and Ohio on Lakes Michigan, Huron and Erie. The order of the lighthouses in the book is as follows: We begin in Michigan City, Indiana at the bottom of Lake Michigan. From there, the route follows the west coast of Michigan to the Straits of Mackinaw and then down the east coast to Port Huron, Michigan. Finally, the lights of Lake Erie on Ohio's north coast are reviewed.

In addition to the sample images, the chapter for each light will include the following information to assist photographers in their pursuit of that "winning" image:

Distinguishing Features—What makes it special and picturesque?

Best Time of Day—Morning or afternoon, considering the position of the lighthouse and accessibility by land.

Suggested Compositions—Some ideas to get started. There are always more to discover.

Sunset/Sunrise—Can the lighthouse be included in the foreground of a sunset or sunrise shot from land?

Directions—Including access from parking areas and whether any vehicle entrance fees are charged. GPS coordinates are also noted.

Hopefully, the material contained herein will be instructional and easy to follow for beginning photographers and also useful to those with more advanced skills.

There are many fine publications that cover the history, keepers and detailed physical descriptions of these lighthouses and that information will not be repeated here. Regarding entrance fees, Michigan State Parks charge a vehicle fee and six of the Michigan lighthouses featured here are in state parks. Either a daily permit or an annual pass is required (prices slightly higher for out-of-state residents). The annual pass is currently about four times the daily permit. So, visits to several of the six lighthouses in the same year or spending more than one day at some of them make the annual pass the best buy.

Photographic Tips for Lighthouses

Without trying to cover the multitude of general photographic guidelines that apply to all landscape images, there are some principles that are specifically applicable to lighthouses.

VERTICAL OR HORIZONTAL FORMAT   Owing to the very shape of lighthouses, there is a tendency to think that a vertical (portrait) format is always appropriate. When close to tall lights, this is usually the case. However, many times a horizontal (landscape) format works well also. This is especially true of shorter lights. So, where possible, try both formats on every composition and decide later which is better.

FRAMING   Look for elements to "frame" the light, such as tree limbs, overhanging rocks, flag poles, etc. Such framing can be overhead, along the sides or both. Framing gives perspective to the image and adds a pleasing compositional element.

LEADING LINES   Always look for something that leads the viewer's eye to the subject. It can take the form of a shoreline, fence, path, railing, catwalk or row of rocks.

FOREGROUND INTEREST   Lighthouse settings include many objects that can be included in the foreground, such as rocks, sea gulls, tall grasses, driftwood, boats or keeper's houses. Such items add scale and interest to what otherwise would be a "record" shot.

WATER   Whenever possible, position your camera to include some part of the water near the light. This can add considerably to the feeling of "place." If the water is relatively still, try to capture a reflection. If you are lucky enough to be there when waves are crashing, it will create a dramatic effect. Again, a shoreline (especially with waves) can be a very effective leading line or provide foreground interest.

Shutter speed can significantly affect the look of waves. A faster speed of 1/500 or 1/250 second will "freeze" the water's action. A longer speed such as 1/8 or 1/4 second will create a blurred appearance. This is a personal choice, but a good compromise is about 1/50 second that will give some motion to the water. Also, a shutter speed of about 1/250 second should freeze the movement of flying sea gulls so they are not blurred.

STRAIGHT VERTICAL AND HORIZONTAL LINES   Shooting tall subjects like lighthouses can often result in a condition known as "keystoning"—the lighthouse in the image is leaning from vertical. This is more pronounced when up close and/or using a wide-angle lens. One way to correct it is to move further away and use a longer lens. But sometimes this is not possible or the desired composition can't be achieved further back. There are special "shift" lens that can make the correction in the camera, but they are generally very expensive. In today's digital world, the most practical way to correct it after the image is captured is by digital editing. This is fairly easy using any one of the software systems available.

Horizontal lines need to be kept straight also, especially horizons. The simple principle here is to hold the camera level. This is one of the reasons to use a tripod. To be sure of being perfectly straight, attach a bubble level to the hot shoe of the camera. If the image is not level after capture, it also can be corrected through digital editing.

SUNSETS AND SUNRISES   Lighthouses make ideal subjects for sunset and sunrise photos. Check the local paper, television, or Internet for the time of a sunset or sunrise. Plan to arrive about 30 minutes early and stay 30 minutes after. With scattered clouds to diffuse the light, dramatic results can occur. If you have to squint while looking at the sun, it is too early (sunset) or too late (sunrise) to begin shooting. Meter the sky well away from the sun, and then bracket your exposures. If it is a working light, time the shutter release to capture the flashing light.

WINTER SEASON   For several reasons, winter can be the best season for lighthouse photography.

> Light – The sun is relatively low in the southern sky all day, resulting in softer light and longer shadows from dawn to dusk. This contrasts with the rest of the year when the best light is available only in early morning and late afternoon hours.

> No Crowds – Other people are rarely present, resulting in unobstructed views. Only avid photographers are crazy enough to brave the conditions – but it's worth it!

> Snow and Ice – The snow cover can create a beautiful scene totally different from the warm weather months. In many cases, there are dramatic ice formations on the lighthouse itself, rocks, catwalks, etc. This is especially true for the lights on piers, which stretch out into the lake. CAUTION: There are several lighthouses on the east side of Lake Michigan situated on long piers. Do not venture out on these piers when they are slippery or if it is extremely windy. This is especially true in winter with snow and ice underfoot. In these cases, shoot from the shore using longer lenses. Several people have lost their lives from accidents at these lighthouses.

> No Leaves on Trees – Without leaves, compositions not otherwise possible exist. Openings will create different and interesting vantage points.

COLOR VS. BLACK AND WHITE   Don't forget that lighthouse scenes can also make excellent black and white (monochrome) images. This is particularly true of white lighthouses shot against dark or polarized skies. Also the snow in winter opens up more black and white possibilities. Original color images can be converted to monochrome images using digital editing.

TRIPODS AND POLARIZING FILTERS   Although applicable to all landscape photography, tripods and polarizing filters are worth emphasizing when it comes to lighthouses.

 Mounting the camera on a sturdy tripod has several advantages versus hand held. The obvious one is keeping the camera steady when releasing the shutter. In most cases, it is desirable to achieve sharpness throughout the image, from near to far. This often requires a small aperture to achieve the necessary depth of field. In order to get the right exposure, selecting a small aperture (e.g. F16 or F22), results in a slower shutter speed that may or may not be successfully hand held (especially when using a polarizing filter).

The tripod is also a big aid in composition. It allows one to make small adjustments to the frame while looking all around the edges and holding it firmly in the right spot. A tripod makes it much easier to capture the lighthouse in the same position as things change, such as people, light, clouds, etc. It is also important when bracketing for different exposures of the same shot. As mentioned earlier, a tripod is a must in getting the horizontal and vertical lines exactly straight. All the photos in this book were taken with the camera on a tripod.

A polarizing filter can play an important role in photographing lighthouses because the sky is usually included. As the outer ring is rotated while looking through the viewfinder, a dramatic change in contrast and a darkening of the sky takes place. All the colors are richer, especially reds. The polarizer can also eliminate glare in water. It works best when shooting at about 90 degrees to the sun. When rotating the glass, be careful not to overdo this polarizing effect, as it is possible to make the sky almost black. Using a polarizing filter can result in a loss of one to two stops of light. For example, if the shutter speed is 1/100 second without it, it could be 1/50 or 1/25 second with it, thereby increasing the need for a tripod. Nearly all the photos in this book that have sunny skies were taken with a polarizing filter.

Enjoy these beautiful historic landmarks. May you get excited about photographing them. "Happy Shooting!"

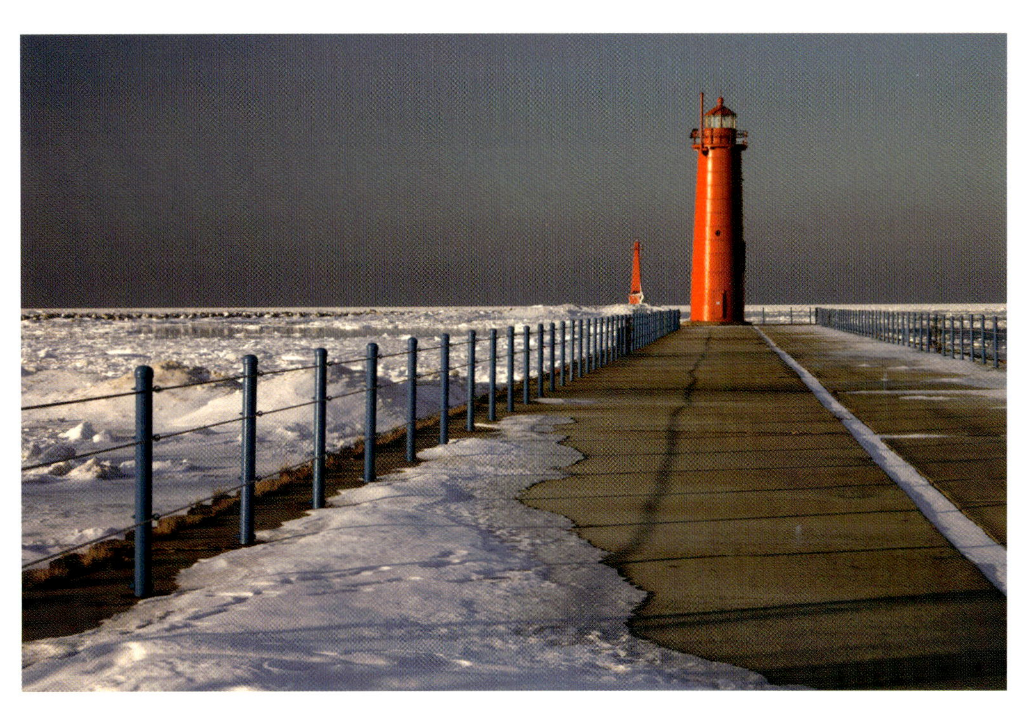

Muskegon 1 *Blue posts as leading line*

Michigan City East Pier Light

Michigan City, Indiana

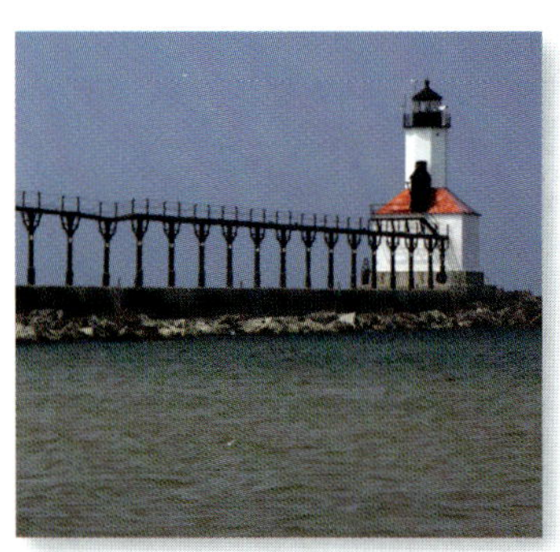

"Crooked Catwalk"

DISTINGUISHING FEATURES

One of several pier lights on Lake Michigan, Michigan City is unique because of a sharp bend in the pier and catwalk. This creates the potential for different perspectives versus those piers that extend straight out into the lake. The lighthouse itself has an interesting shape with a red roof.

BEST TIME OF DAY

Good lighting conditions are possible both morning and afternoon.

SUGGESTED COMPOSITIONS

From the beach east of the pier, compose images that include the shoreline and, if present, sea gulls **(1)**. Up closer to the pier, use one of the openings in the catwalk for framing while making the pier and catwalk a curved leading line **(2)**. Where the catwalk begins, try images from both sides and continue to move closer including some very close to the lighthouse **(3) & (4)**. Remember the warnings about slippery piers or high winds. This is a busy marina; watch for boats to add to your compositions **(5)**.

SUNSET/SUNRISE

There is very good sunset potential from the beach or from the pier where it turns west, especially in the summer months when the sun sets in the northern sky.

OTHER

Back some distance from the beach area is the original Michigan City Light (1858) that resembles a city dwelling with a short tower on top. It is now a lighthouse museum **(6)**.

DIRECTIONS

From I 80/I 90 or I 94, go north on Rt. 421 that becomes Franklin St. Continue through town to 4th St. and turn right. Go one block to Pine St. and turn left. Cross Rt. 12, follow the curve to the left, and turn right on Franklin St. across the bridge into Washington Park. Turn right to parking area for beach and pier light (parking fee) or left to the old lighthouse museum.

GPS coordinates: 41.729N, 86.911W.

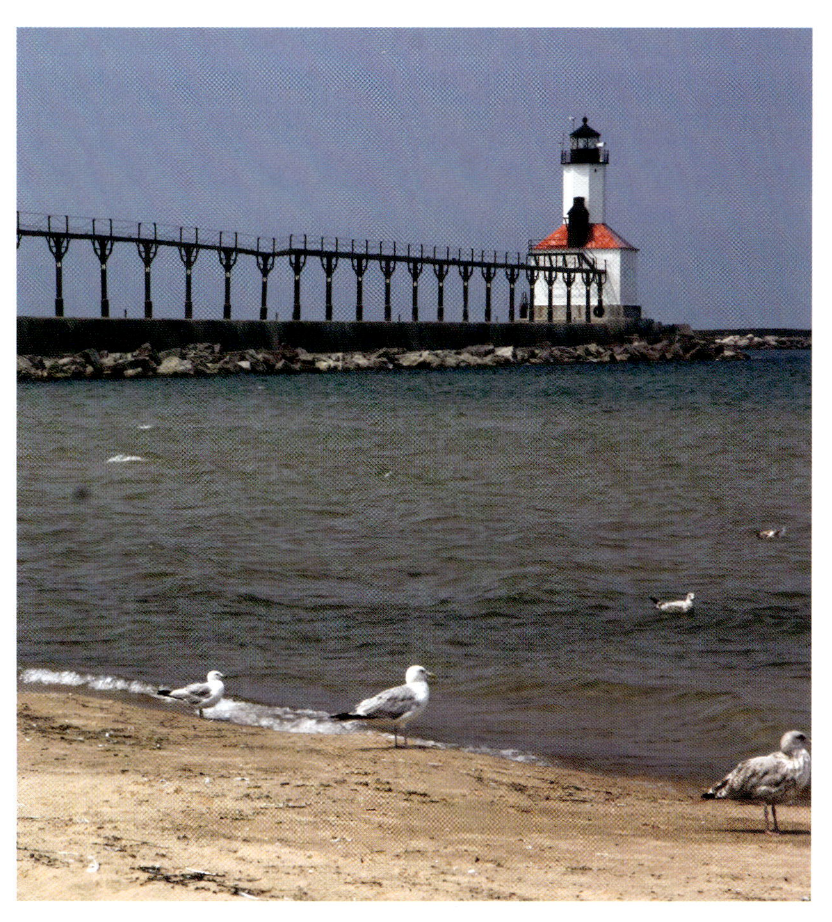

Michigan City 1 (left)

*View from
the beach, east
of the pier*

Michigan City 2 (below)

*The crooked
catwalk*

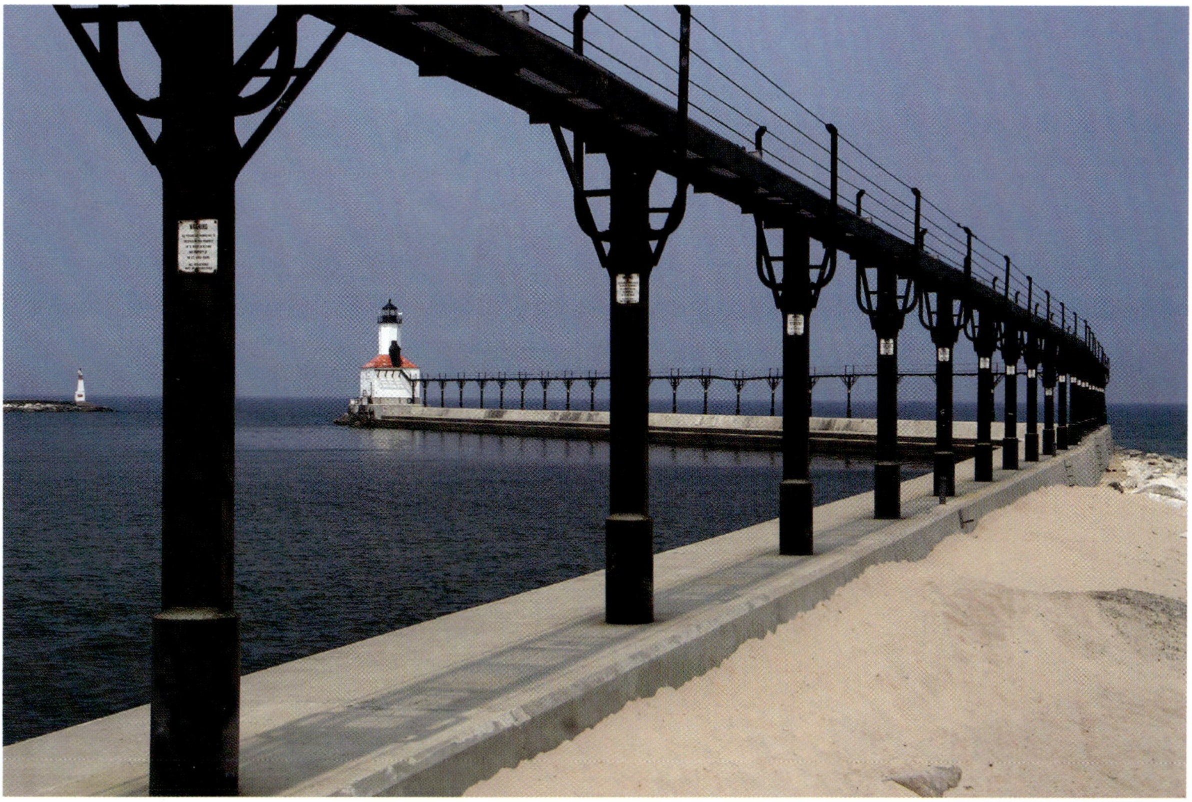

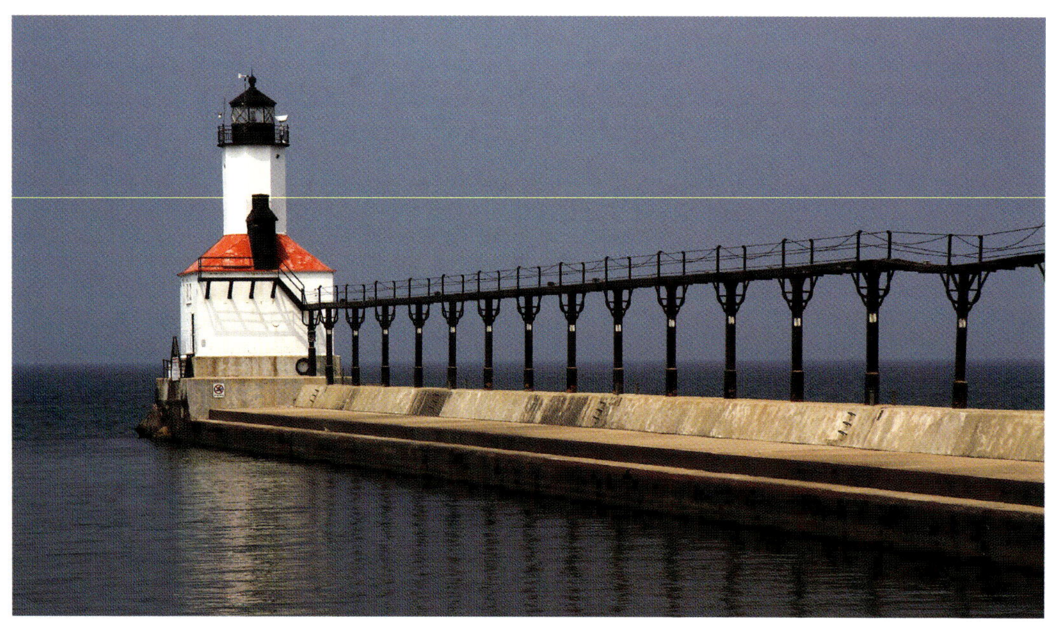

Michigan City 4 *View along the catwalk*

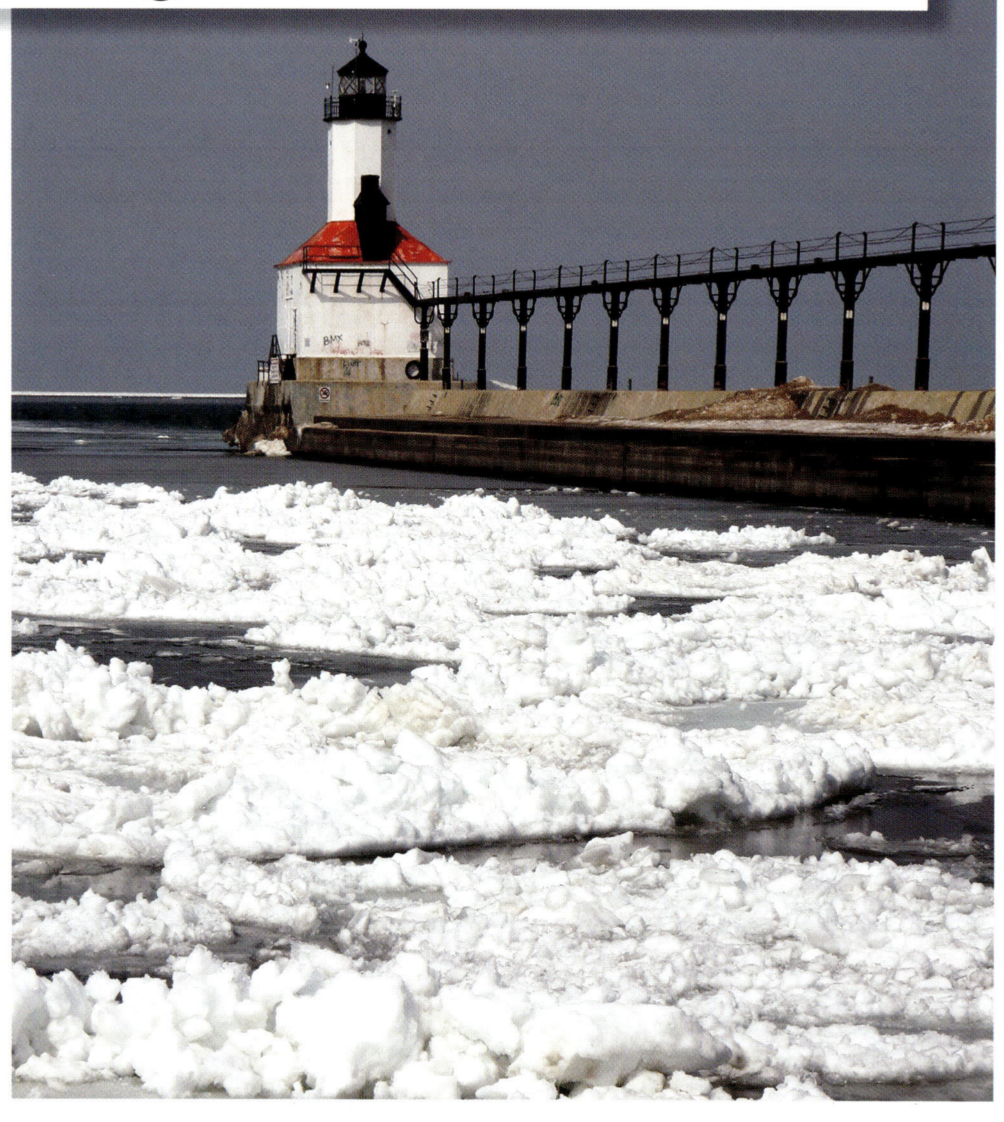

Michigan City 3 *View along the catwalk*

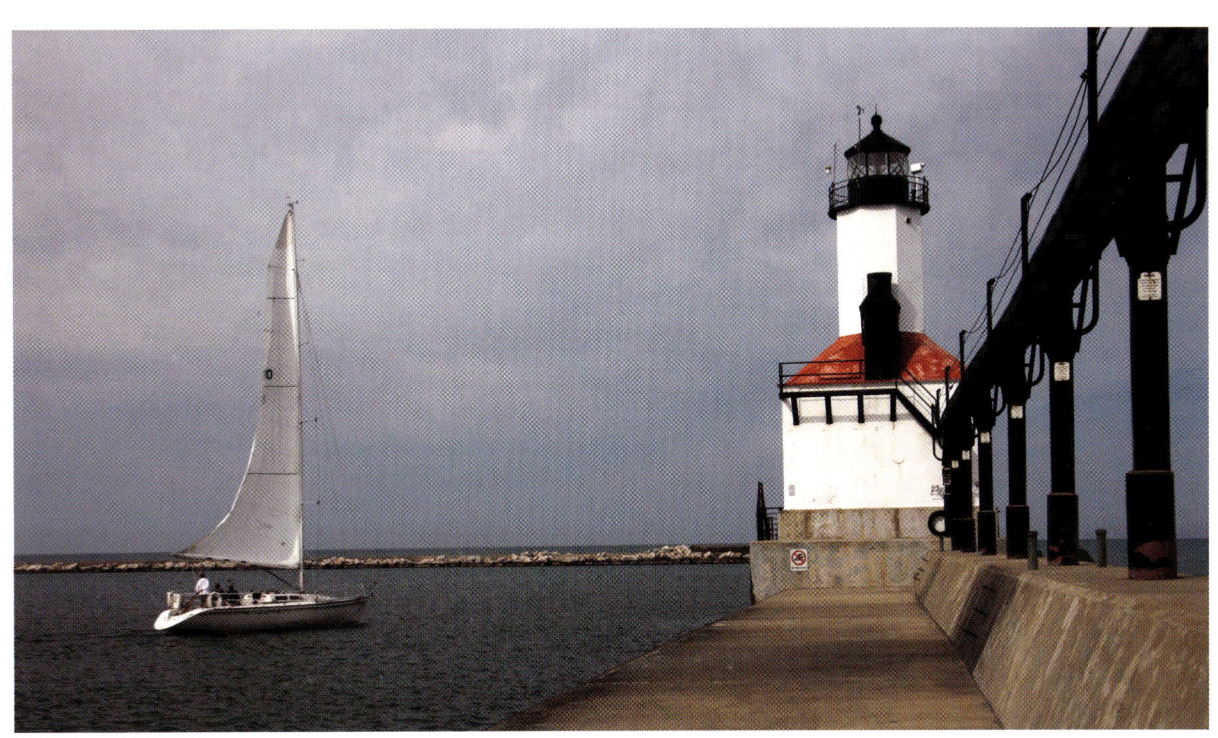

Michigan City 5 *This is a busy marina*

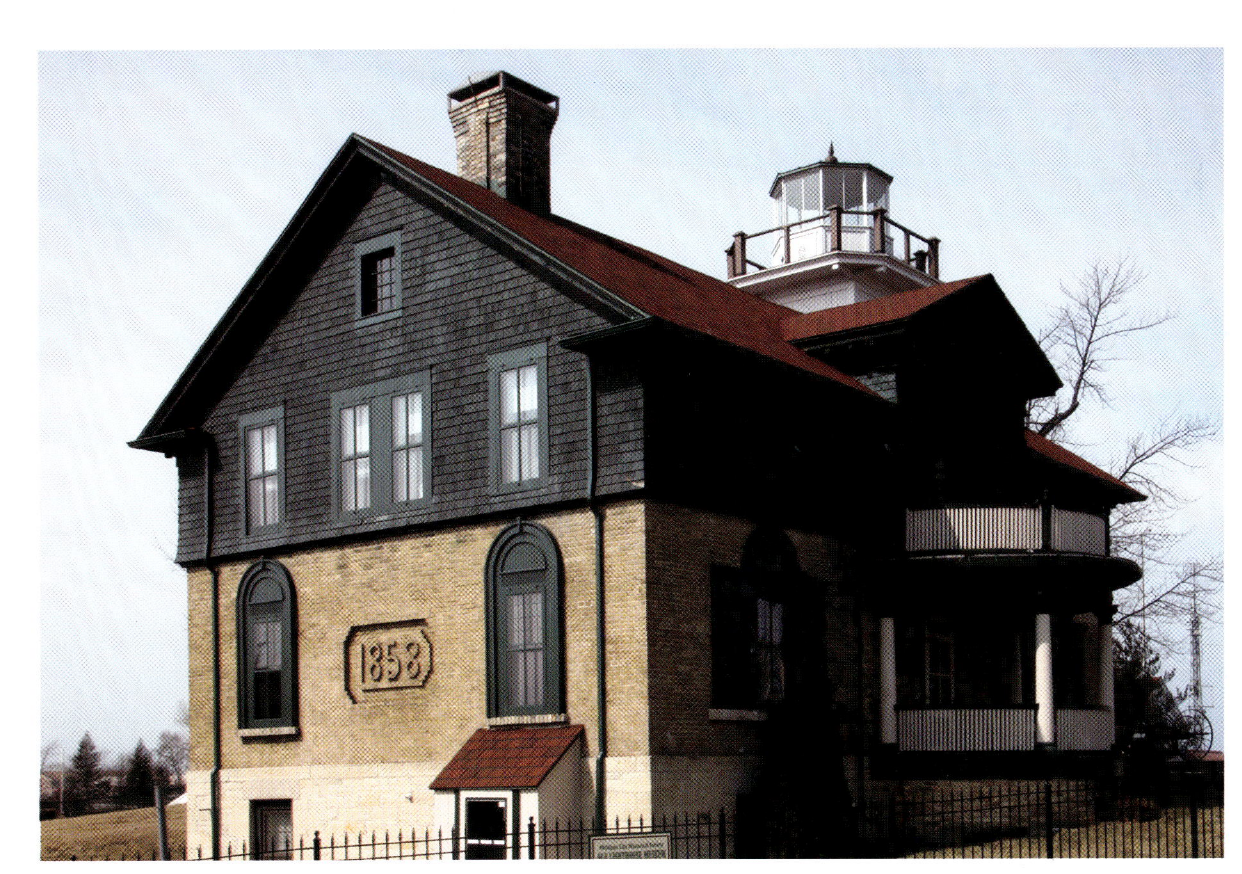

Michigan City 6 *The lighthouse museum*

St. Joseph North Pier Lights

St. Joseph, Michigan

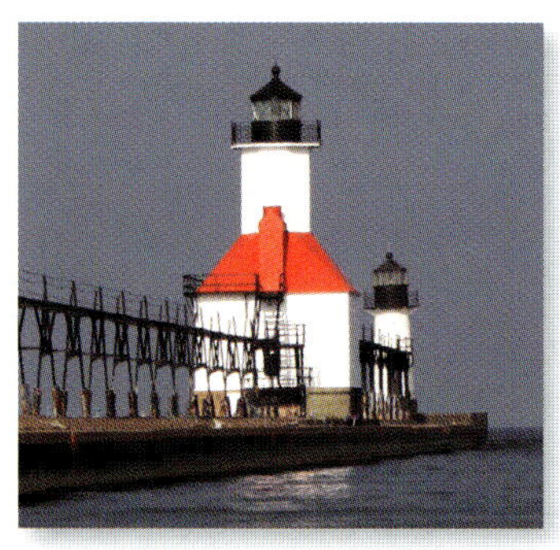

"Picture Perfect Pair"

DISTINGUISHING FEATURES

St. Joseph Light Station is distinguished by the presence of two photogenic lighthouses on a single pier. The outer light is a short white tower topped in black while the inner light is larger and taller with a red hip roof. An elevated catwalk extends the length of the pier.

BEST TIME OF DAY

Good light is possible morning and mid afternoon, with early morning being the best time.

SUGGESTED COMPOSITIONS

There are blue railings on each side of the pier for about half its length. Use them and the catwalk for strong leading lines to the inner light **(1)**. Continue walking out on the pier past the railings for closer shots of the inner light **(2)** & **(3)**. Walk around it for views of the outer light. For all of the foregoing, try horizontal and vertical formats and different lenses at various distances from the lights. For safety sake, remember to stay off the pier when slippery or when very windy.

From the beach, north of the pier, catch incoming waves in the foreground **(4)**. Begin close to the pier and gradually move further away for different perspectives. Look for sea gulls at water's edge to provide interest and scale **(5)**. From the sand dunes to the northeast, there are small trees and beach grasses to include in compositions while looking down on the lights **(6)**.

SUNSET/SUNRISE

Excellent sunset images are possible from the beach year around **(7)**.

DIRECTIONS

From the north: From US 31(I 196), exit at M 63 and follow it south for 9.5 miles to Momany Dr, turn right through an Industrial Park to stop sign at Upton. Turn left to next intersection and continue straight on Marina Dr. (brick street). Follow it to the entrance to Tiscornia Park on the right and the parking area near the beach and pier.

From the south: From I 94 (south of St. Joseph and Benton Harbor), exit at M 63 and take it north through town. Cross the bridge over the St. Joseph River, turn left on Momany Dr and follow the directions above.

GPS coordinates: 42.116N, 86.494W.

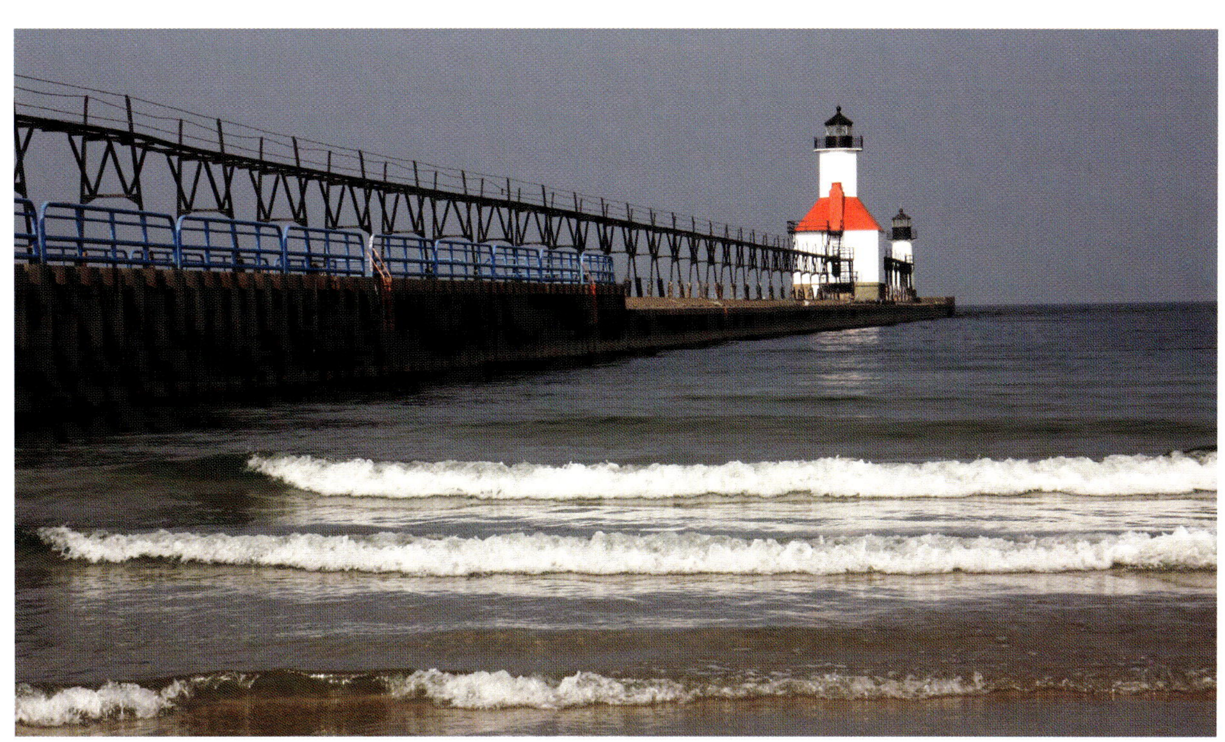

St. Joseph 4   *From the beach, north of pier*

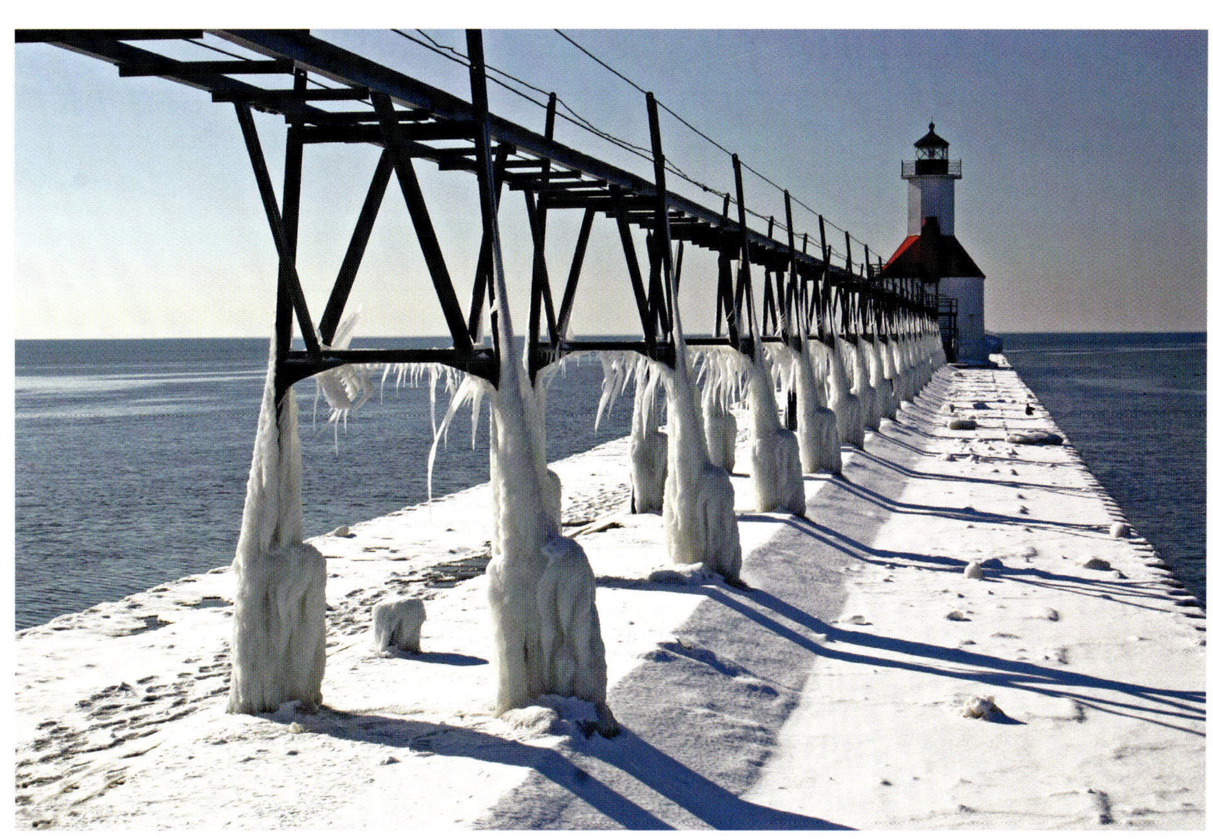

St. Joseph 2   *Catwalk as leading line*

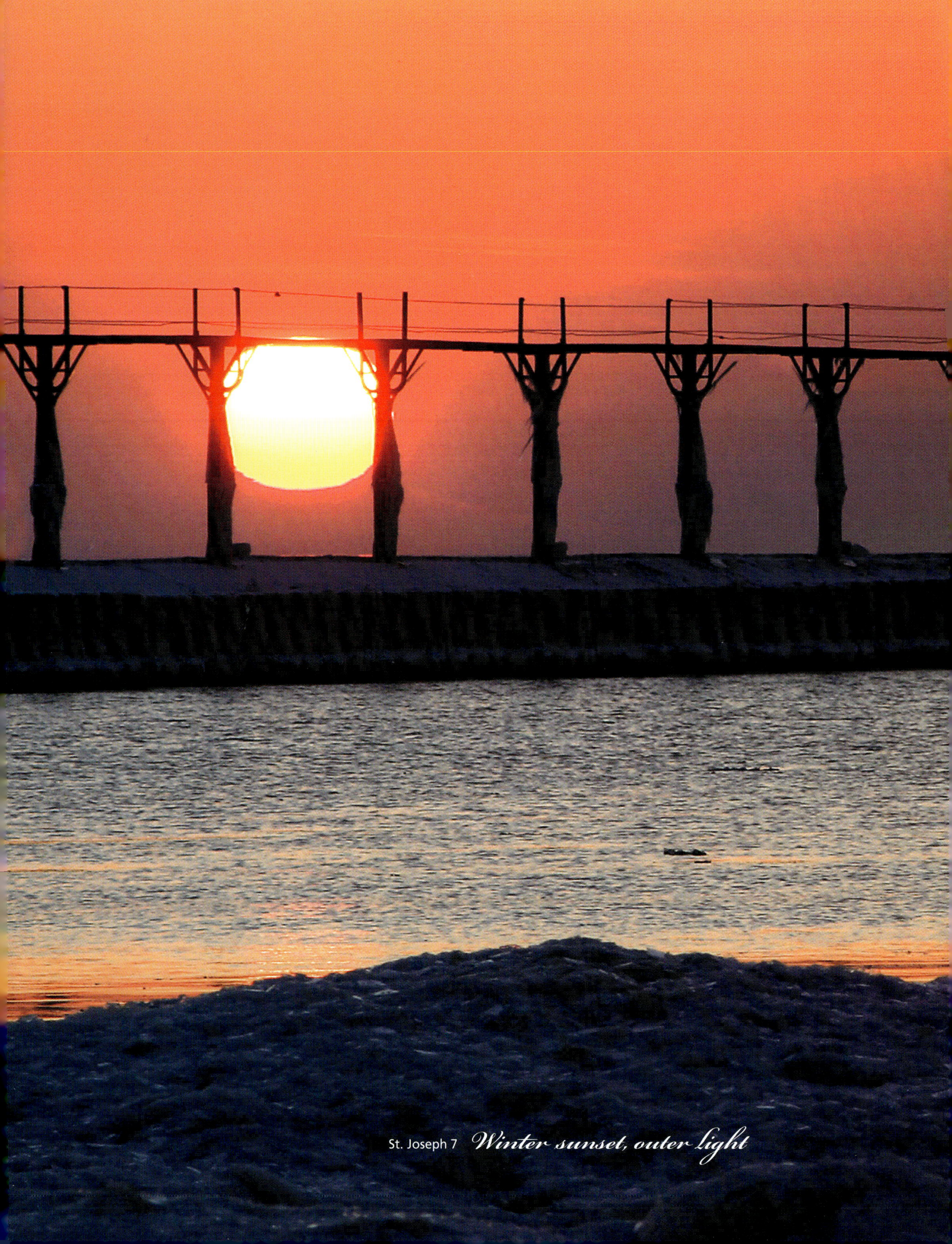

St. Joseph 7 *Winter sunset, outer light*

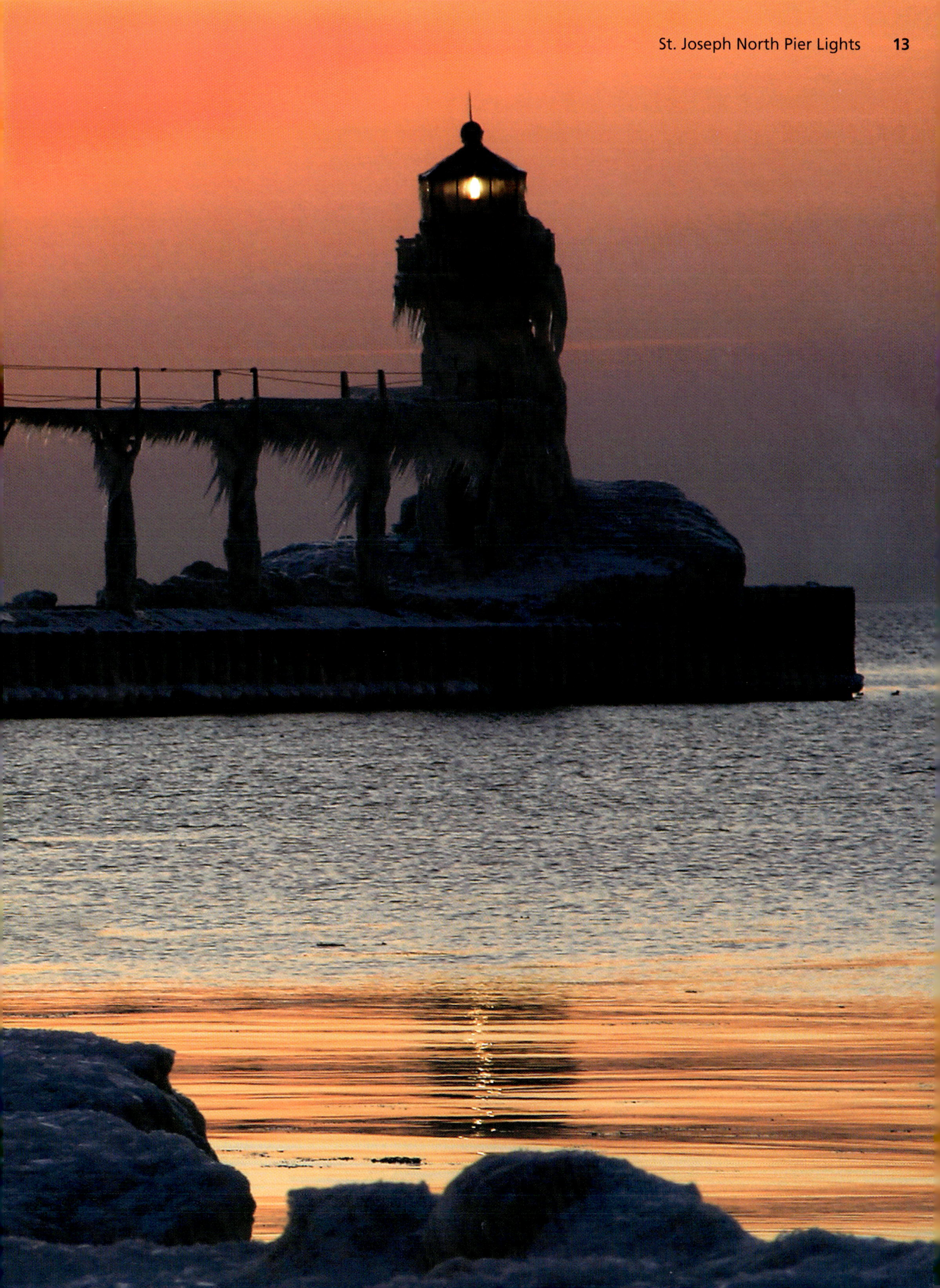

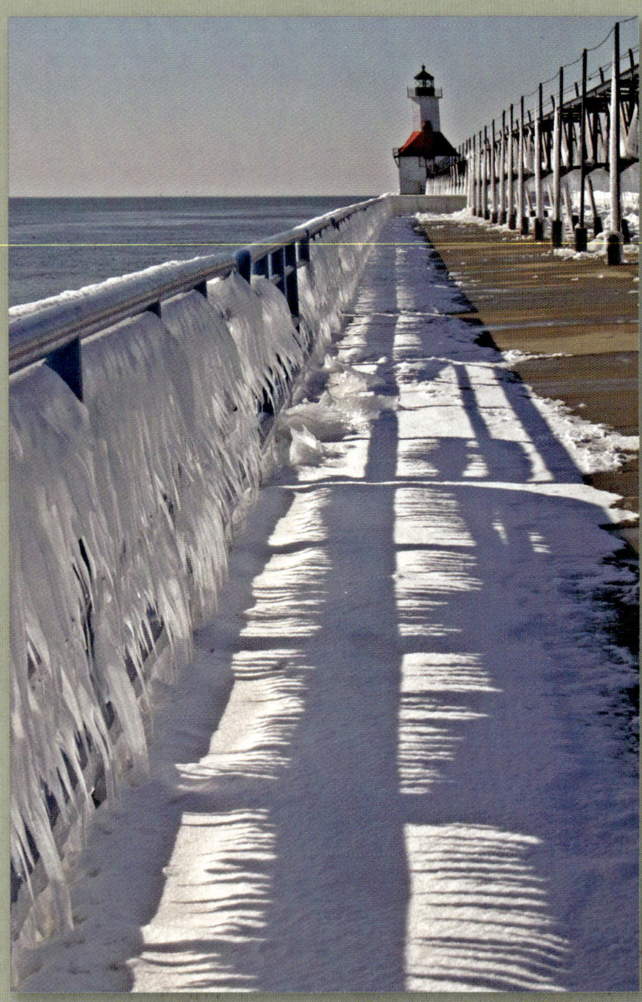

St. Joseph 1 *Railing as leading line*

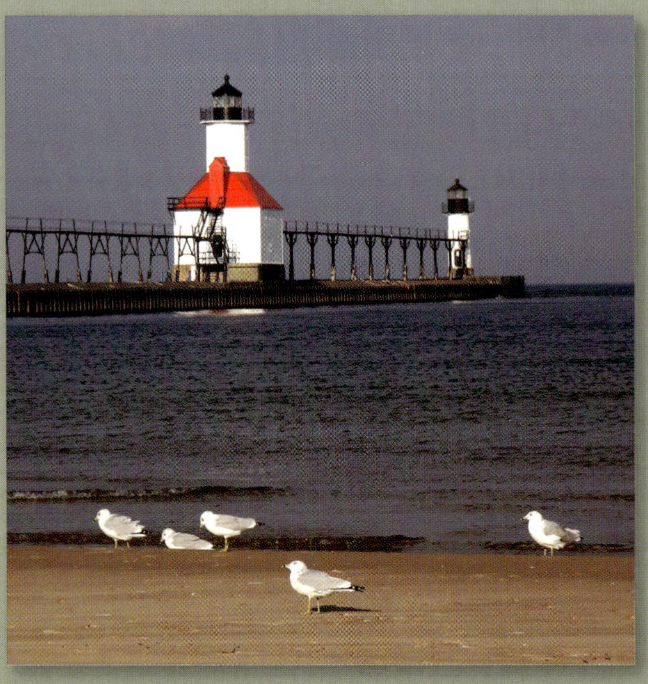

St. Joseph 5 *From the beach, with gulls*

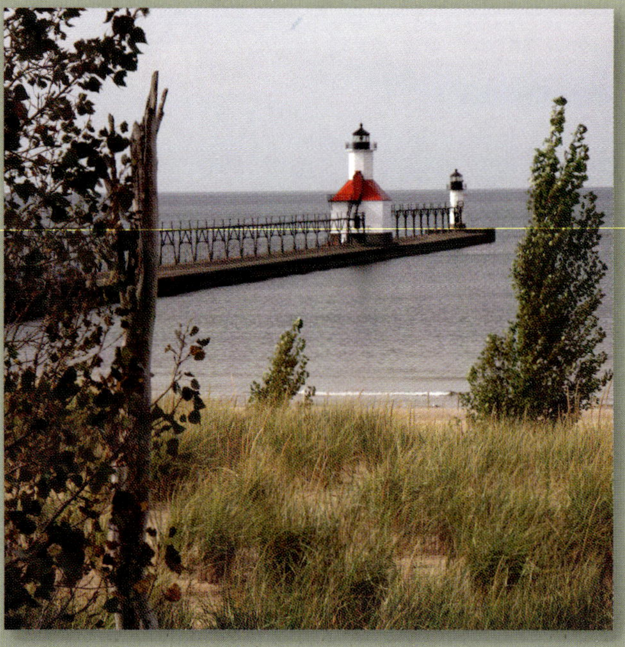

St. Joseph 6 *From top of dunes*

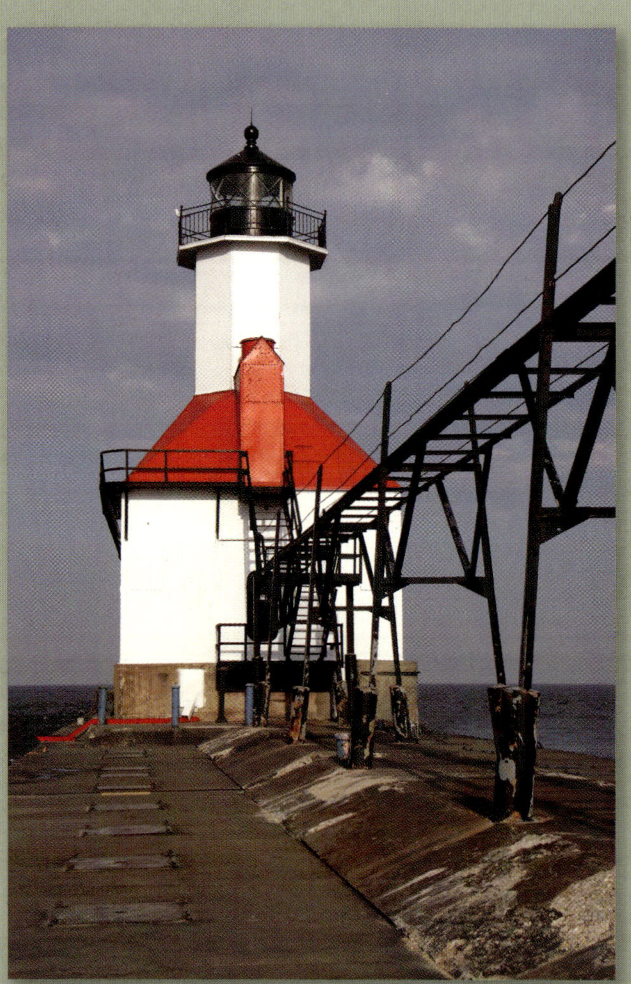

St. Joseph 3 *Close to inner light*

South Haven South Pier Light

South Haven, Michigan

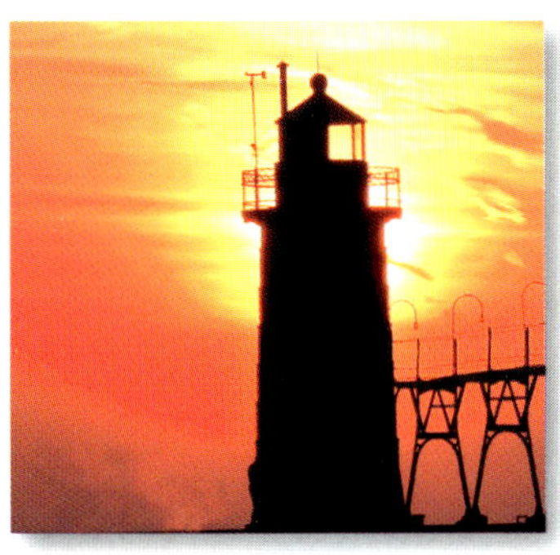

"Colorful Pier Light"

DISTINGUISHING FEATURES
This cherry red lighthouse sits at the end of a pier complete with a black metal catwalk. Like some of the other pier lights, it can be very dramatic in winter with snow and ice formations coating the catwalk and tower **(2) & (3)**.

BEST TIME OF DAY
Favorable light is available morning and afternoon, with early morning being the best time of day.

SUGGESTED COMPOSITIONS
From the beach south of the pier, the catwalk leads to the lighthouse from right to left. If nice white- capped waves are rolling in, place the lighthouse in the upper left of your frame and minimize the sky **(1)**. If the water is rather calm, but the sky is interesting, change the composition so the lighthouse is in the lower third, emphasizing the sky and minimizing the water. Then start walking the pier (when it's safe), using the catwalk as a leading pattern, at different distances with various focal length lenses (horizontal and vertical formats) **(4)**. Go all the way out near the end and include some close ups of the bright red lighthouse **(5)**.

SUNSET/SUNRISE
Excellent sunset shots can be taken from the beach all year **(6)**. Also, there are white lights across the top of the catwalk that are turned on after sunset, providing an illuminated leading line to the lighthouse.

DIRECTIONS
From I 196 (US 31), go west on BR 196 (exit 20) thru the downtown business district to parking near the beach and pier. BR 196 is also Phoenix St., which changes to Water St. near the lake.
GPS coordinates: 42.401N, 86.288W.

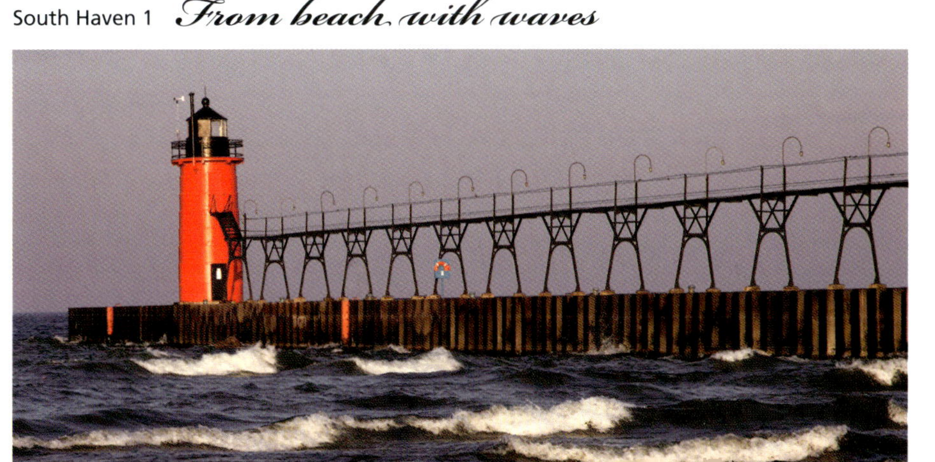

South Haven 1 *From beach, with waves*

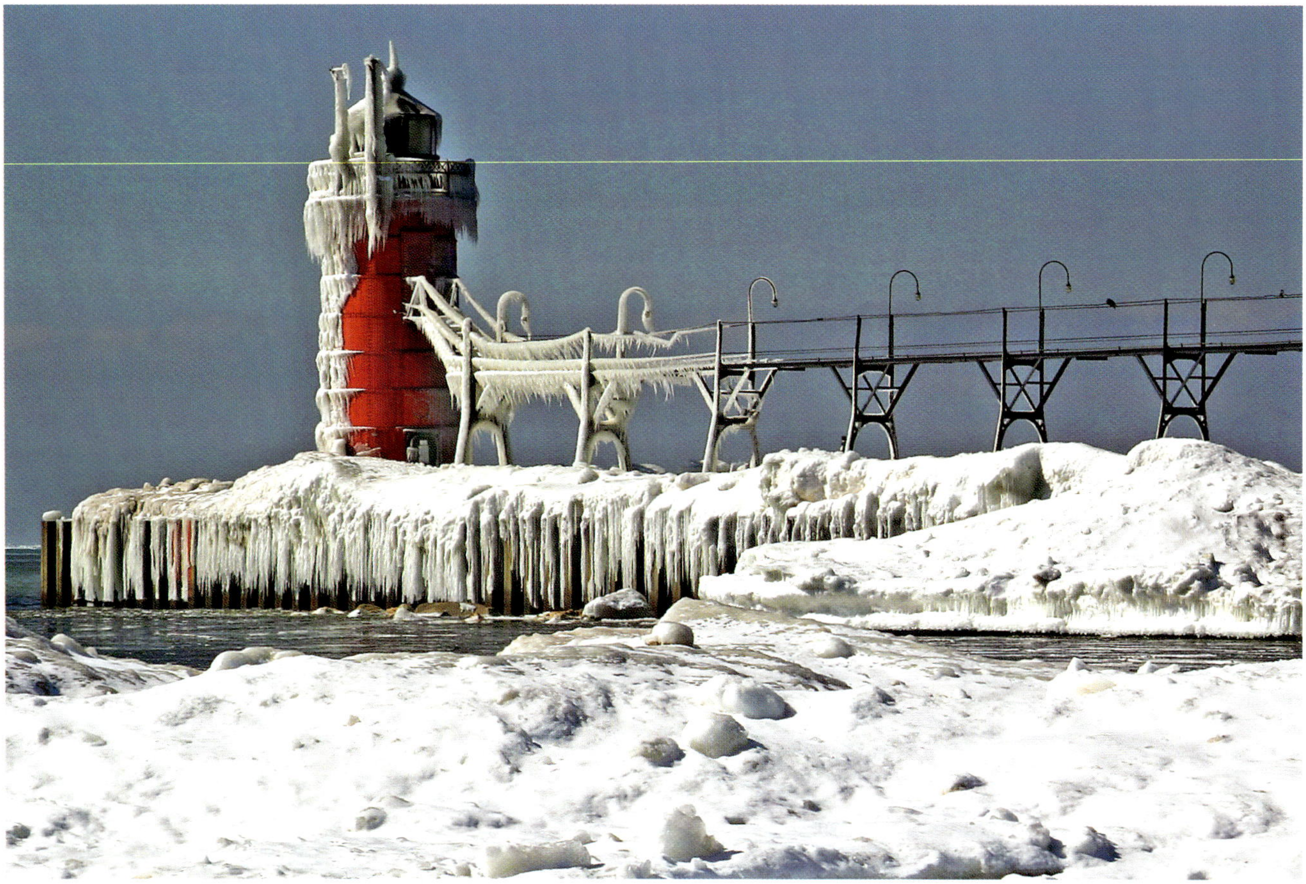

South Haven 2 *From beach, snow and ice formations*

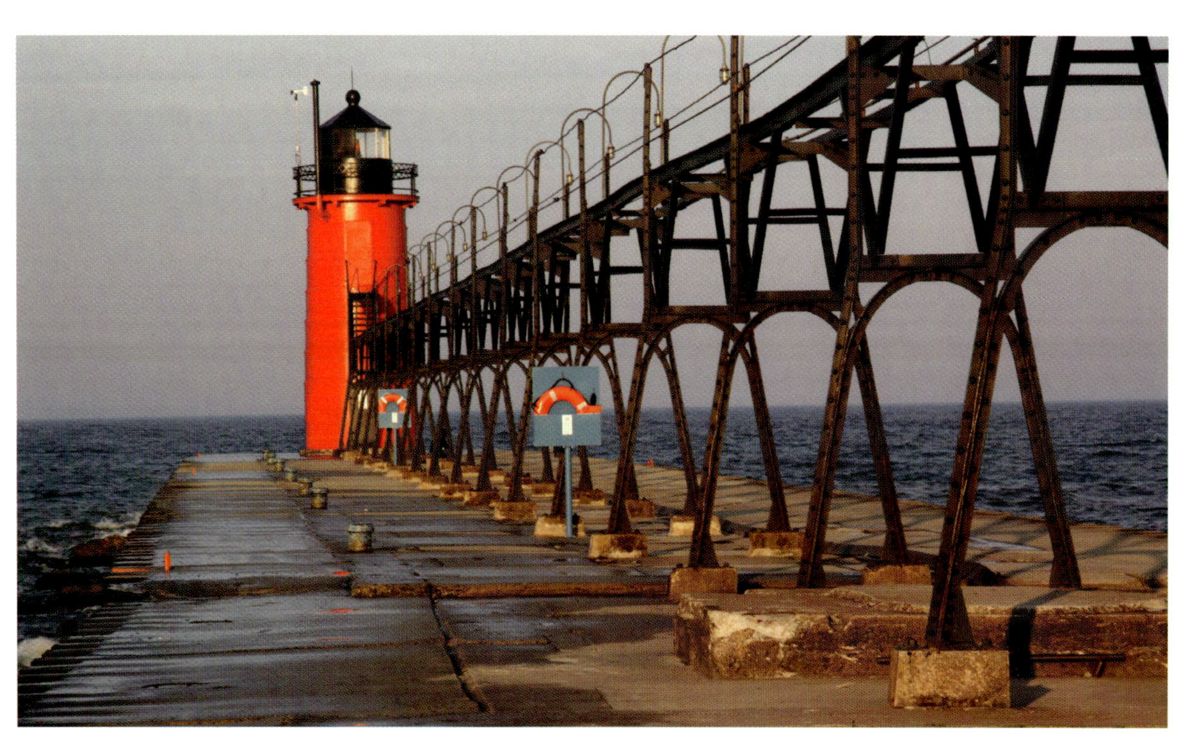

South Haven 4 *Catwalk as leading line*

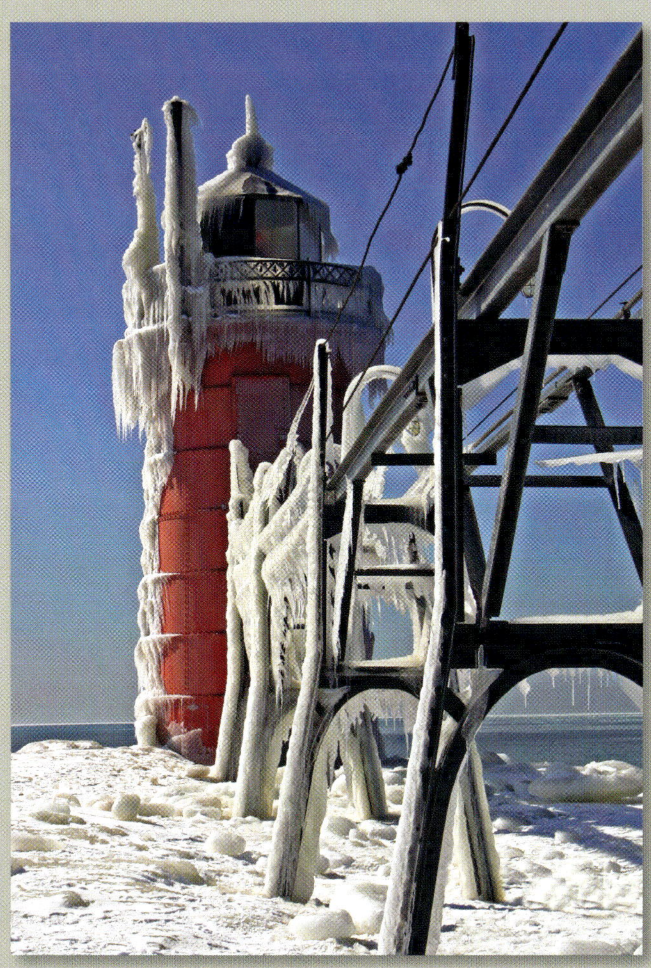

South Haven 3 *Ice formations, close up*

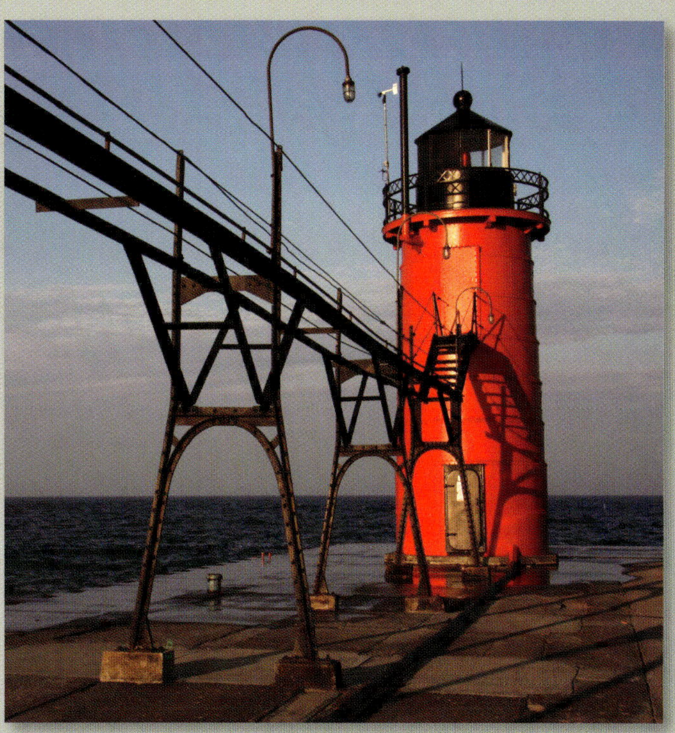

South Haven 5 *End of catwalk, close up*

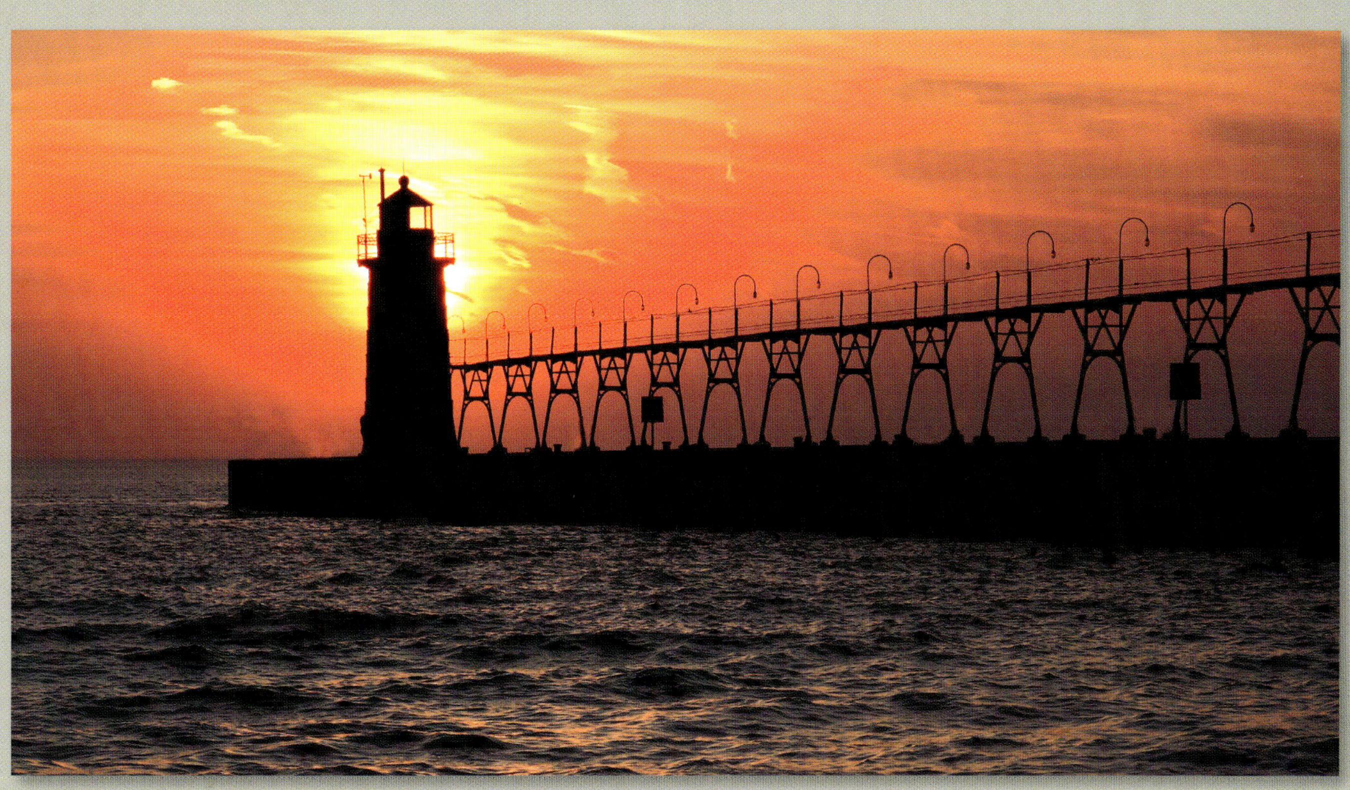

South Haven 6 *Sunset from beach.*

Holland Harbor Light

Holland, Michigan

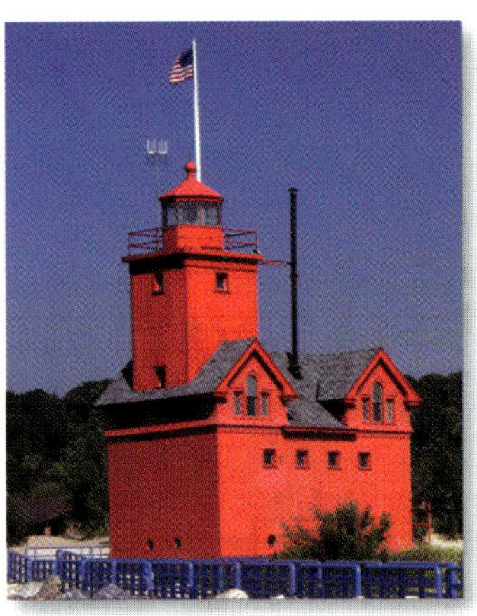

"Big Red"

DISTINGUISHING FEATURES

Big Red, as it's known locally, is truly a picturesque lighthouse. It boasts vivid red color and unique architecture with a twin peaked roof. It can be viewed from the beach, a walkway with blue railings or across the canal.

BEST TIME OF DAY

South of canal where the lighthouse is located—Good light is available morning and afternoon.

North of canal in Holland State Park—The majority of the year the north side of the lighthouse is shaded with only the east side (morning) or west side (afternoon) exposed to the sun. Early morning is usually the best time, looking southwest.

SUGGESTED COMPOSITIONS

South side of canal—There is a walkway running south of the light with blue railings on each side. Use these for strong leading lines or foreground color and interest **(1)**. Also walk down by the beach and include beach grasses or shoreline in compositions from there **(2) & (3)**. Take some close up shots of this unusual and beautiful structure: examples include the lantern room with flag and peaked roof sections **(4)**.

North side of canal—View the lighthouse across the canal using small trees for framing with sand and grasses in the foreground **(5) & (6)**.

SUNSET/SUNRISE

Colorful sunset images are possible from either side of the canal.

DIRECTIONS

From US 31 on the north side of town where there is a sign "To Holland State Park", go west on Lakewood a short distance and then take the curve to the left onto Douglas Ave. (which later changes to Ottawa Beach Rd.) to arrive at Holland State Park, a total of about 6.5 miles. This is a Michigan State Park with entrance fee.

To reach the south side of the canal, return from the State Park on Ottawa Beach Rd./Douglas Ave. to River Ave. Turn right and cross the bridge. Stay to the right onto Pine St. Turn right on 16th St., which later becomes S. Shore Dr., for about 5 miles to the end of the road at a gate to private residences. Only members are allowed to drive into this area. However, you are permitted to walk in. Follow signs on the path to "Big Red" lighthouse (about a 15 minute walk).

GPS coordinates: 42.772N, 86.212W.

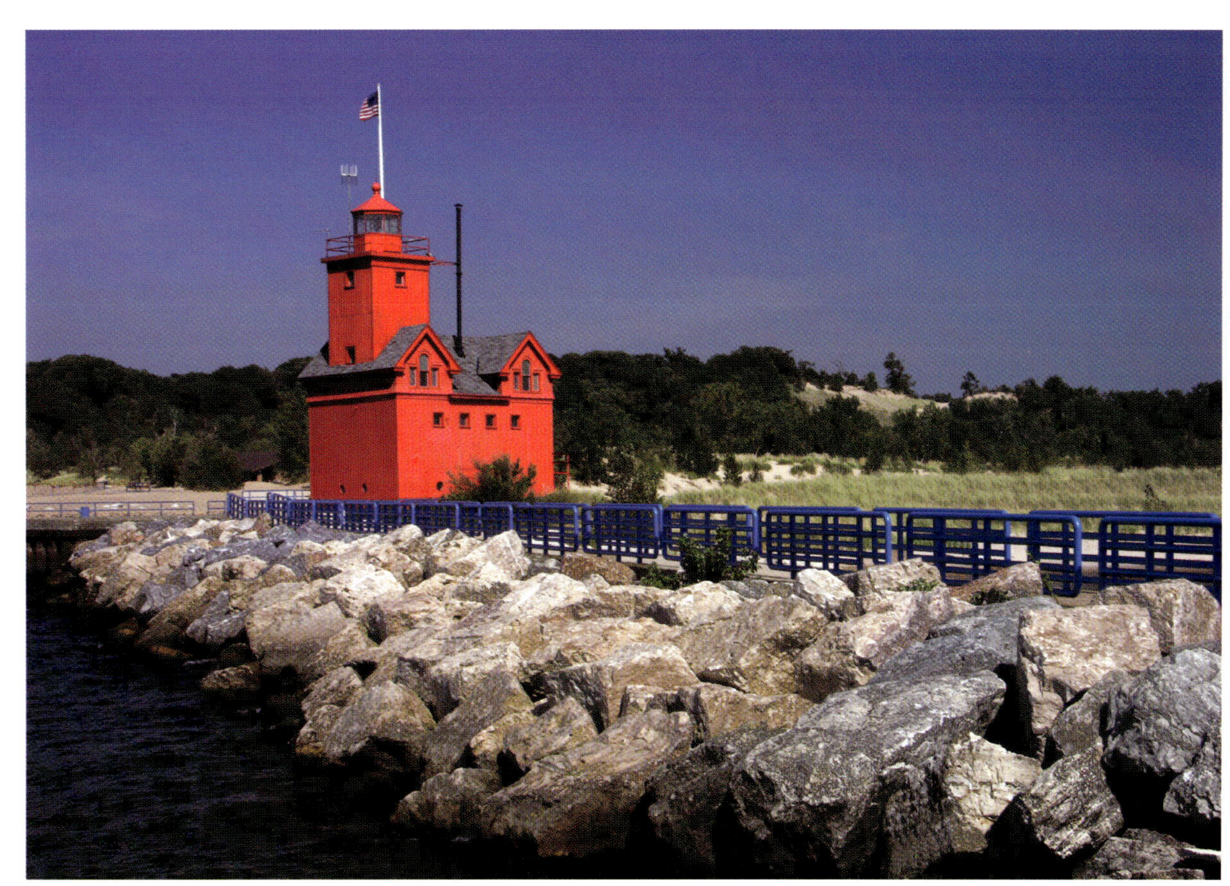

Holland 1   *Blue railing as leading line*

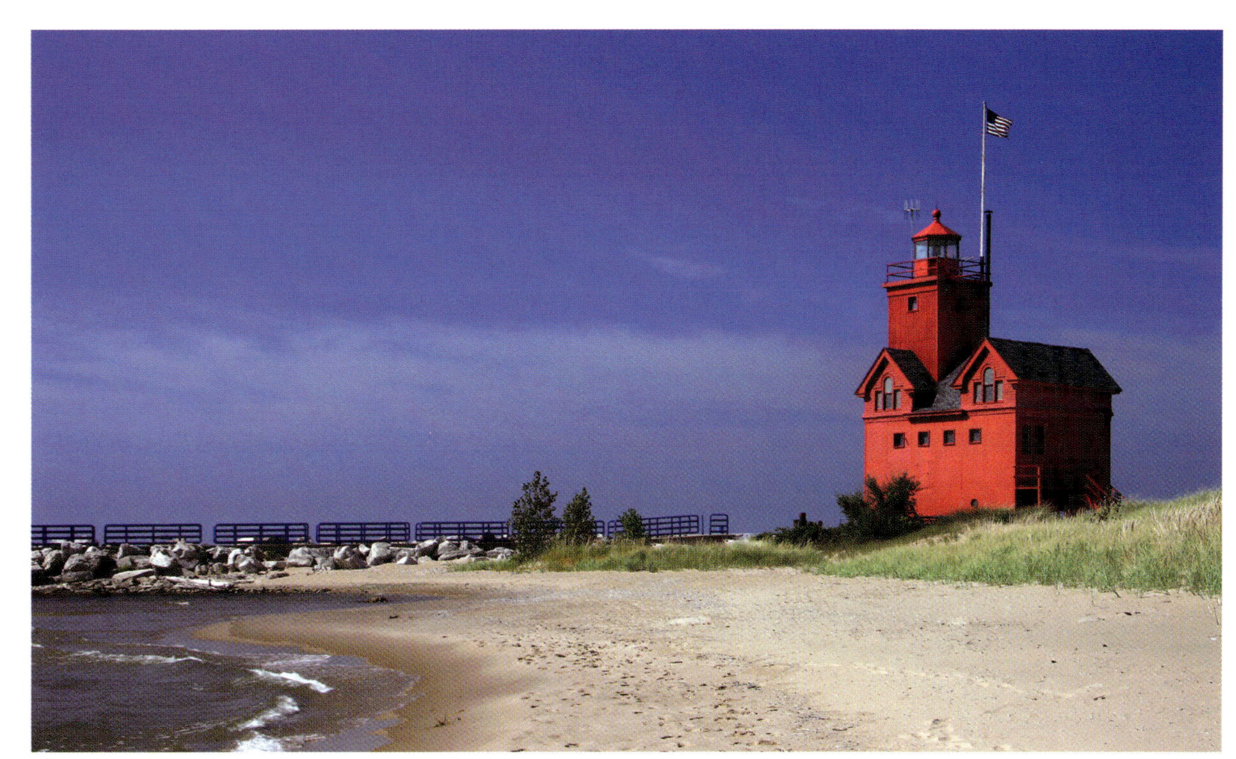

Holland 3   *From beach with shoreline*

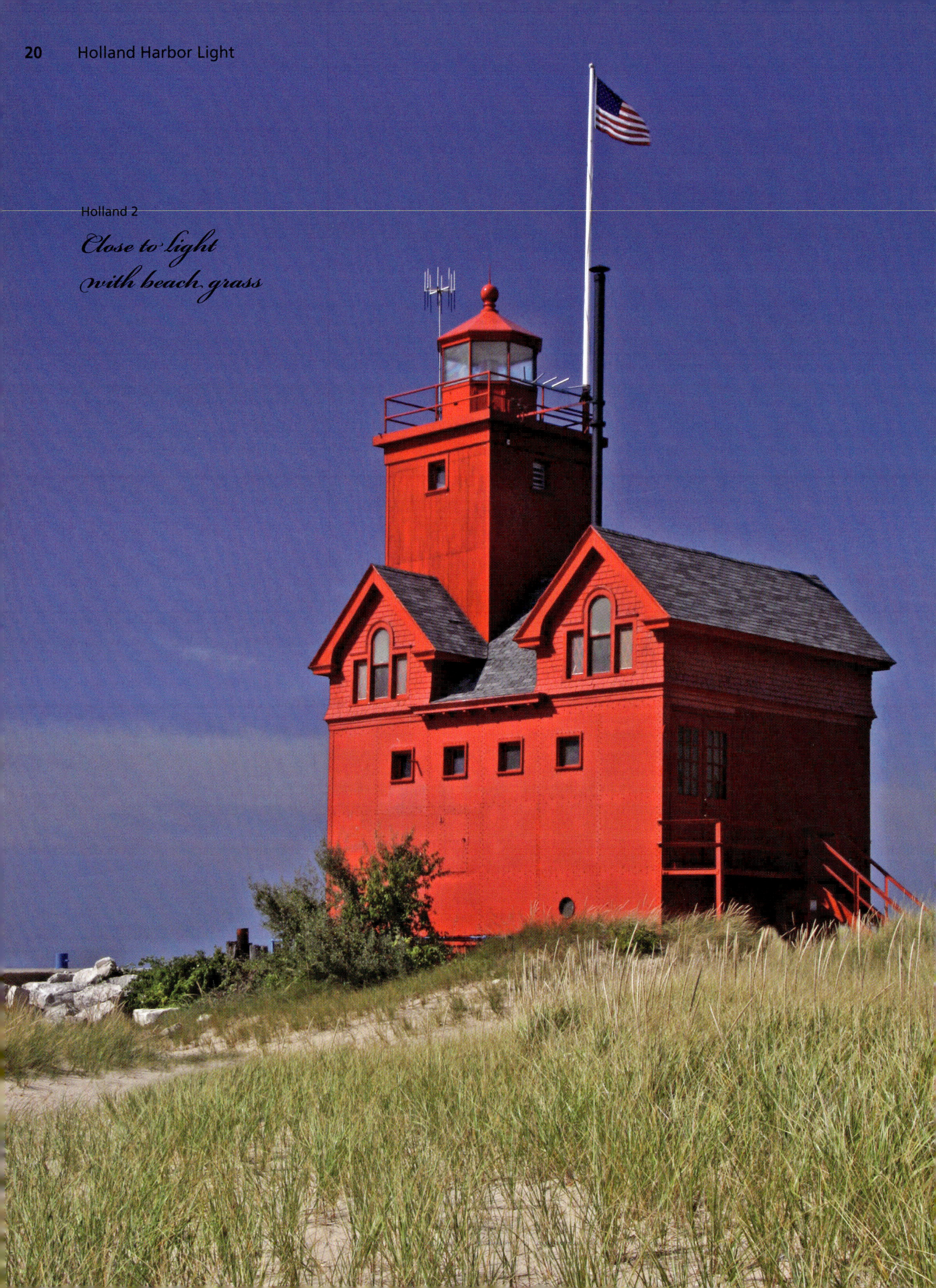
Holland 2
Close to light
with beach grass

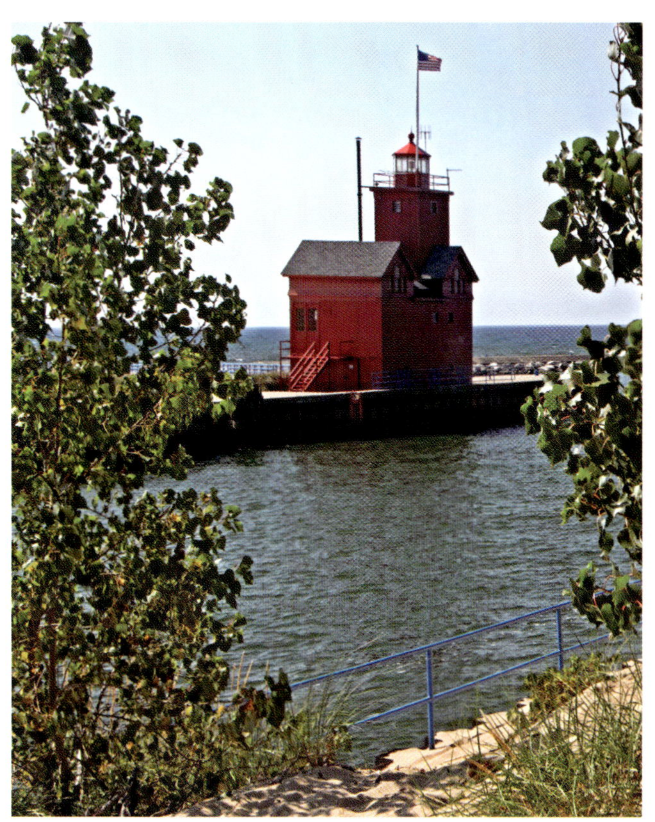

Holland 5 *Across canal, framed by trees*

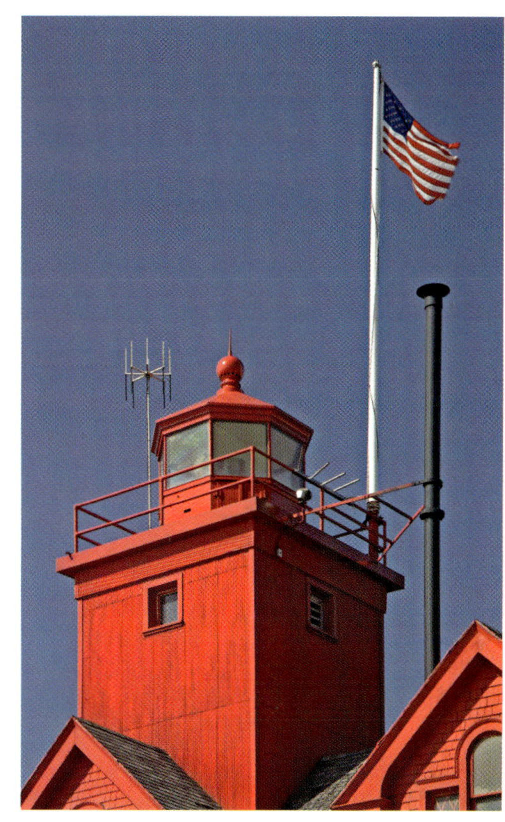

Holland 4 *Lantern room / roofline*

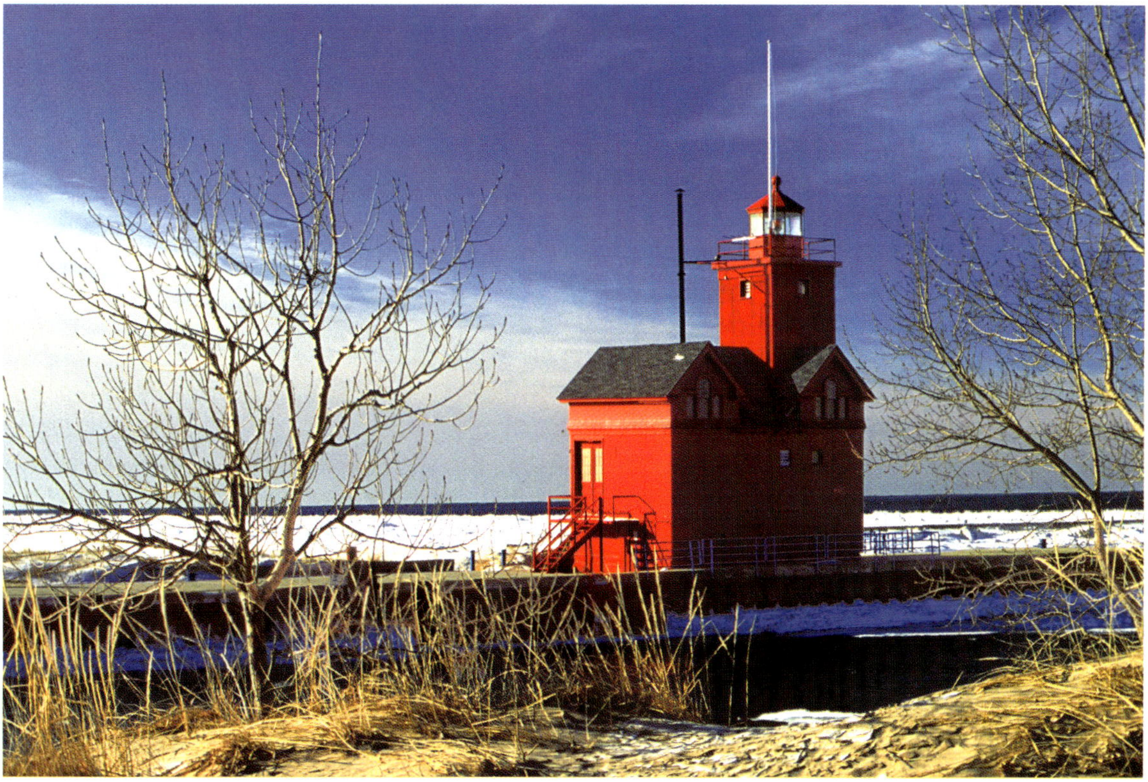

Holland 6 *Across canal, winter*

Grand Haven South Pier Lights

Grand Haven, Michigan

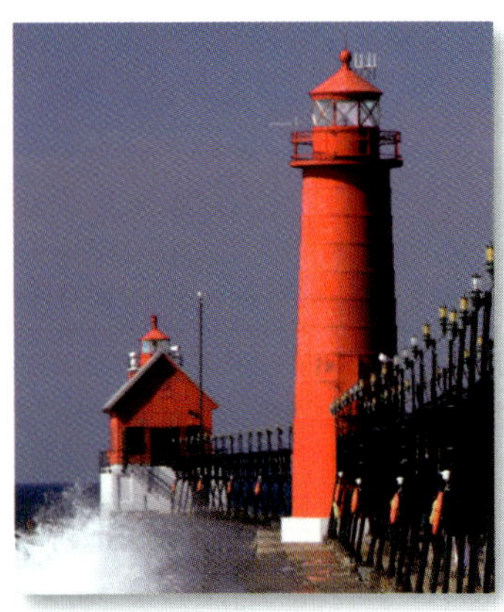

"Dynamite Duo"

DISTINGUISHING FEATURES

Not one, but two bright red lighthouses on a long breakwater with an elevated catwalk provide a great setting for photographers. There's even small lights stretched across the top of the catwalk for some eye-catching sunset and night shots.

BEST TIME OF DAY

Morning and afternoon are both good times to be here with the early morning being the best.

SUGGESTED COMPOSITIONS

The catwalk is a great aid to effective compositions. Try a variety of shots at different angles from the beach **(1)**. Take some that include both lights as well as some of each light individually **(2) & (5)**. Also walk the pier (except when slippery or windy) and sight along the catwalk supports using focal lengths ranging from wide angle to telephoto, using both vertical and horizontal formats **(3)**. Include close ups of both lighthouses **(4)**.

An alternate viewing area with the pier/catwalk running left to right is available to the north across the river (see directions).

SUNSET/SUNRISE

Excellent sunset images can be obtained from the beach or across the river. Regardless of weather, dramatic nights shots are possible, particularly just after sunset, when the white and yellow lights on the catwalk are illuminated. Both lighthouses have working red lights that are reflected in the water along with the catwalk lights. Time the shutter release to capture both red lights when they flash in your direction **(6)**.

DIRECTIONS

From US 31 in town, turn west on Franklin Ave. go less than a mile to S. Harbor Dr., turn left and go a short distance to the entrance to Grand Haven State Park on your right. This is a Michigan State Park with vehicle entrance fee.

To reach the area north of the lighthouses across the river, take US 31 north over the Grand River to the Ferrysburg exit and turn left at stop sign on 3rd St. Go about one half mile and turn left on N. Shore Dr. Continue about 3 miles to the end and turn right to parking area.

GPS coordinates: 43.056N, 86.256W.

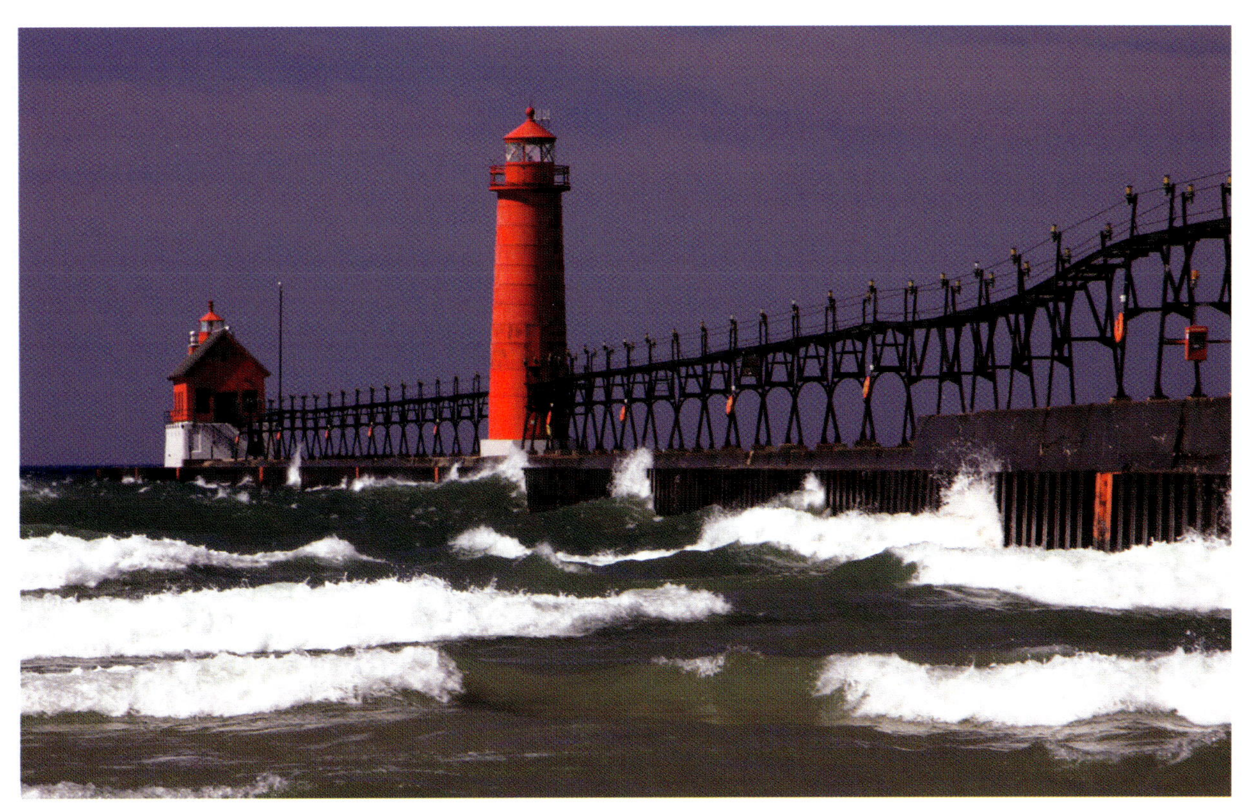

Grand Haven 1 *From the beach, with crashing waves*

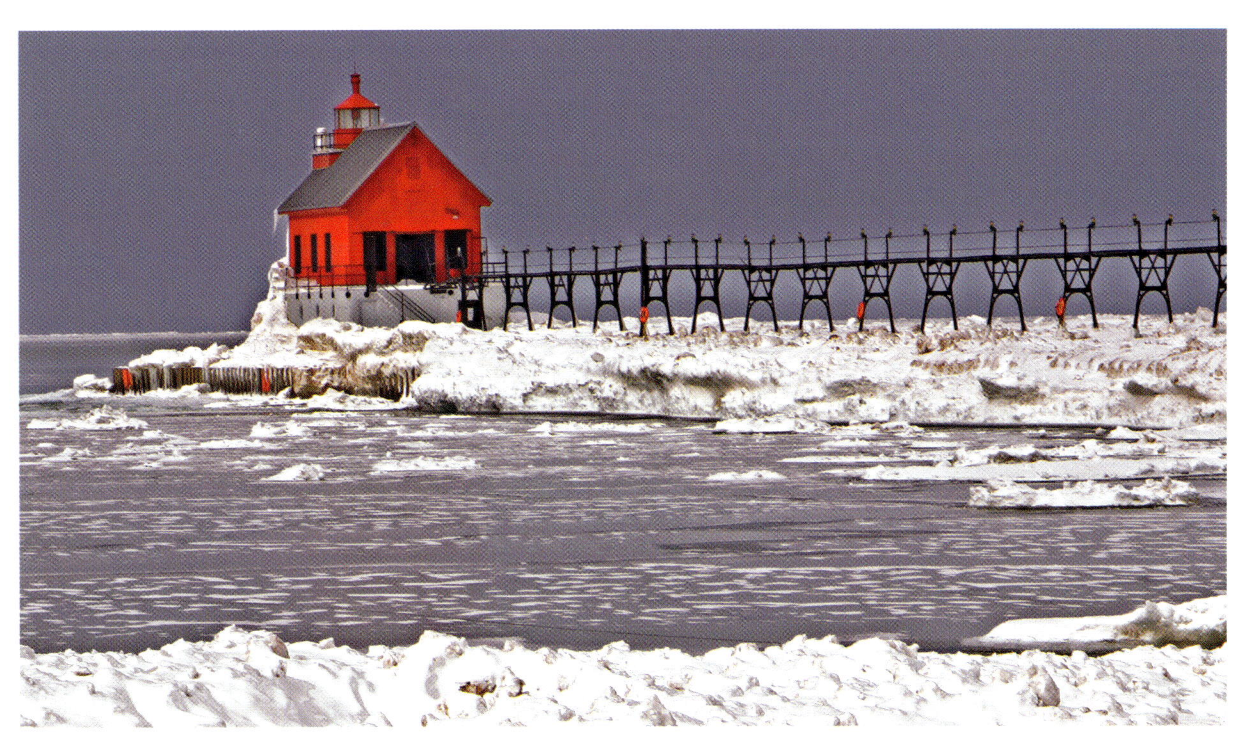

Grand Haven 2 *From the beach, outer light in winter*

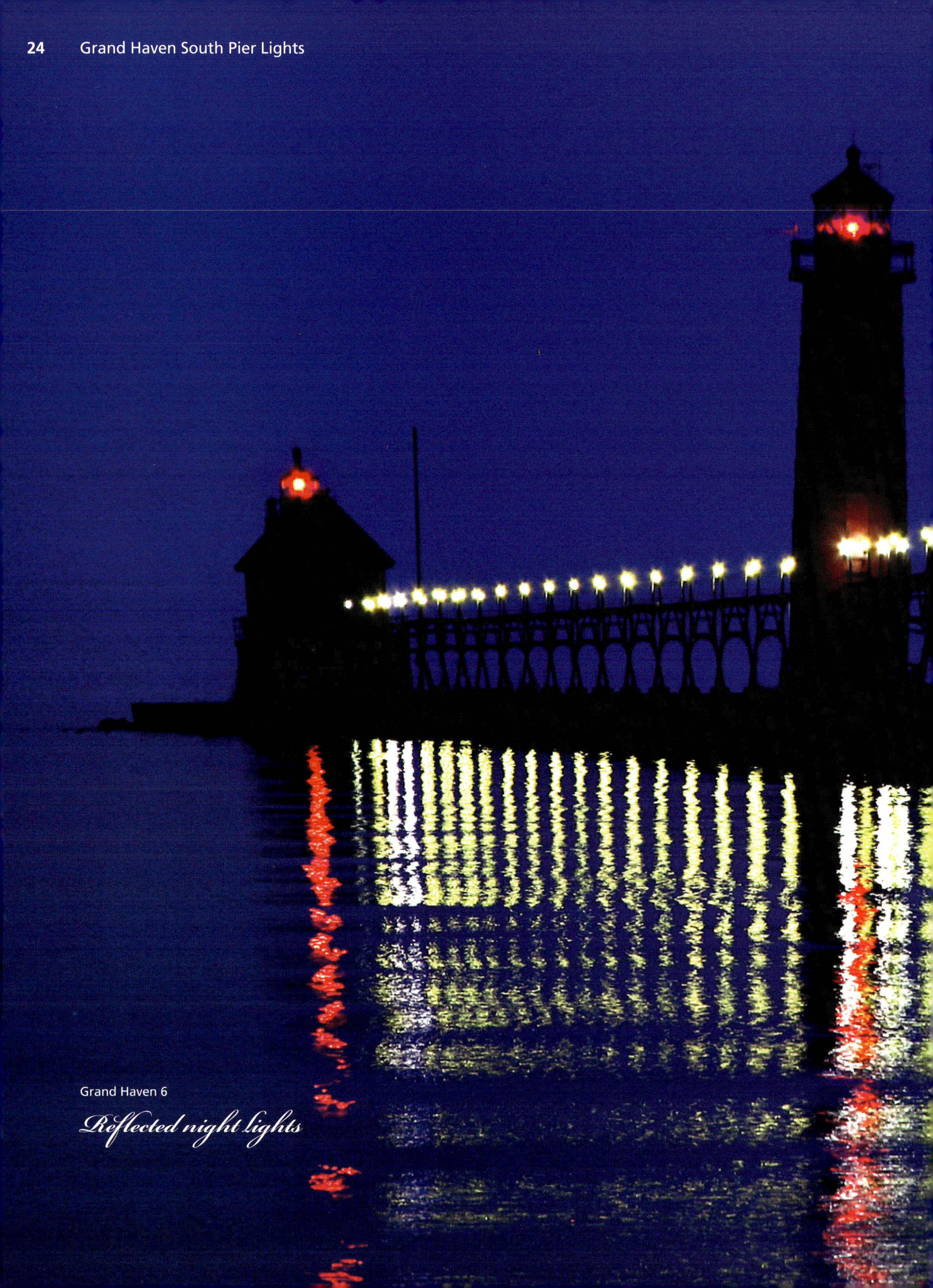

Grand Haven 6

Reflected night lights

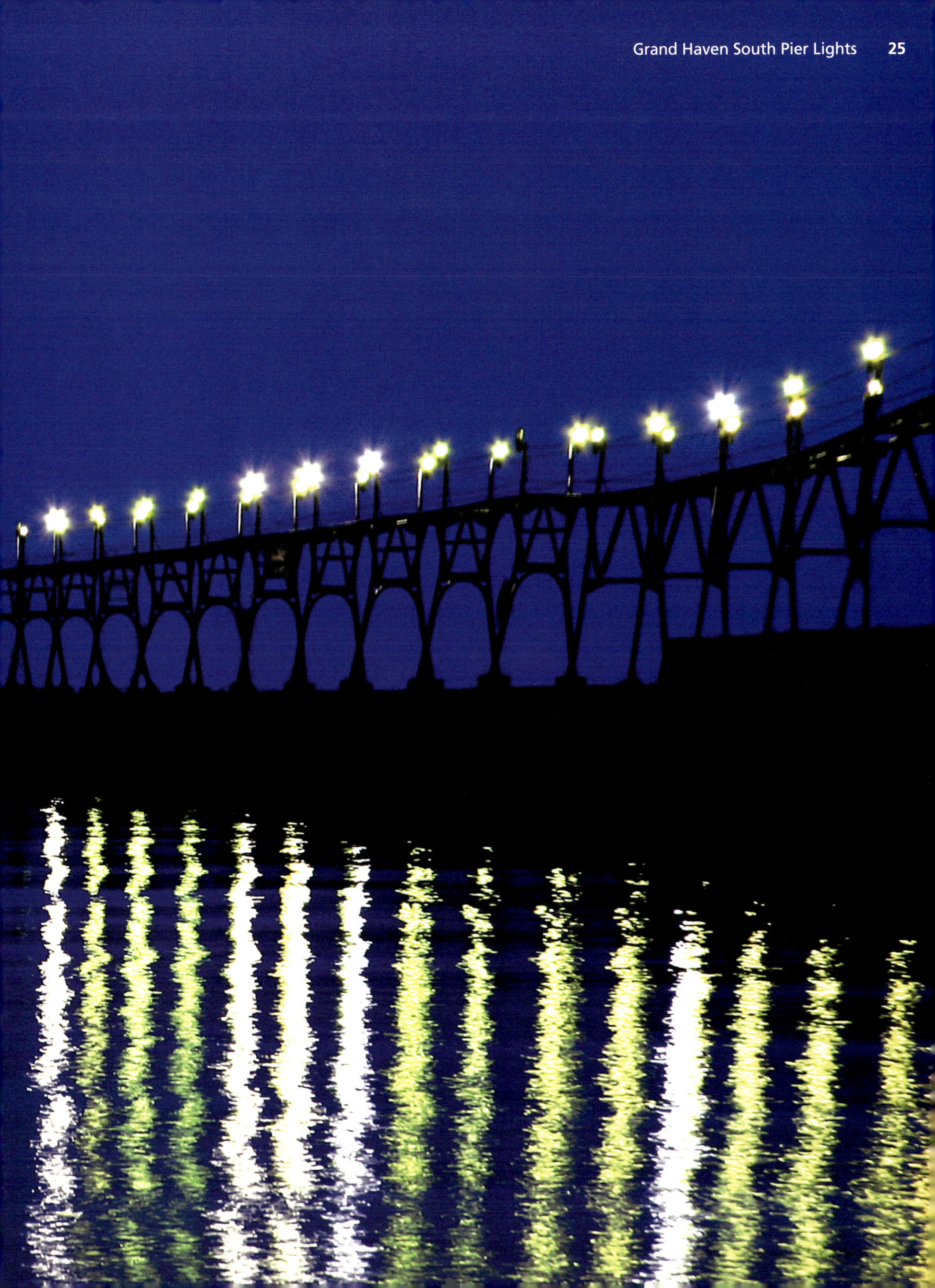

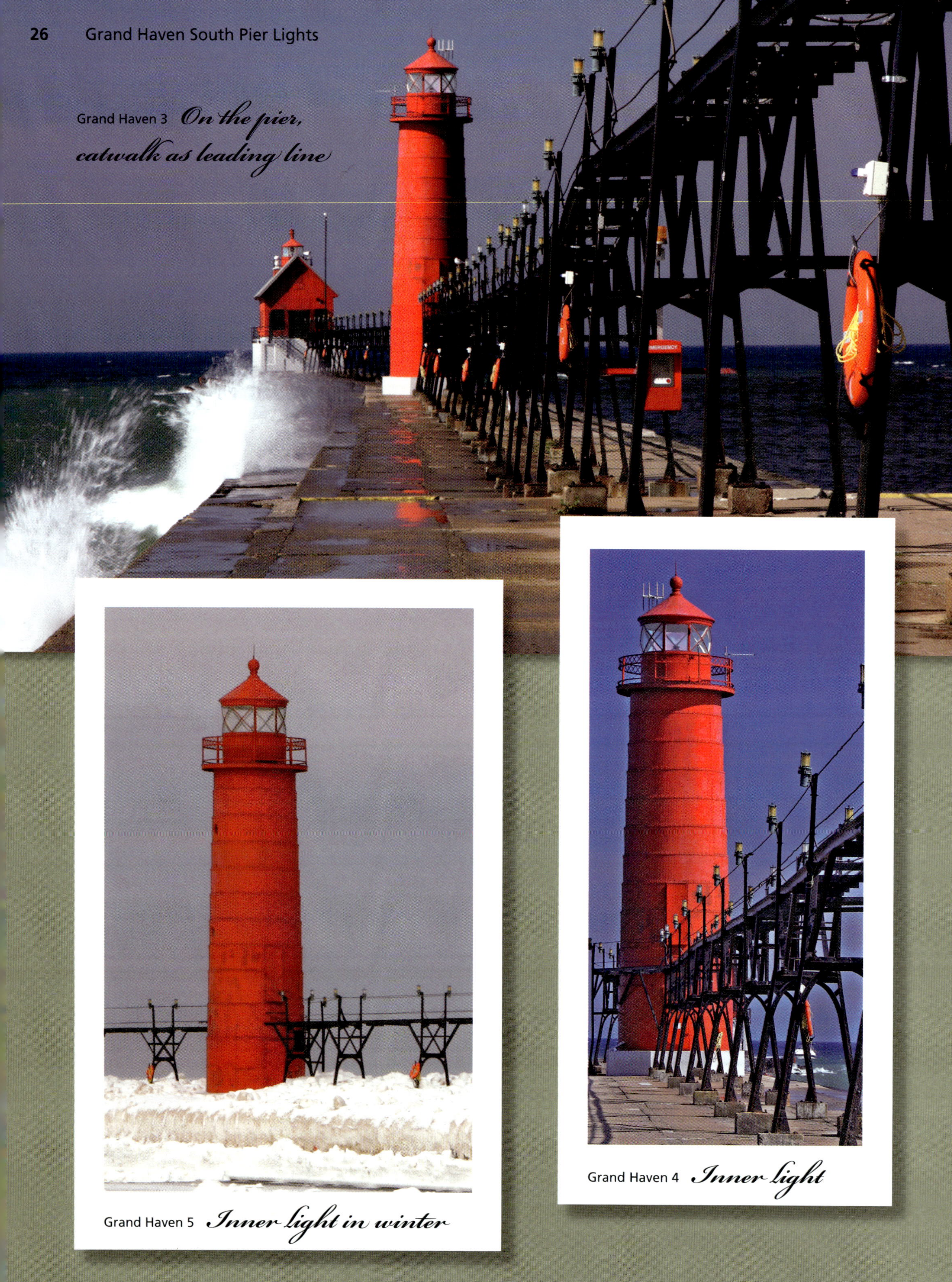

Grand Haven 3 *On the pier, catwalk as leading line*
Grand Haven 5 *Inner light in winter*
Grand Haven 4 *Inner light*

Muskegon South Pier Light

Muskegon, Michigan

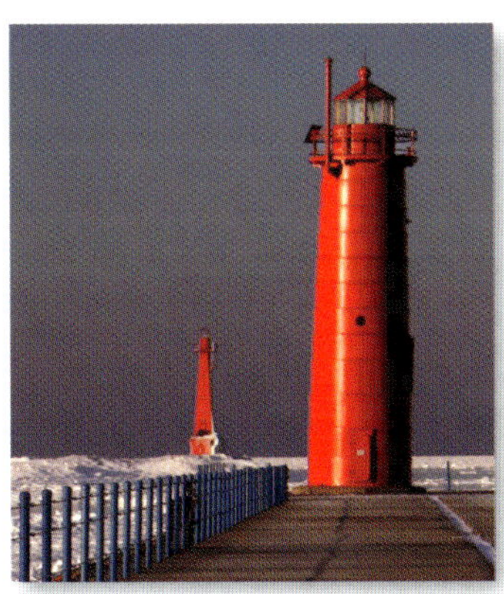

"Ruby Red Beacon"

DISTINGUISHING FEATURES

A crimson steel tower stands at the end of a short pier by the channel connecting Muskegon Lake and Lake Michigan. Blue posts supporting cable railings provide more color leading to the light.

BEST TIME OF DAY

Good lighting conditions exist in the morning and afternoon hours, with early morning being the best time.

SUGGESTED COMPOSITIONS

On the pier, use the blue posts with the cable railing as a leading line **(1)**. This works best close to the left side, minimizing the amount of the wide concrete walkway. Try various distances from the light, using different focal lengths as well as horizontal and vertical formats **(2) & (3)**. On the shore, just left of the pier, include the large rocks in the foreground **(4)**. Near the beach parking spaces, there are several small trees that can be used for framing **(5)**. This is also a good spot to catch the rolling waves **(6)**.

SUNSET/SUNRISE

There is excellent sunset potential from the pier or the beach.

DIRECTIONS

From US 31, exit at Sherman Blvd. and go west about 5.5 miles to Beach St. Turn right and go about 2 miles to Pere Marquette Park. Just past the Coast Guard Station, park in the public spaces facing the Lake.

To reach the lighthouse pier, walk down the driveway between the buildings headed by the sign "Great Lakes Environmental Research Laboratory". This leads to the pier that is open to the public.
GPS coordinates: 43.227N, 86.341W.

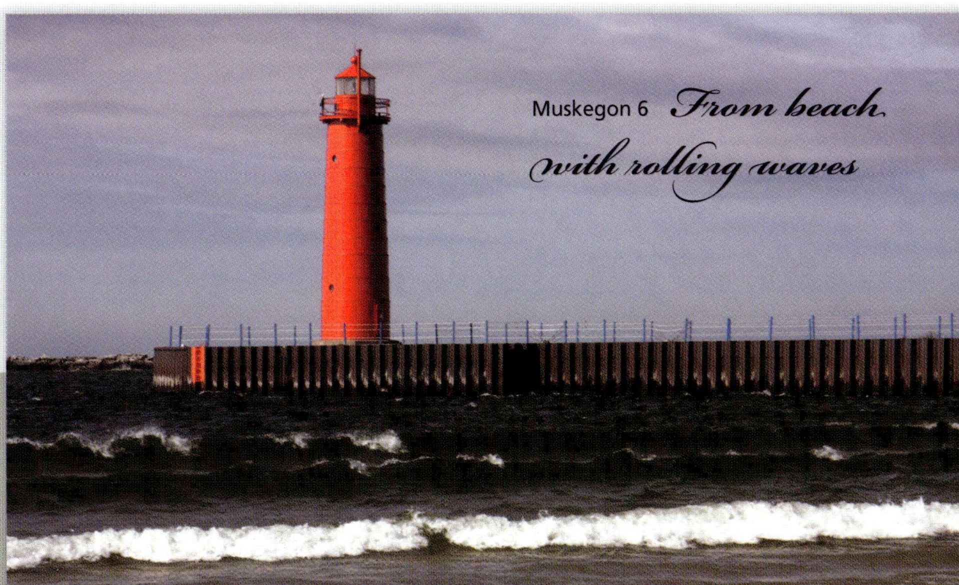

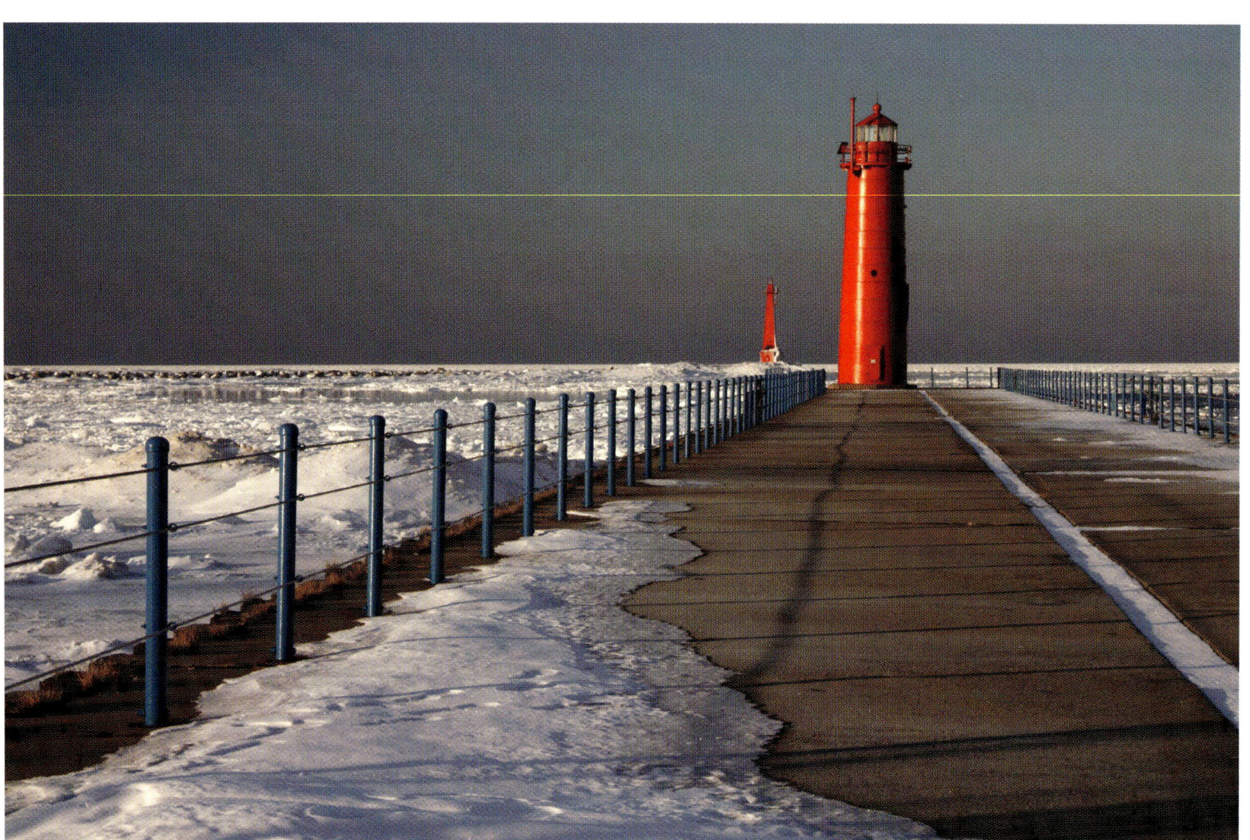

Muskegon 1   *Blue posts as leading line*

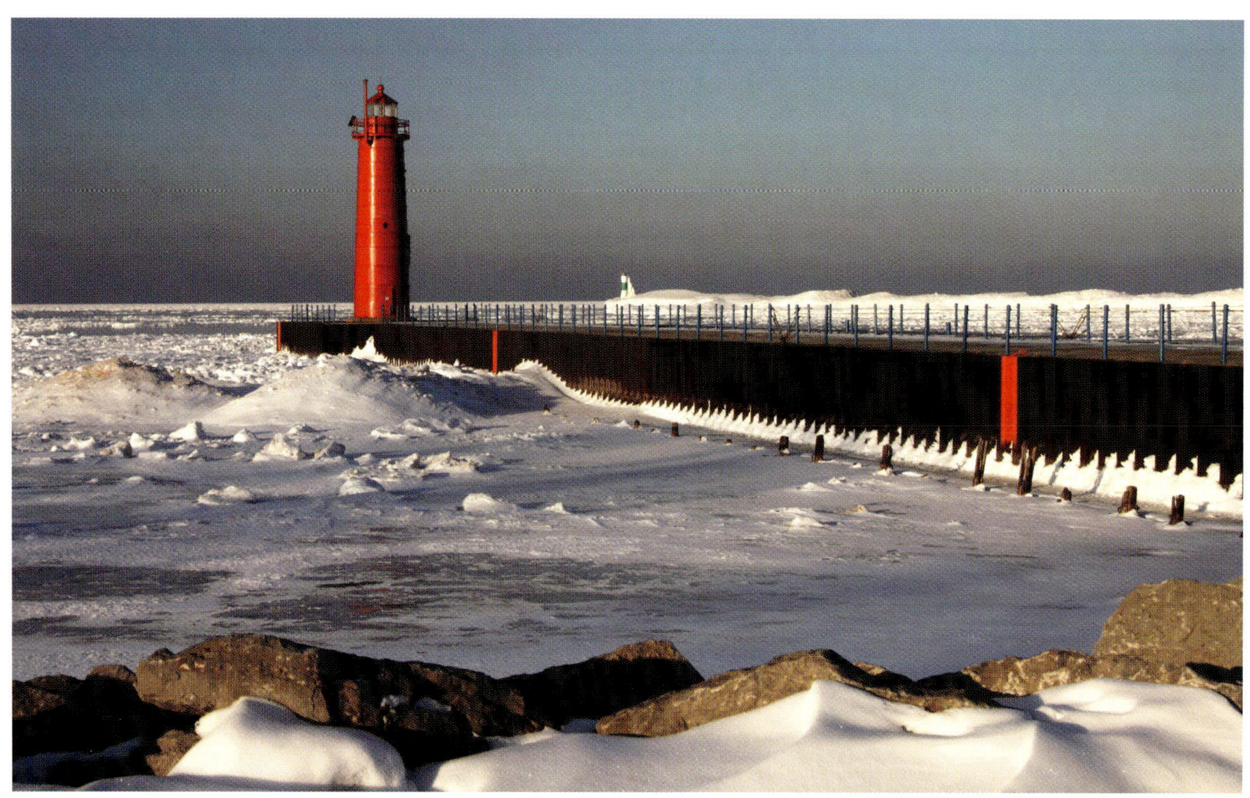

Muskegon 4   *Large rocks in foreground*

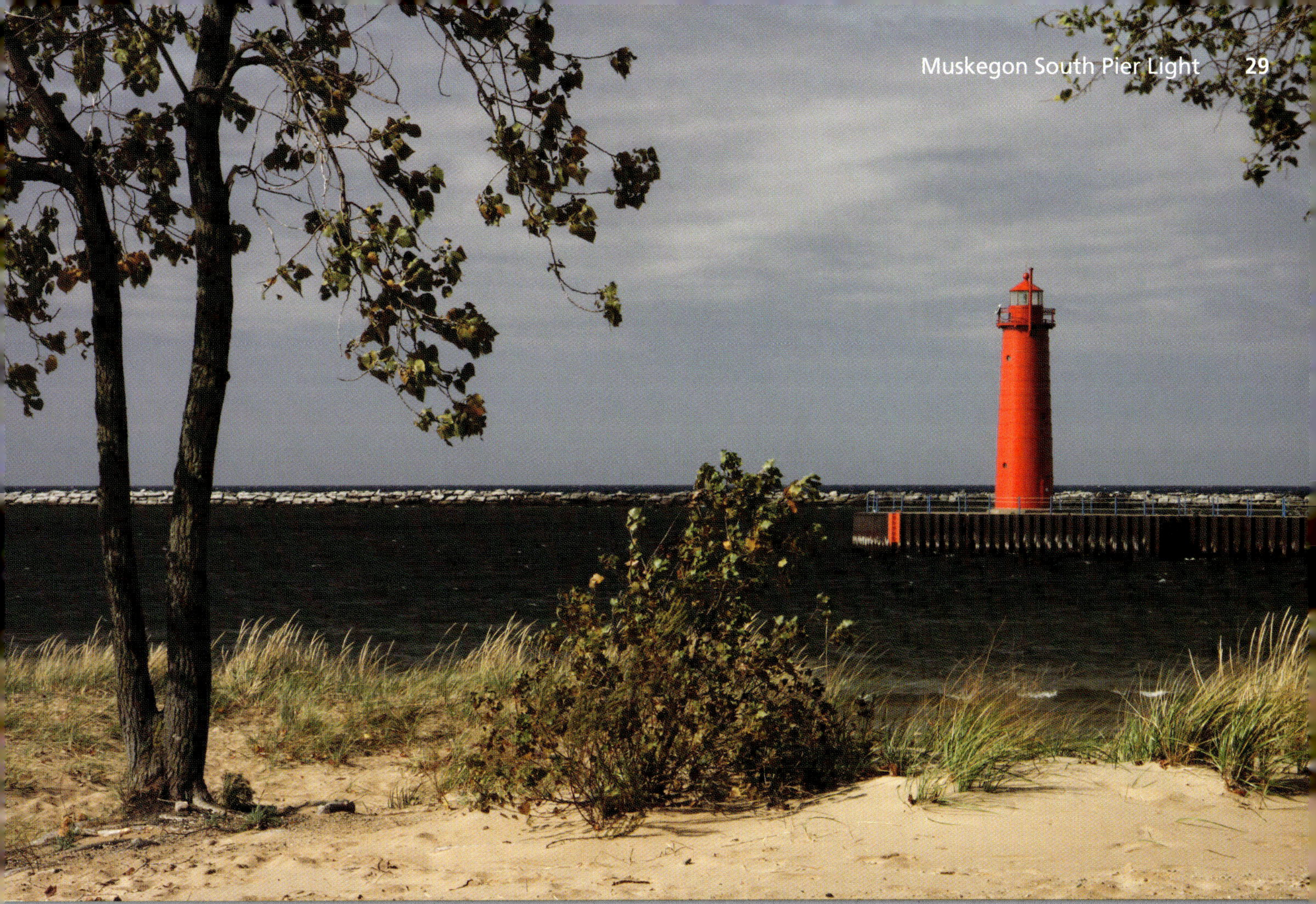

Muskegon 5 *From beach, framed by trees*

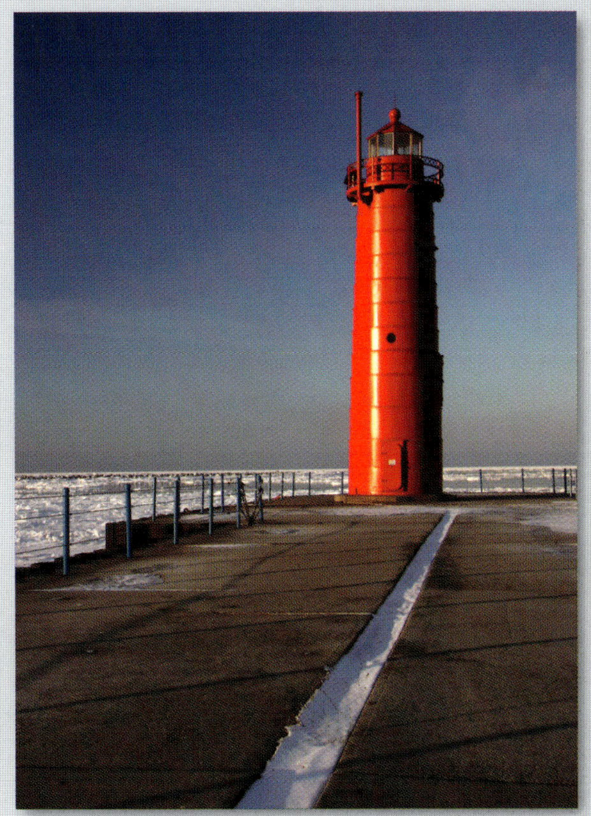

Muskegon 2 *Snow channel as leading line*

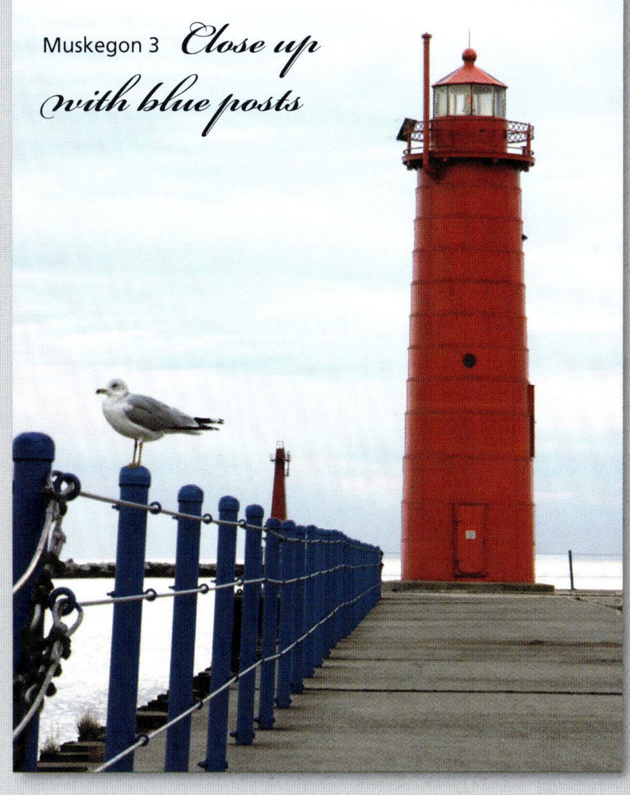

Muskegon 3 *Close up with blue posts*

White River Light

Whitehall, Michigan

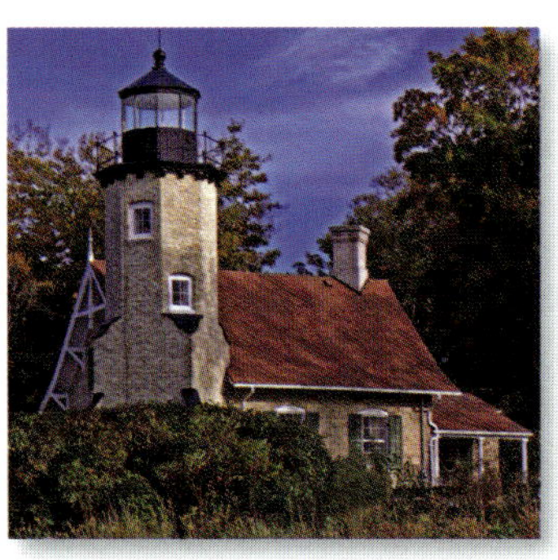

"Just Like Home"

DISTINGUISHING FEATURES

White River Lighthouse looks like a brick cottage on Main Street USA, including the lawn and shade trees around it. There is even a picket fence around the back yard. It also has very interesting architectural features and trim.

BEST TIME OF DAY

This is primarily an afternoon shot. The large trees east of the lighthouse heavily shade the building in the morning.

SUGGESTED COMPOSITIONS

There are good vantage points from the walkway along the channel north of the lighthouse. Walk the full length and look for pleasing angles and compositions **(1)**. On the west side of the light is a white picket fence that can provide a diagonal foreground **(2)**. Be sure to take some close up shots of the distinctive features of the light tower and keeper's house **(3)**. There is an alternate viewing area across the channel that connects White Lake and Lake Michigan. This will allow you to include the channel water in the foreground **(4)**. Although there are maple trees in the yard just east of the lighthouse, they are of a type that produces mostly muted colors in the fall **(1)**.

SUNSET/SUNRISE

There are practically no sunset possibilities here due to the large trees obscuring the view of the lighthouse as you look west.

DIRECTIONS

From US 31, exit at White Lake Dr. and take it west about 4.5 miles to S. Shore Rd. Turn left and go about 3.5 miles to a four way stop. Go straight ahead onto Murray Rd. and continue for about 1 mile. Turn left on the narrow road that leads to the lighthouse.

To reach the north side of the channel starting from the lighthouse, follow S. Shore Rd to BR 31 in Whitehall. Cross the bridge to Montague and take Dowling St. a short distance to a sign leading left to Old Channel Trail. Go about 3 miles to a stop sign, turn left (still on Old Channel Trail) and drive about 2 miles to Lau Rd, where there is a sign pointing left for Medbury Park. After a short distance, go right at the fork in the road to a parking area across from the lighthouse.

GPS coordinates: 43.374N, 86.424W.

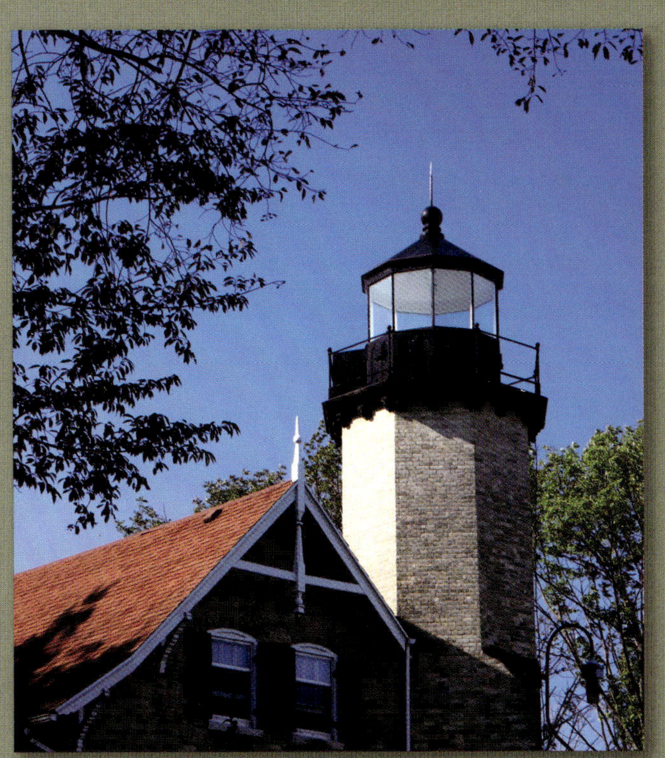

White River 3 *Framed tower with long lens*

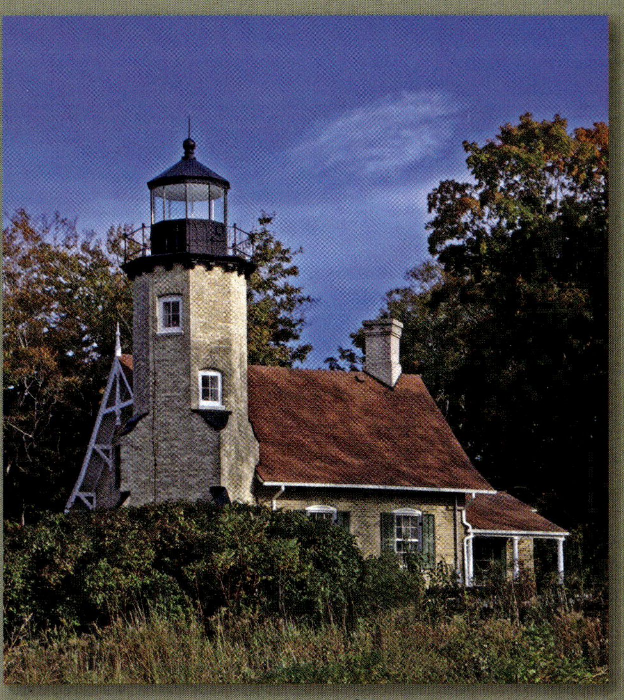

White River 1 *From walkway along channel*

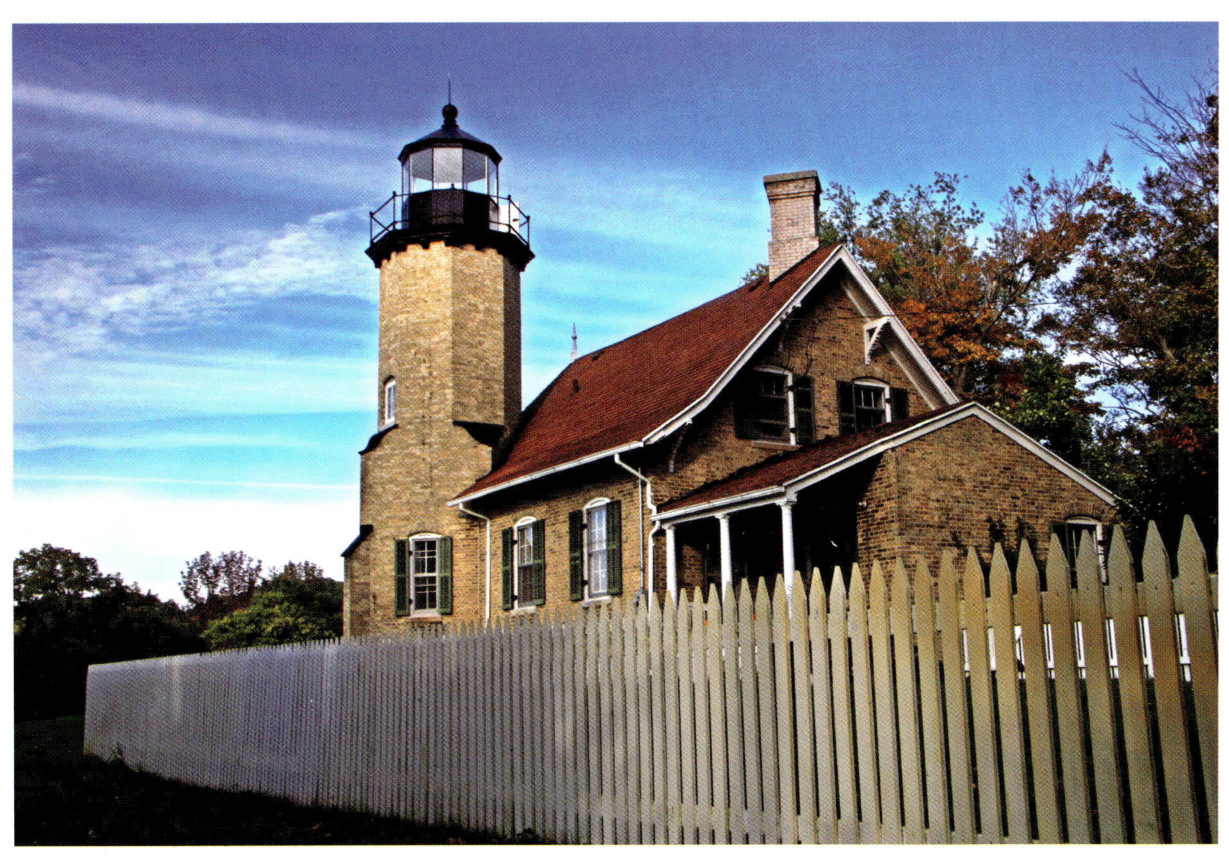

White River 2 *Down low in back yard*

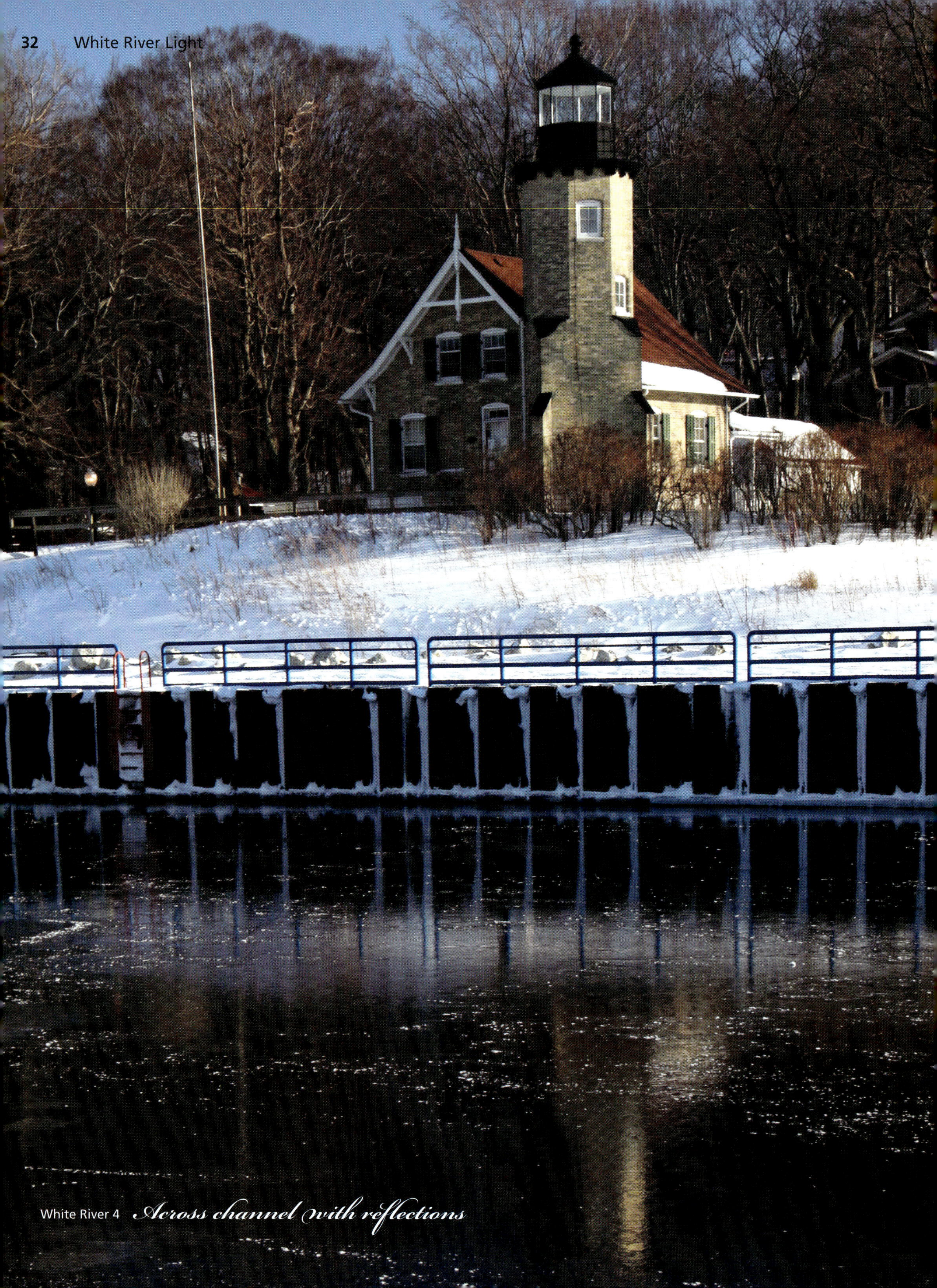

White River 4   *Across channel with reflections*

Little Sable Point Light

Near Mears, Michigan

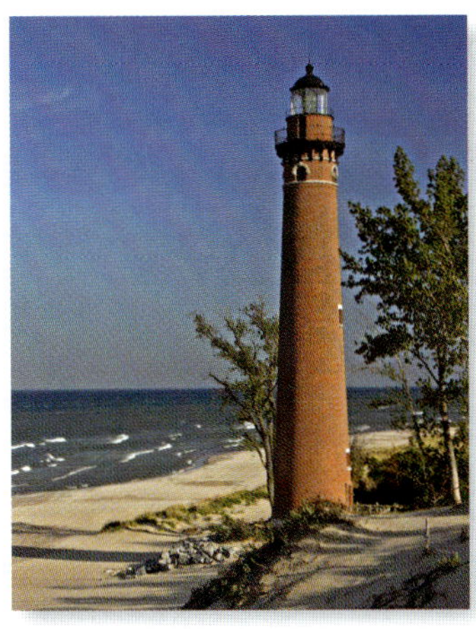

"Solitary Sentinel"

DISTINGUISHING FEATURES

Set beside a sprawling beach and rolling sand dunes is the distinctive Little Sable lighthouse. This tall brick tower stands alone in a remote area. The keeper's dwelling was removed years ago. There are many small to medium sized poplar trees scattered throughout the dunes close to the light.

BEST TIME OF DAY

Best lighting conditions are usually found in mid morning and the afternoon. The beach is in heavy shadows from the sand dunes in the early morning hours.

SUGGESTED COMPOSITIONS

The rise and fall of the sand dunes with trees and vegetation provide many opportunities for interesting compositions. Use the trees for framing with the dunes and grasses in the foreground **(1) & (2)**. The views from north and south of the light are especially nice with the lake included in the frame **(3) & (4)**. Look for positions where a sand dune runs diagonally **(5)**. In the fall, the leaves of the poplar trees turn yellow to add more color.

SUNSET/SUNRISE

The lighthouse is well positioned for lovely sunset scenes.

DIRECTIONS

From US 31, exit at Shelby Rd. (south of mile marker 145) and go west about 6 miles to a "T" at Scenic Dr. (also 16th Ave.). Turn right and drive about 3.5 miles (there are turns in the road and it changes to 18th Ave.) to another "T" at Silver Lake Road. Turn left and follow the winding road about 1.5 miles to the parking area of Silver Lake State Park, which has a state park entrance fee.
GPS coordinates: 43.650N, 86.539W.

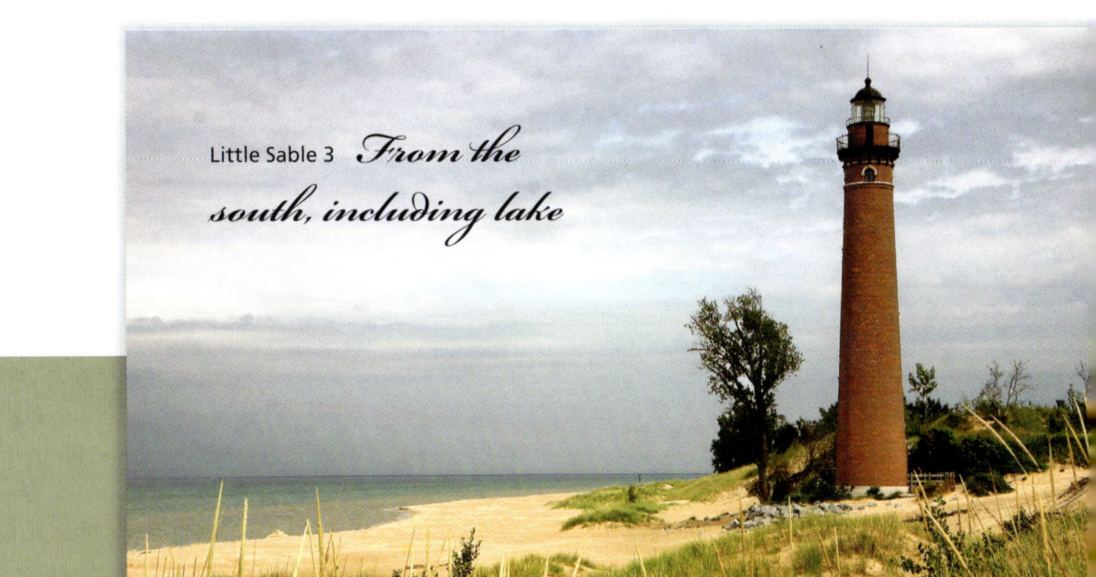

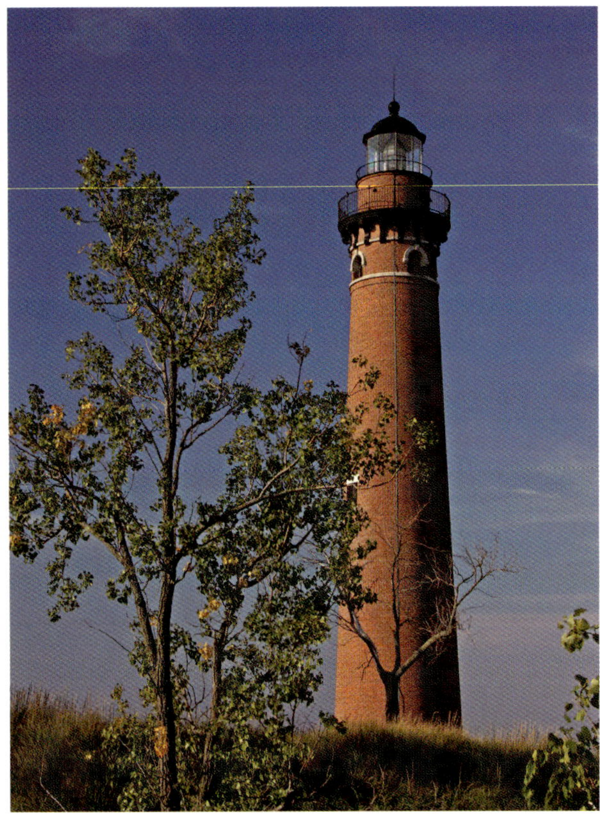

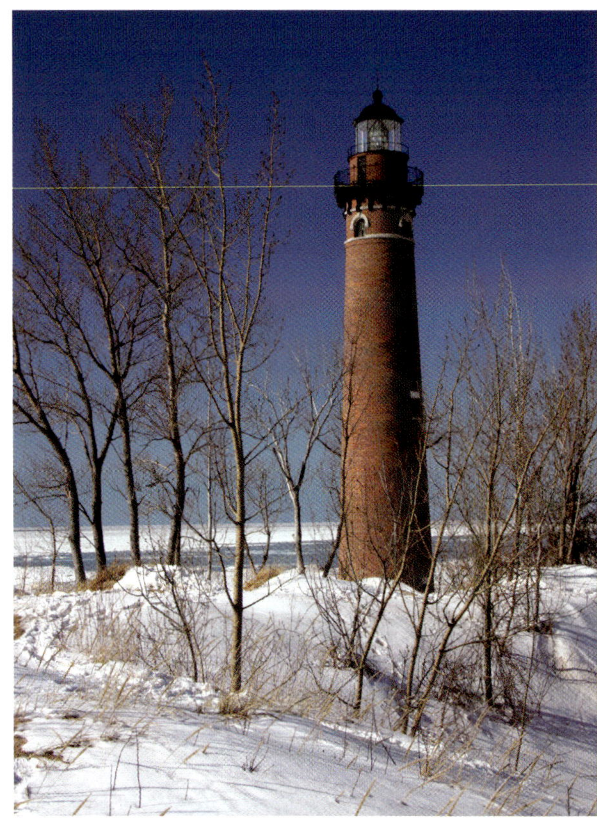

Little Sable 1 *Framed by poplars, summer* Little Sable 2 *Framed by poplars, winter*

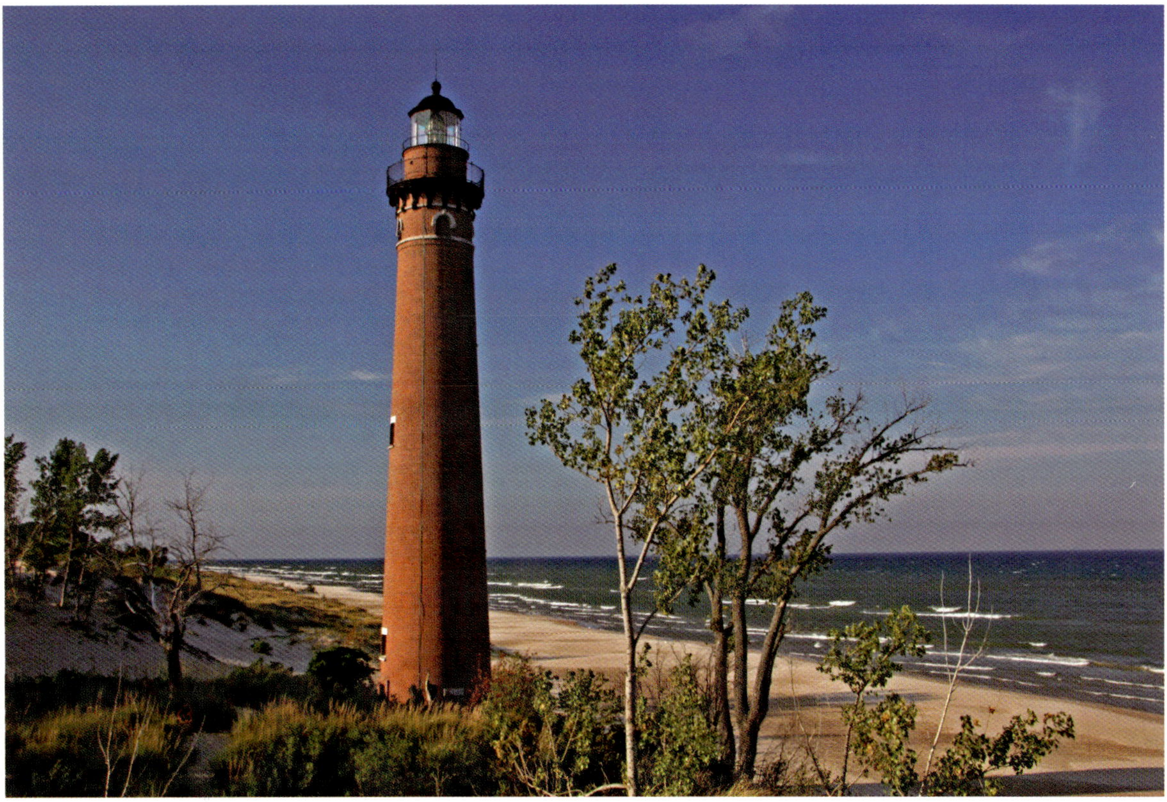

Little Sable 4 *From the north, including lake*

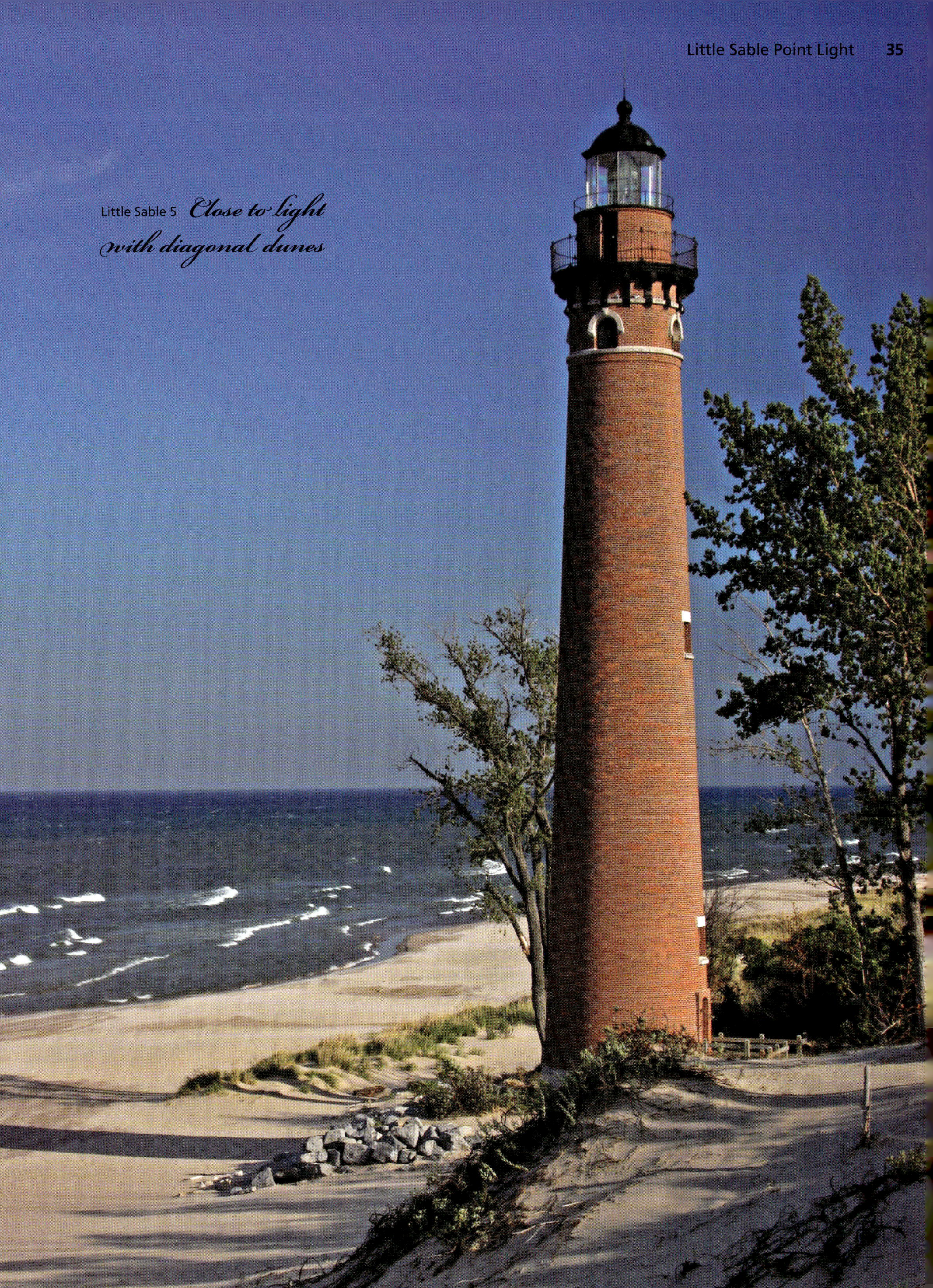

Little Sable 5   Close to light
with diagonal dunes

Big Sable Point Light

Near Ludington, Michigan

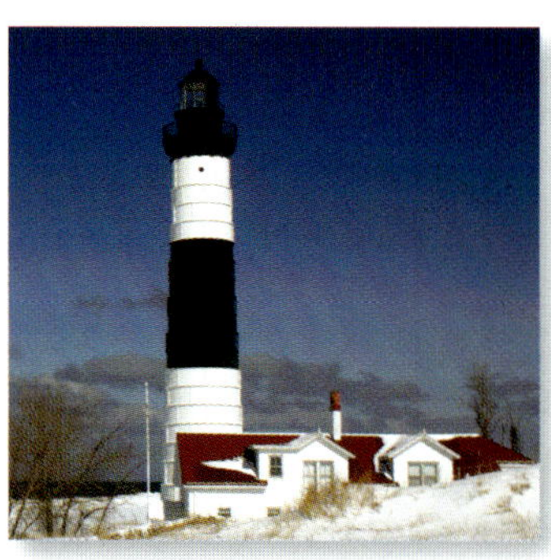

"Majesty Among the Dunes"

DISTINGUISHING FEATURES

The majestic Big Sable lighthouse set among sand dunes is one of the most scenic light stations on the Great Lakes. The tall and unusual black and white tower has steel plates that give it a nice texture. The red roof of the attached keeper's house adds vibrant color.

BEST TIME OF DAY

There is favorable sunlight on the lighthouse in the morning and afternoon.

SUGGESTED COMPOSITIONS

The sand dunes surrounding the lighthouse in all directions provide many opportunities for creative compositions. Perhaps start at the path from the campground and use it as a leading line **(1)**. Then walk around the light on the dunes and where possible, include the lake in the background **(2)**. Look for openings in the small trees or breaks in the grasses to provide "lead-ins" **(3)**. There are several boardwalks running out from the lighthouse (some with "S" curves) that can enhance your images **(4)**. Take some shots with the dunes running diagonally in the foreground **(3)**. Sweeping beach perspectives can be taken from the north side. When the lighthouse is open, capture a pattern shot of the iron circular stairs from the bottom of the tower. This makes a good black and white image **(5)**.

SUNSET/SUNRISE

There is excellent sunset potential looking out to Lake Michigan.

DIRECTIONS

From the junction of US 31 and US 10, take US 10 west into Ludington to M 116 (Lakeshore Dr.) and go north about 6.5 miles to Ludington State Park. From the gatehouse, go straight ahead to a parking area. It is an easy walk of 1.75 miles from here to the lighthouse (about 30–35 minutes at a steady pace). Start at the "Lighthouse Trail" sign and follow the road through the campground. The trail itself begins between campsites No. 58 and 59 and is mostly flat and firm as you hike along the sand dunes. Bicycles are allowed on the trail and can be rented at the camp store. This is a Michigan State Park with entrance fee.

GPS coordinates: 44.057N, 86.514W.

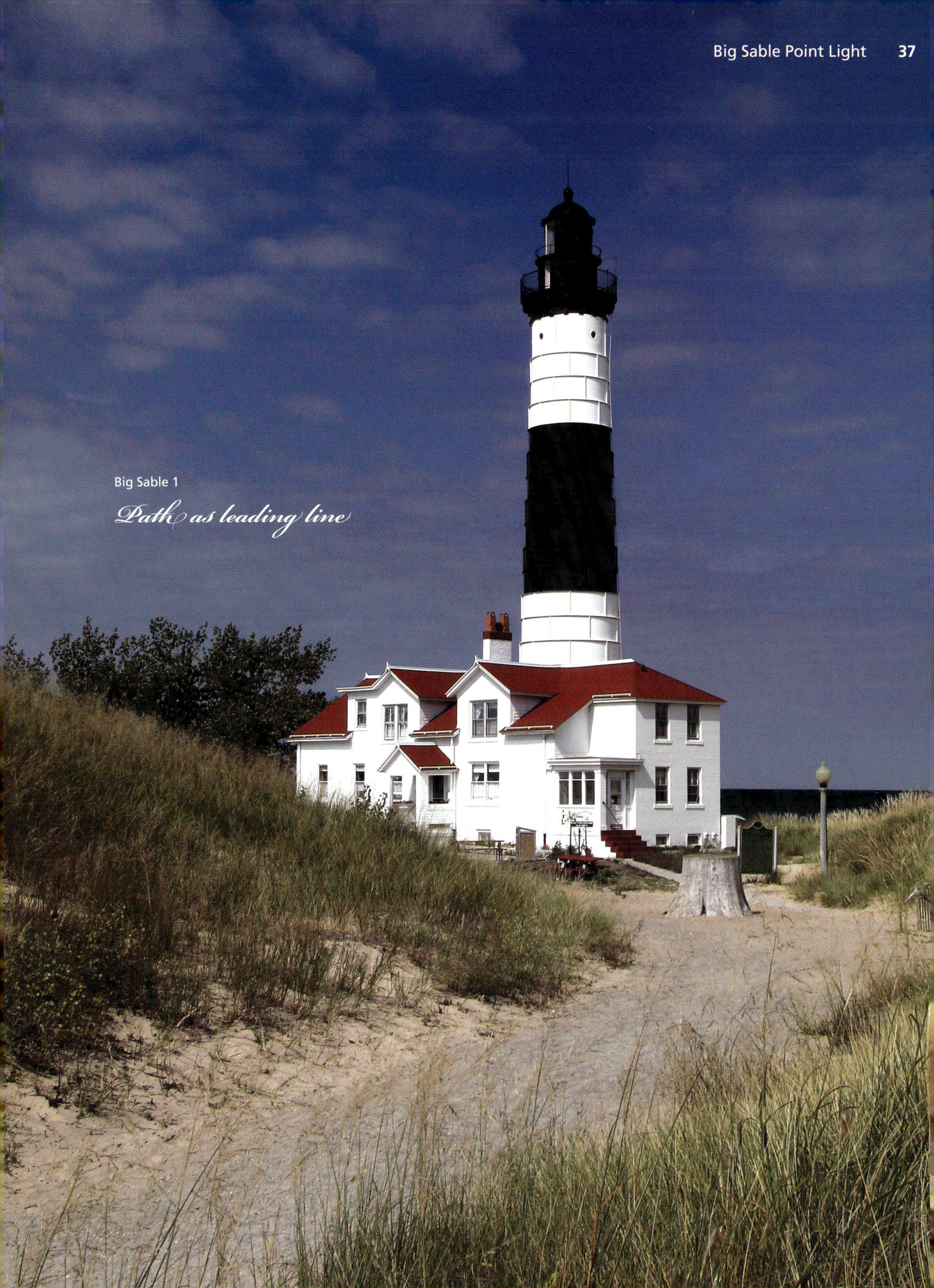
Big Sable 1
Path as leading line

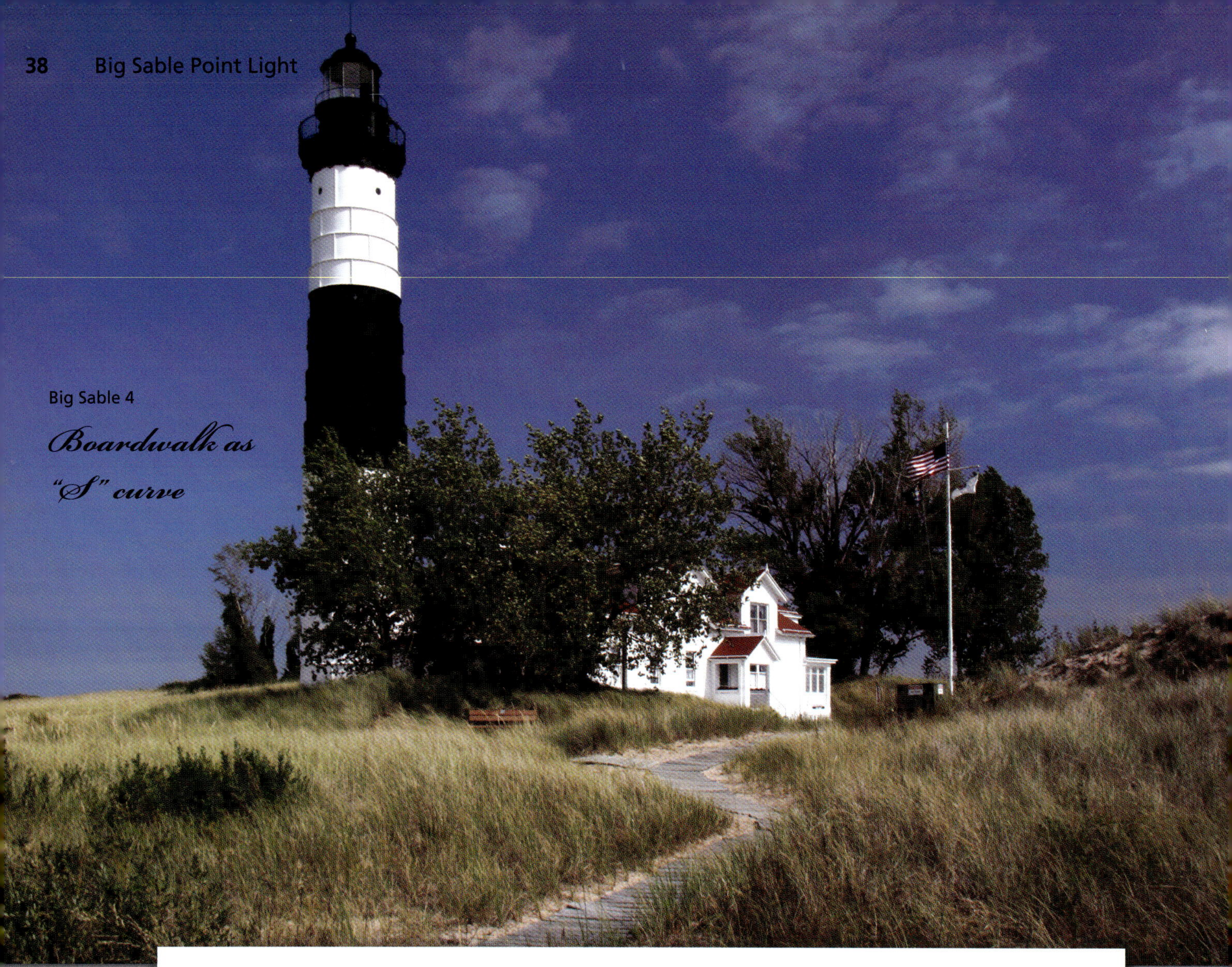

Big Sable 4

Boardwalk as "S" curve

Big Sable 3

Framed by trees with diagonal dunes

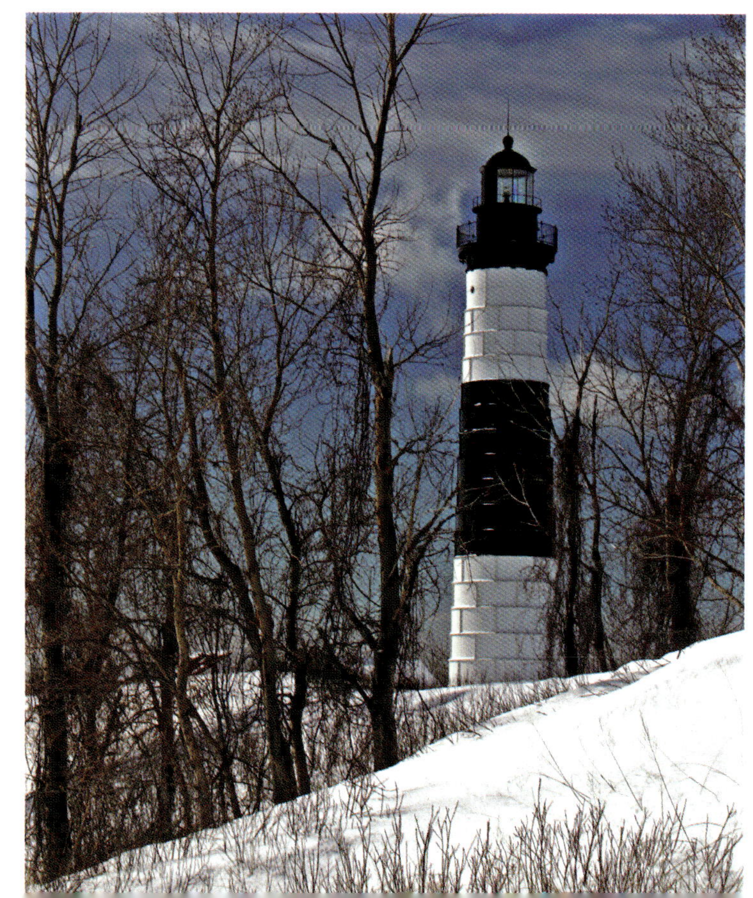

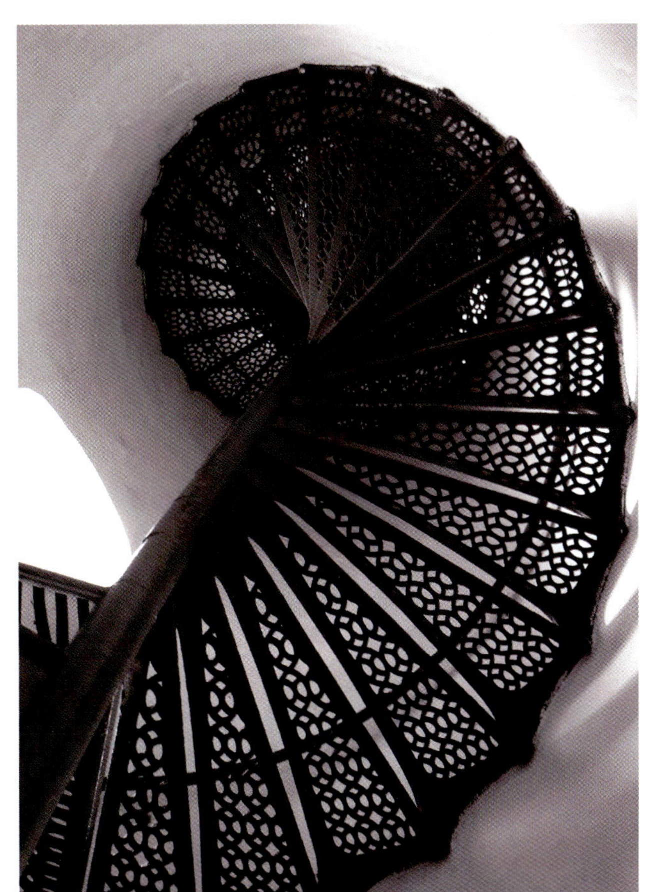

Big Sable 5

From bottom of circular stairs

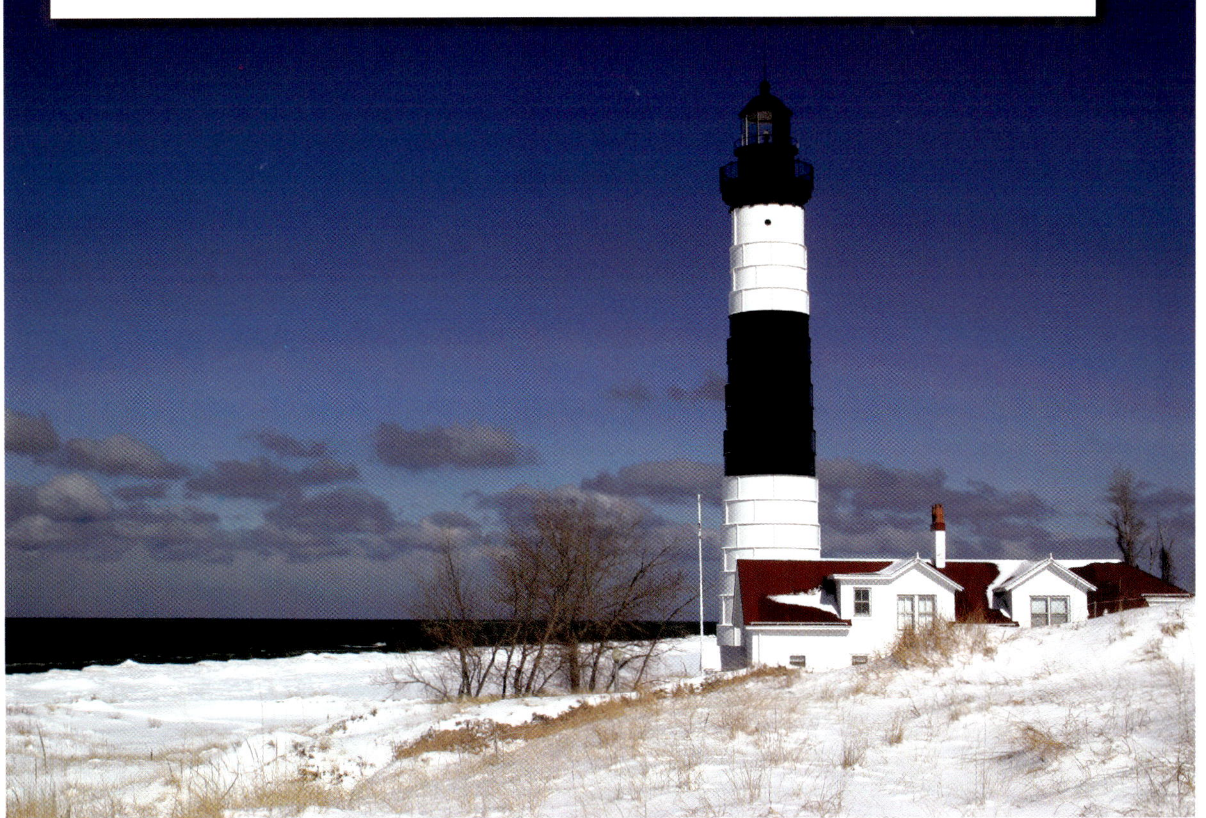

Big Sable 2   *From south dunes, including lake*

Point Betsie Light

Near Frankfort, Michigan

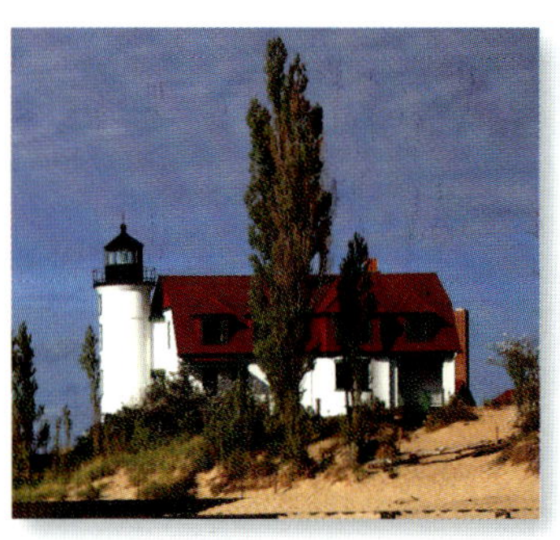

*"Elegance on
the Lake"*

DISTINGUISHING FEATURES

One of the most attractive lighthouses on the Great Lakes, Point Betsie sits on a prominent point providing breathtaking views from the long sandy beach. It consists of a large barn shaped keeper's house with a sloping red roof and an attached white tower topped by a black lantern room.

BEST TIME OF DAY

Morning and afternoon light are both good. The beach is in heavy shadows from the sand dunes in the early morning hours.

SUGGESTED COMPOSITIONS

Classic compositions can be obtained from the beach south of the lighthouse. Position yourself as close as possible to the water's edge to include the shoreline and rolling waves as leading lines **(1)**. Use different focal lengths from various distances to find the one that seems to work best. Close to the lighthouse, use the steel breakwaters for foreground interest **(2)**. Up close, the nearby trees can be used for framing **(3)** & **(4)**. Also, use a long lens to capture the lantern room and include part of the red roof and gable **(5)**.

SUNSET/SUNRISE

Due to the elevated position of the lighthouse and surrounding buildings, a favorable sunset image will be difficult.

DIRECTIONS

From M 22, about 5.5 miles north of Frankfort, turn west on Point Betsie Rd. and drive the short distance to the end of the road by the lake. Park along the side of the unpaved road.
GPS coordinates: 44.691N, 86.255W.

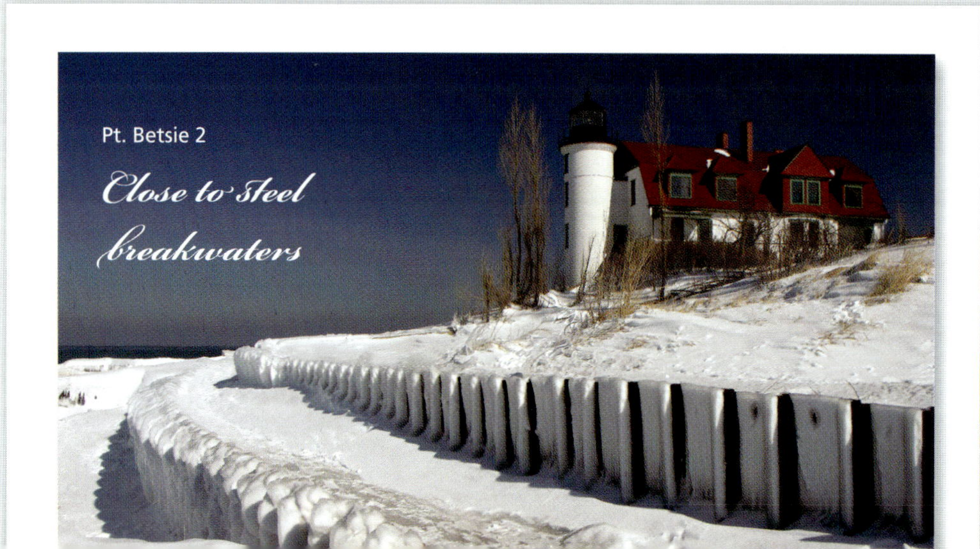

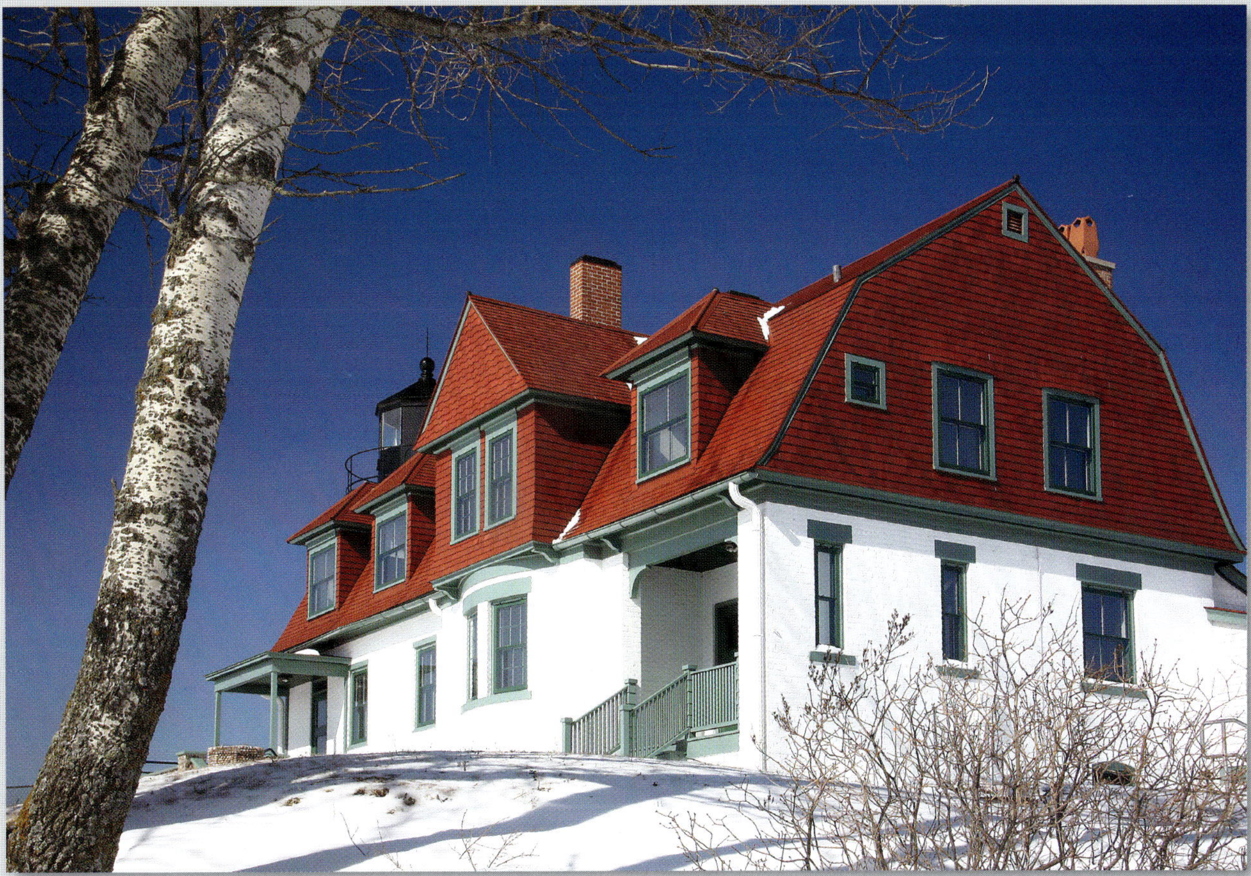

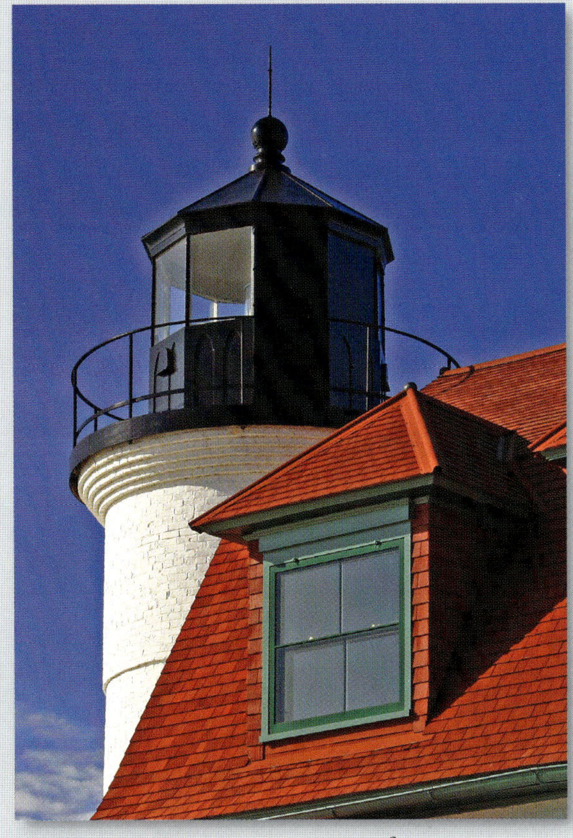

Pt. Betsie 3 *Framed by birch*

Pt. Betsie 5 *Close up with long lens*

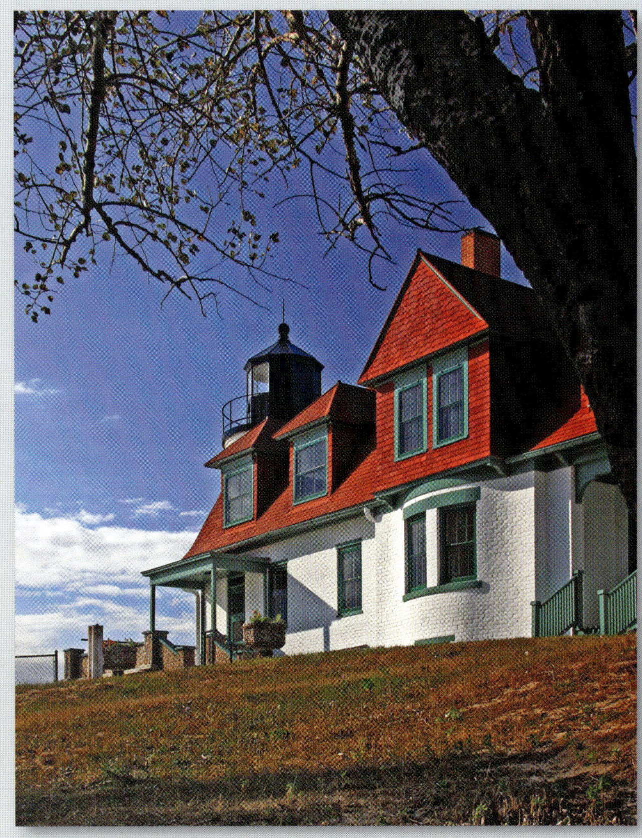

Pt. Betsie 4 *Framed by birch*

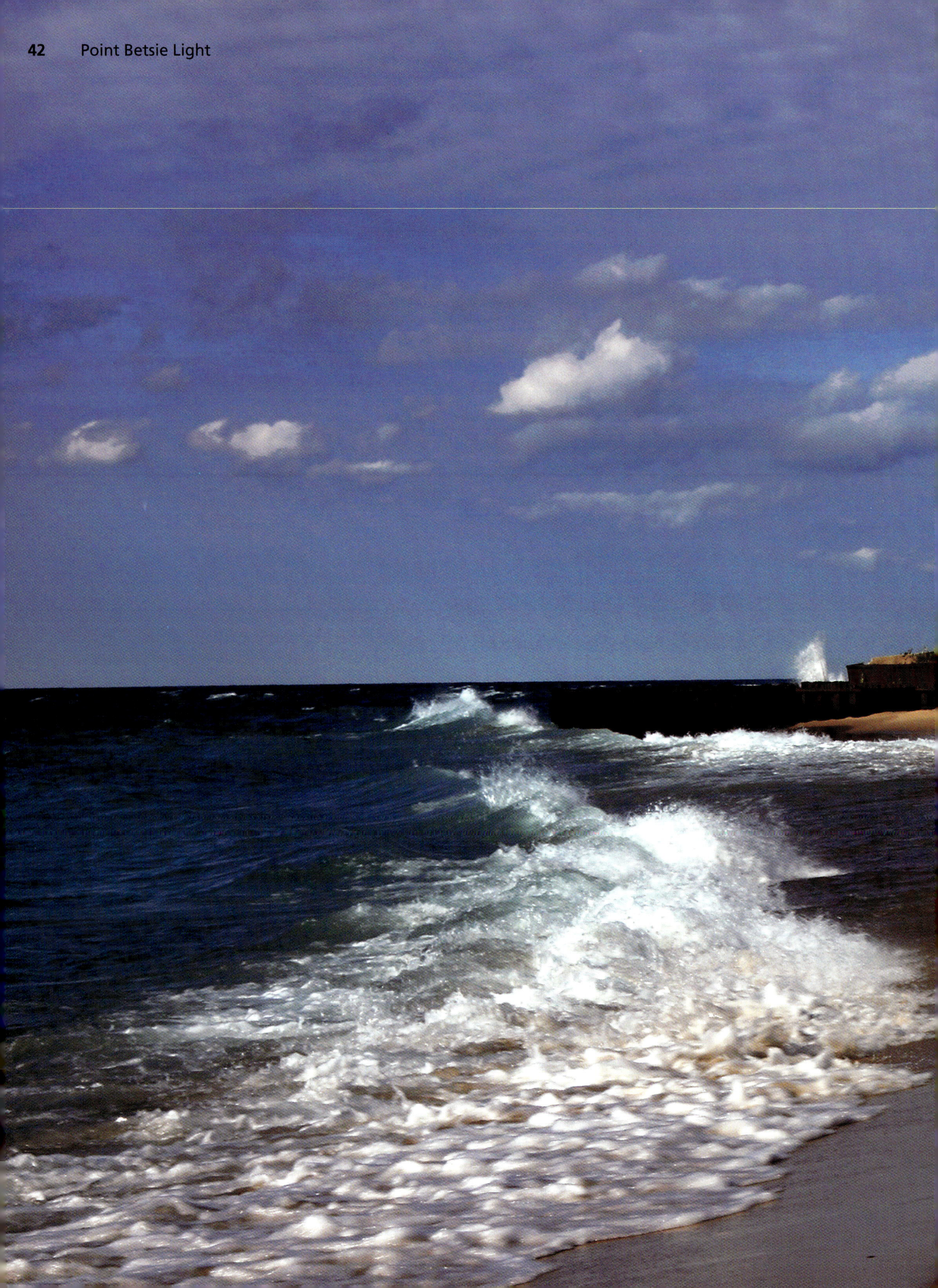

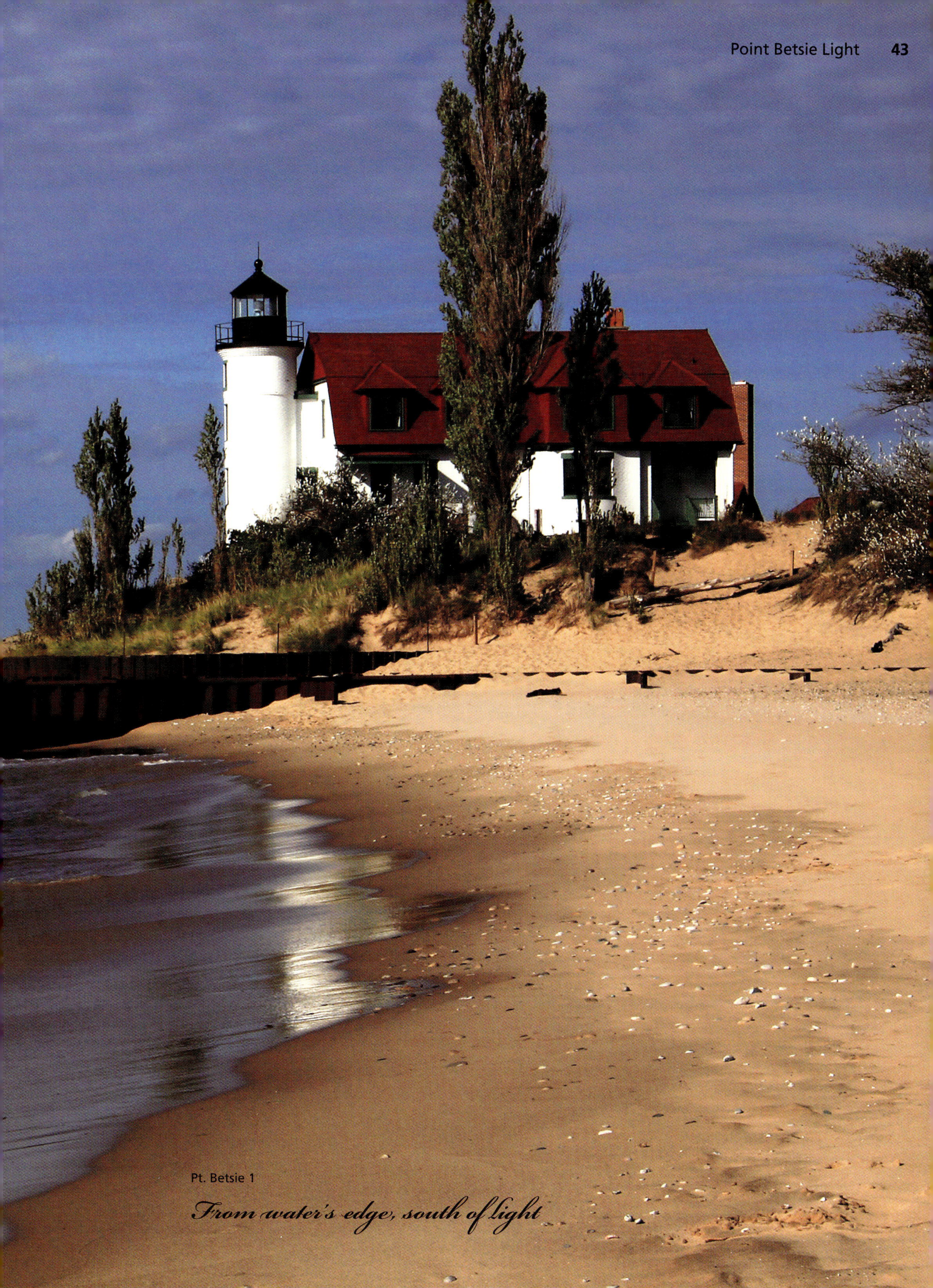

Pt. Betsie 1

From water's edge, south of light

Grand Traverse Light

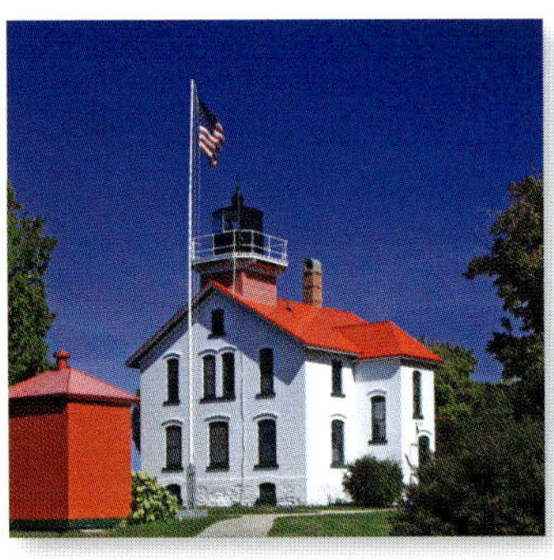

"Cat's Head"

DISTINGUISHING FEATURES

Grand Traverse Light is also known as Cat's Head because it is located at Cat's Head Point at the tip of Leelanau Peninsula. The light tower protrudes through the top of an attractive two-story keeper's house and its bright red roof provides plenty of color.

BEST TIME OF DAY

Lighting conditions are good in the morning and in the afternoon. Afternoon is probably better due to the location of the trees.

SUGGESTED COMPOSITIONS

This lighthouse sits well back from the shore, making it possible to walk around all sides. There are many trees of varying heights surrounding the area that can be used for framing or simply as openings **(1)**. In the afternoon, very nice images can be captured from spots near the fog signal building **(3)**. From the same vicinity, make the sidewalk a strong leading line to the light **(2)**. In the morning, include the old lifeboat on the east side for foreground interest **(4)**. The beach surrounds the lighthouse on two sides. Walk among the rocks and grasses and look for openings in the trees to frame the lantern room.

There are several maple trees near the lighthouse providing fall color in early October.

SUNSET/SUNRISE

Successful sunset or sunrise shots will be very difficult owing to the thick trees and bushes east and west of the lighthouse.

DIRECTIONS

From M 22 in Northport, drive north on M 201 that changes to County Rd. 640 and changes again to County Rd. 629. At the end of the road is Leelanau State Park after a total of about 8.5 miles. The lighthouse is located within the park where there is a large parking lot. This is a Michigan State Park with vehicle entrance fee.

GPS coordinates: 45.209N, 85.550W.

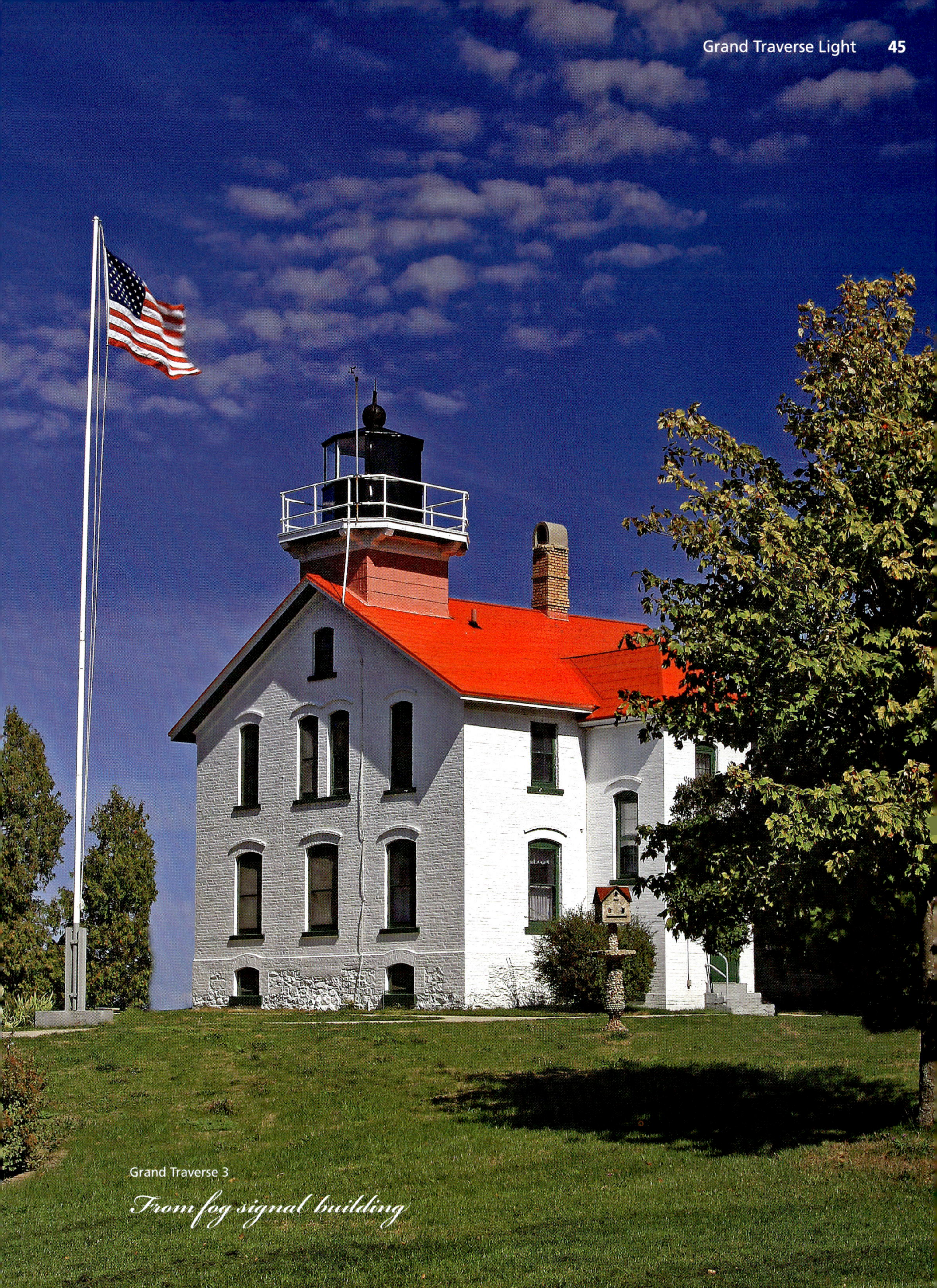

Grand Traverse 3
From fog signal building

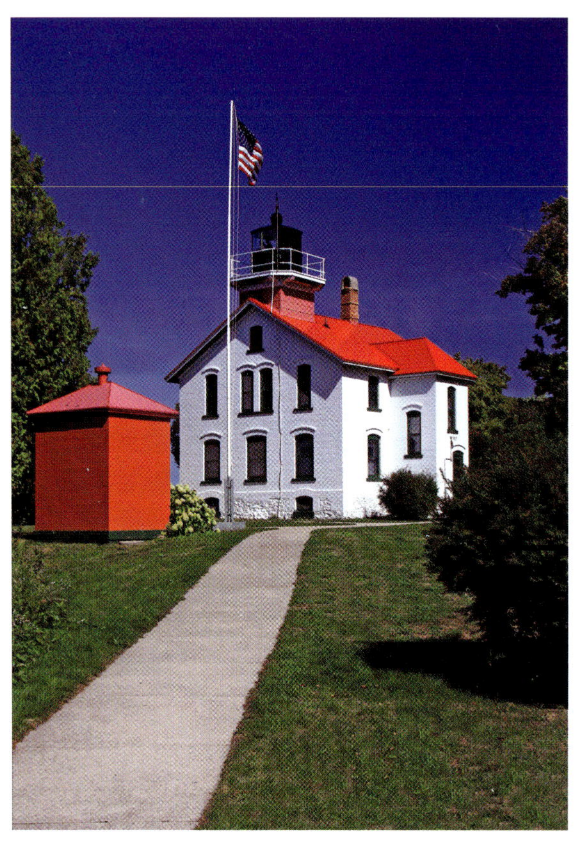

Grand Traverse 2 *With sidewalk as leading line*

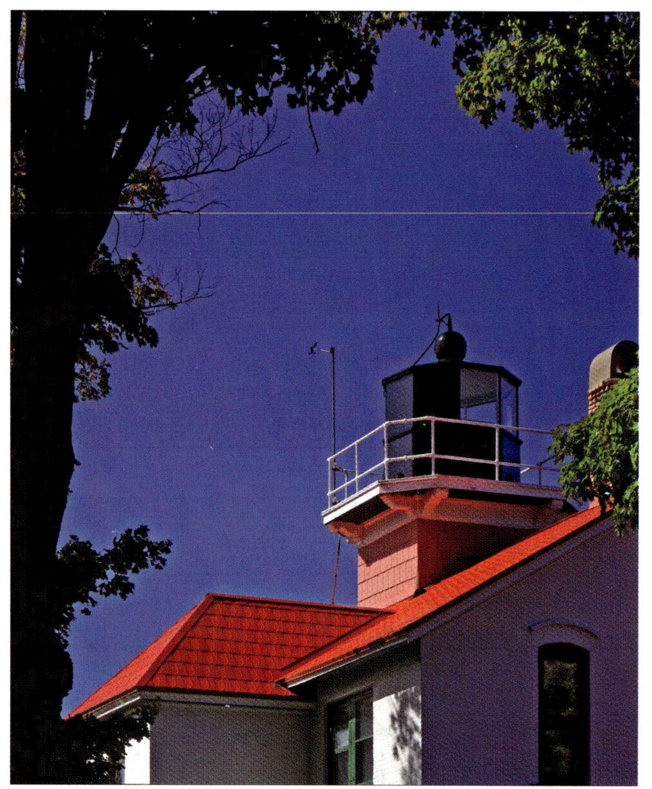

Grand Traverse 1 *Framed tower*

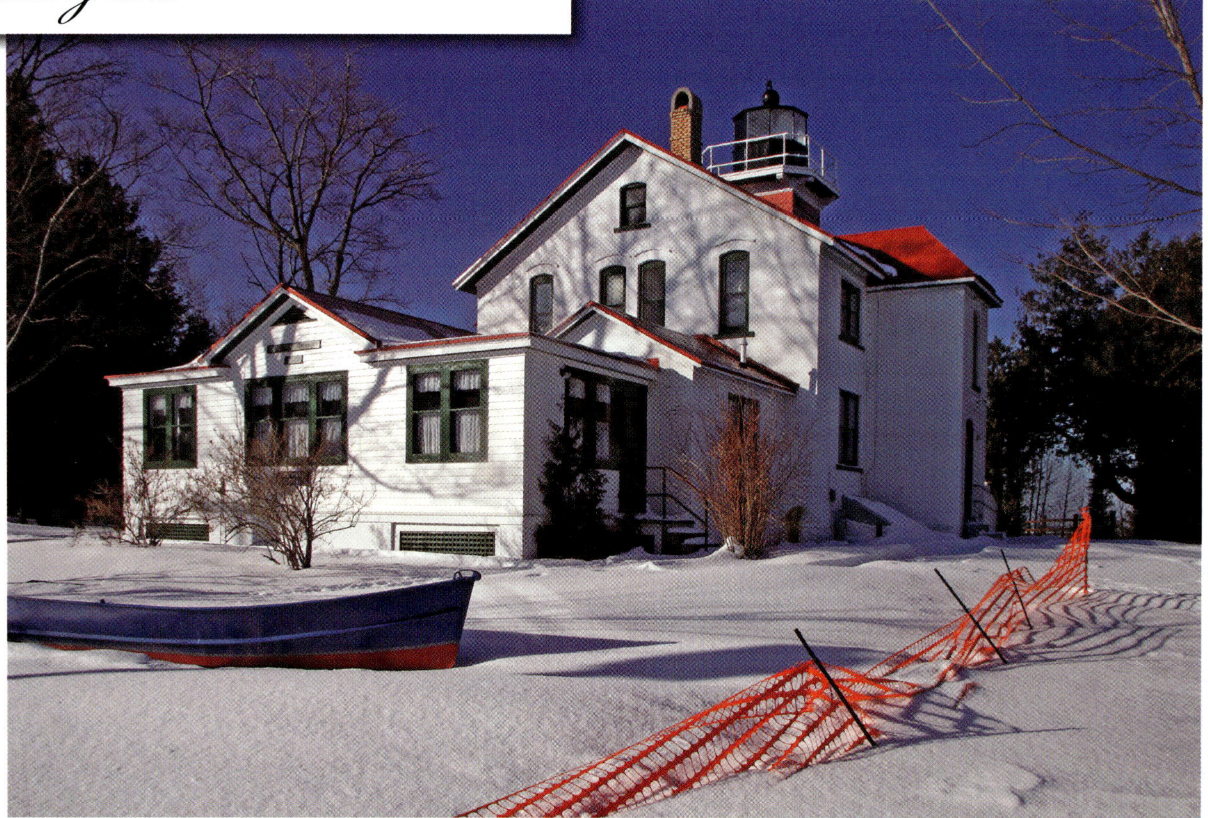

Grand Traverse 4 *East side with lifeboat*

Old Mission Point Light

Near Old Mission, Michigan

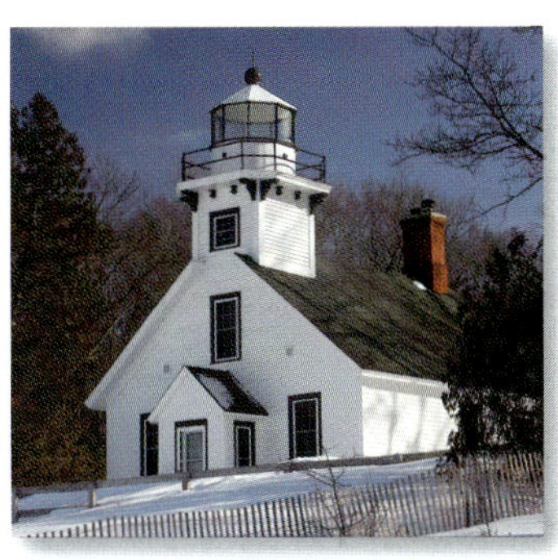

"Schoolhouse"

DISTINGUISHING FEATURES

The simplicity and setting of this small lighthouse make it a fine photographic subject. The shape of the keeper's dwelling and protruding light tower is like an old one room schoolhouse. Surrounded by large trees, it looks down a rather steep embankment to a sandy beach and rock filled shoreline. The pure white siding and black trim provide the components for an excellent black and white image **(5).**

BEST TIME OF DAY

Since the lighthouse faces north, the front is shadowed virtually all day most of the year. On sunny days, morning or afternoon is acceptable, positioning the camera so as not to be shooting into the sun. Bright overcast days would be ideal to capture the details, while   eliminating or minimizing the sky in the frame.

SUGGESTED COMPOSITIONS

From the beach, shoot at an angle to show the front and one side **(1)** & **(2).** Also take some at close range **(3).** Try some shots straight up the wooden stairs from different distances. West of the lighthouse, compose images using the trees for framing **(4)** & **(5).** There are maple trees around the light so fall colors are possible here in early October.

SUNSET/SUNRISE

The short lighthouse is completely surrounded on the east, west and south by tall trees, therefore a decent sunset or sunrise image would be very difficult.

DIRECTIONS

From the junction of US 31 and M 37 in Traverse City, turn north on M 37 and follow it about 18 miles to the end where there is a parking lot close to the lighthouse.

GPS coordinates: 44.991N, 85.479W.

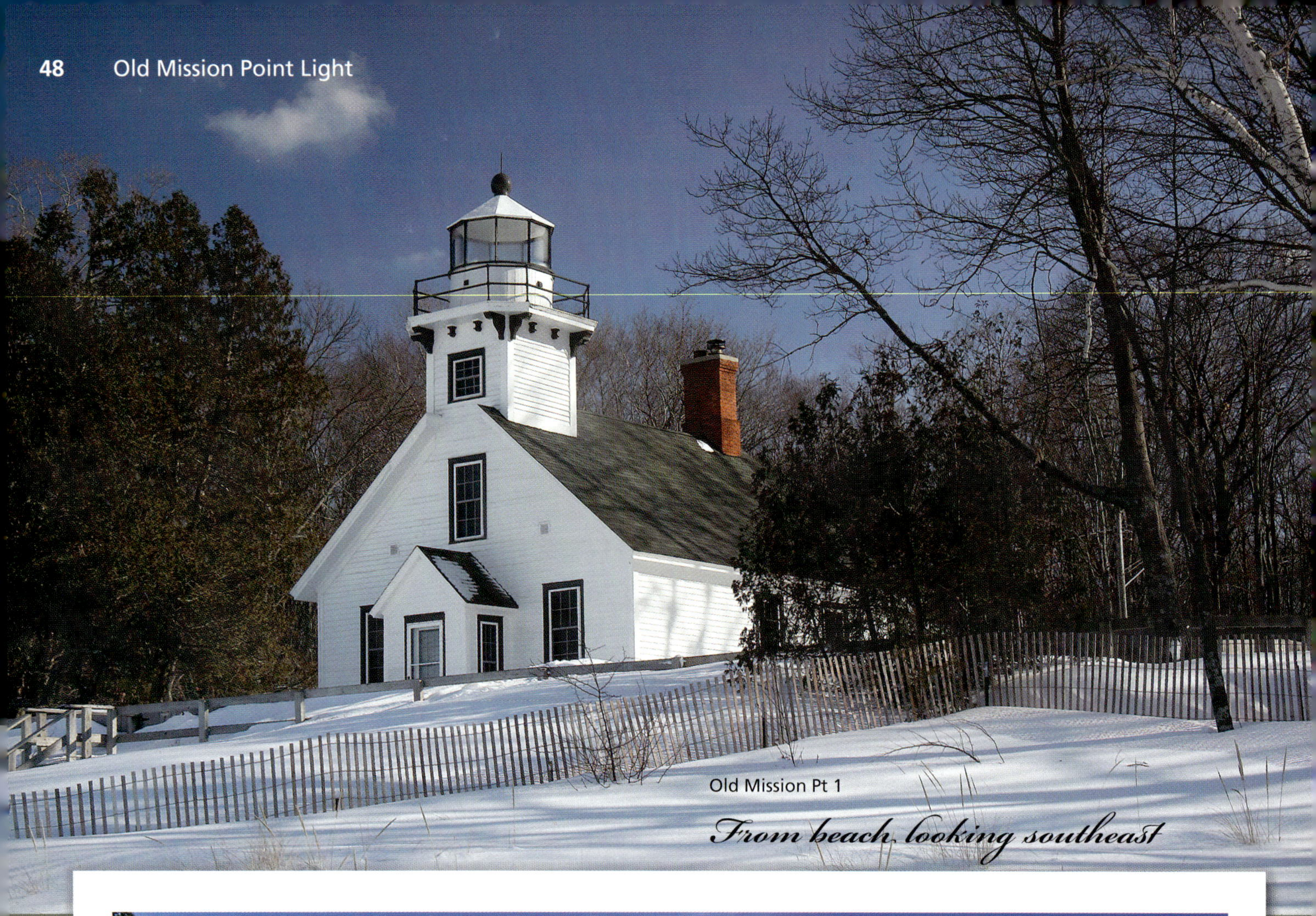

Old Mission Pt 1

From beach looking southeast

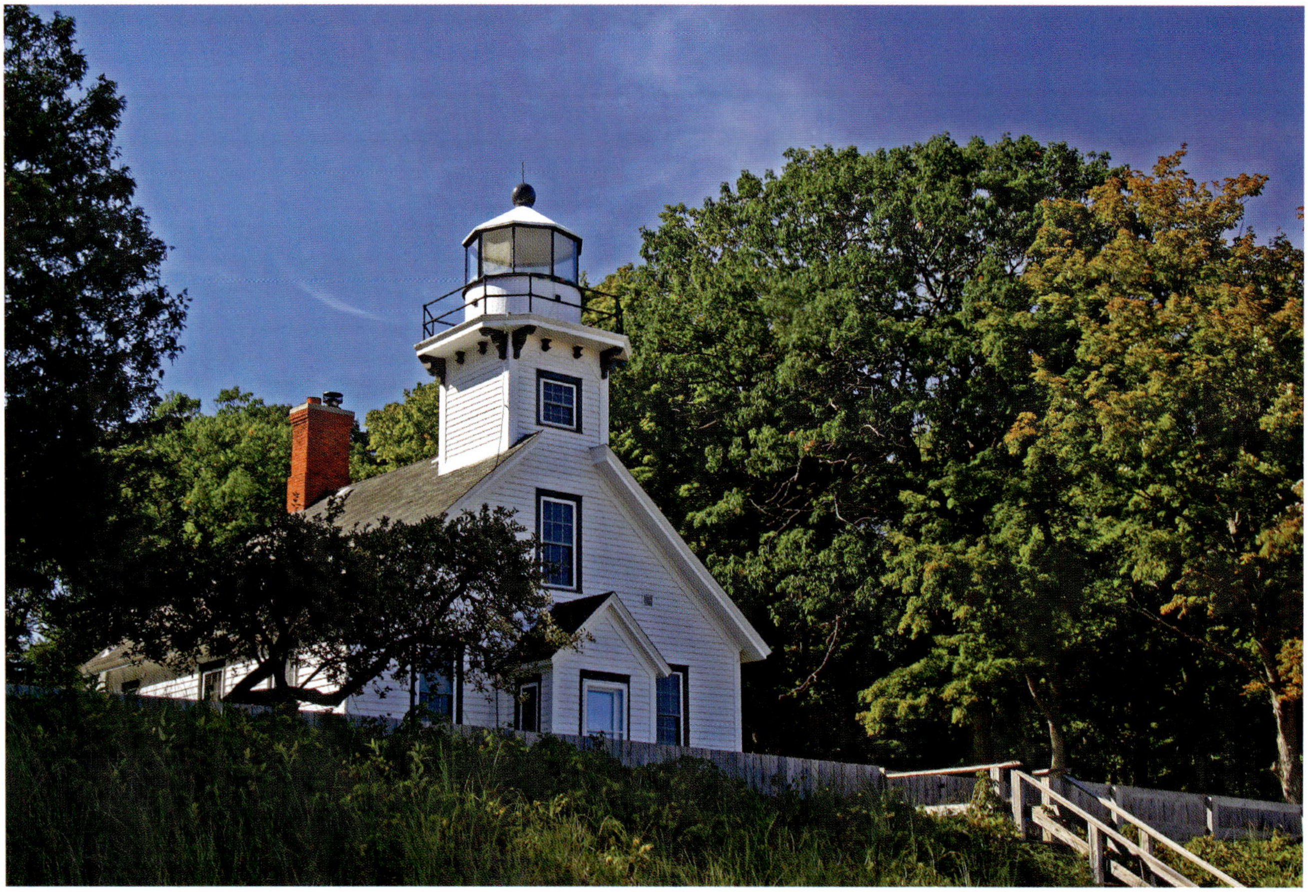

Old Mission Pt 2 *From beach looking southwest*

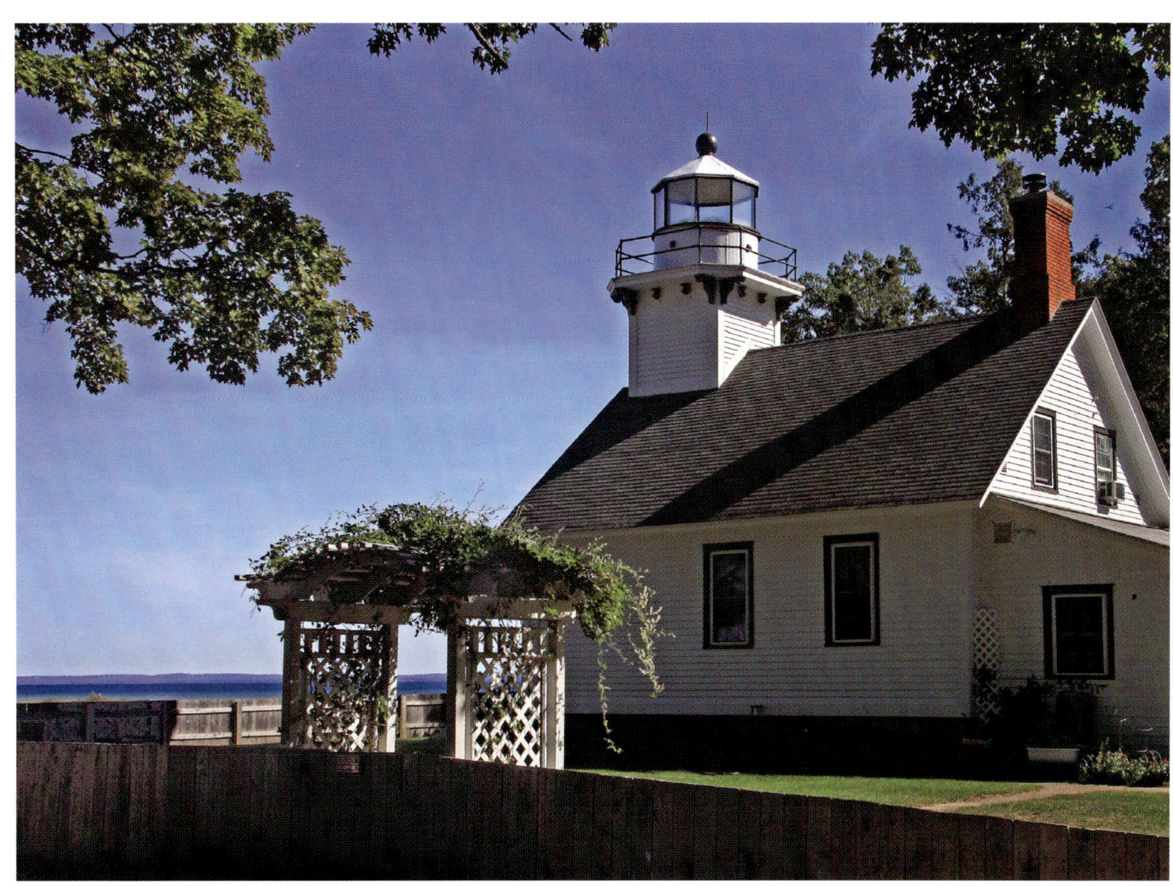

Old Mission Pt 4 *Framed by trees, southwest side*

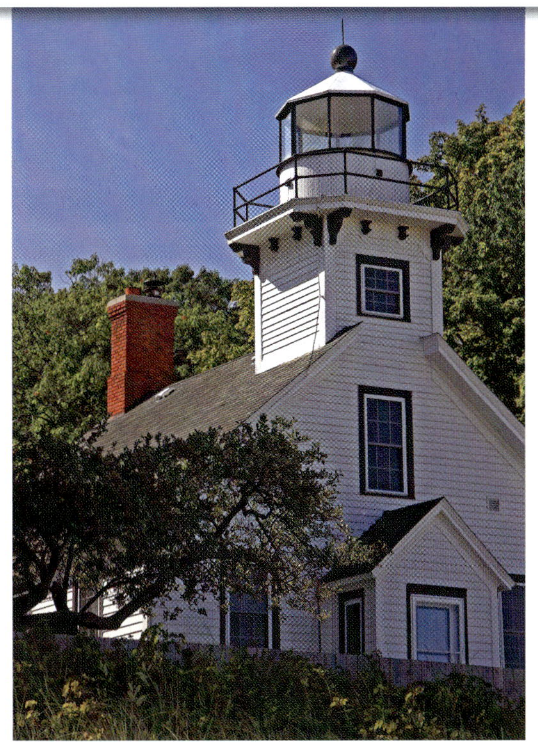

Old Mission Pt 3 *Close to light looking southwest*

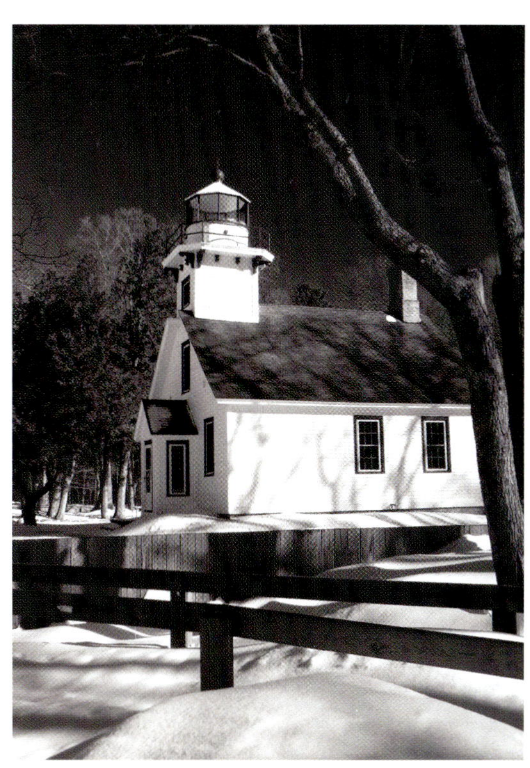

Old Mission Pt 5 *Framed by tree, northwest side*

Old Mackinac Point Light

Mackinaw City, Michigan

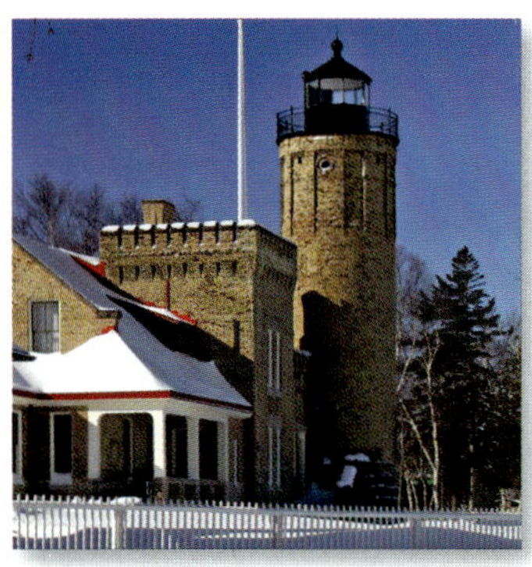

"Fortress by the Bridge"

DISTINGUISHING FEATURES

Looking more like a fortress or a castle, this elegant structure is a popular subject for photographers and travelers alike. The red roof of the keeper's quarters makes it very colorful. It also has the advantage of being accessible from all sides. And who can resist photographing the famous Mackinac Bridge while there **(6)**.

BEST TIME OF DAY

Afternoon and morning light both work well here.

SUGGESTED COMPOSITIONS

A white picket fence surrounds the lighthouse area (fee charged for admission), but it is easy to shoot over the fence. Pleasing compositions of this beautiful light are possible looking northwest or northeast, with or without the picket fence in the foreground **(1)**. There are numerous trees around the perimeter that can be used for framing **(2)** & **(3)**. For images of the entire building, horizontal formats are usually better. Also zoom in close for some of the interesting details. For example, try a vertical shot of the round light tower by itself and include some of the red slanted roof for color **(4)**.

SUNSET/SUNRISE

Both sunset and sunrise images are possible using vantage points between trees or buildings **(5)**.

DIRECTIONS

From I 75 south of the bridge, take exit 339 to Nicolet Avenue. Follow it north to the end at Huron Avenue, turn right and go a short distance to the parking area close to the lighthouse.

GPS coordinates: 45.787N, 84.730W.

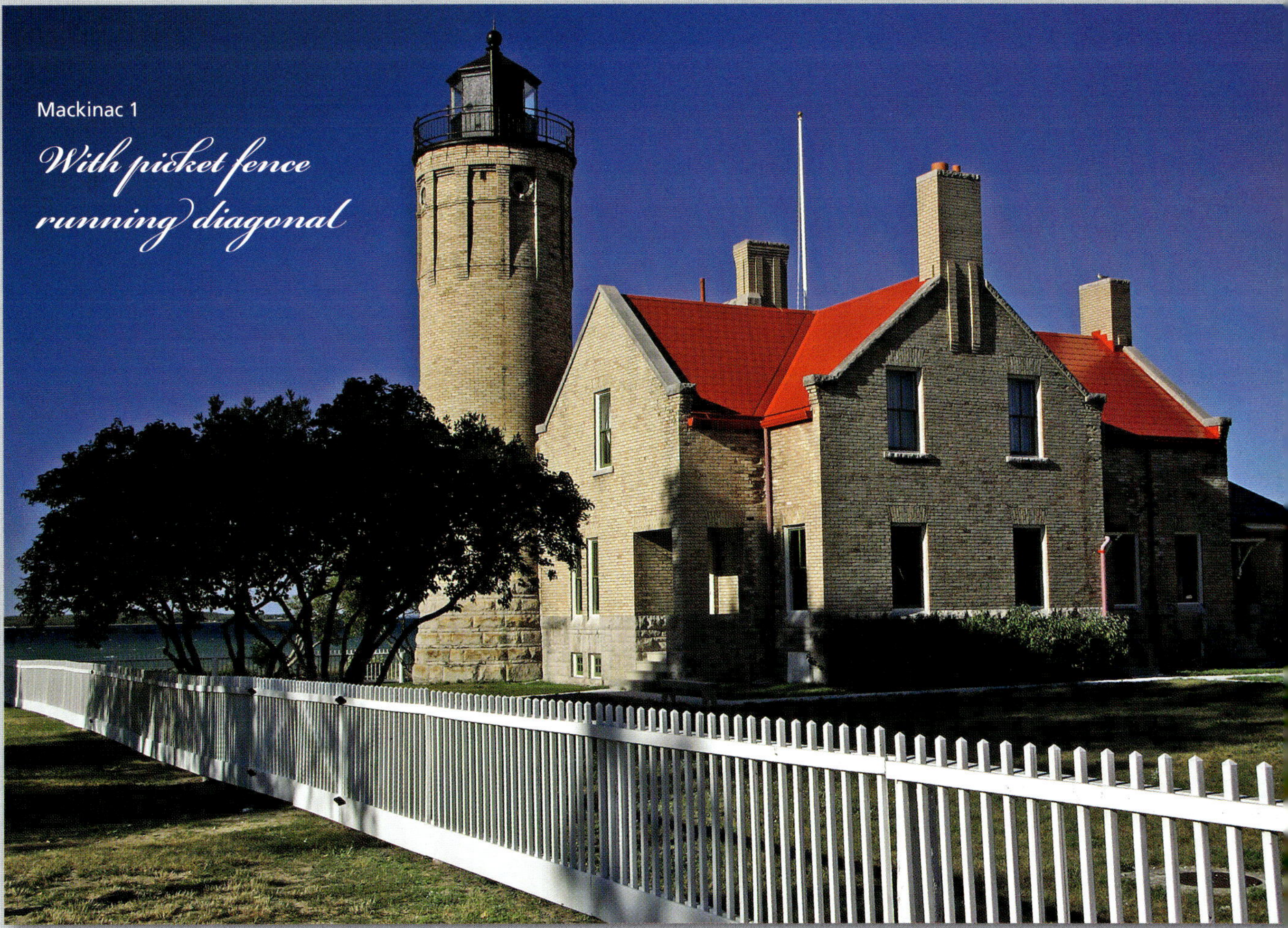

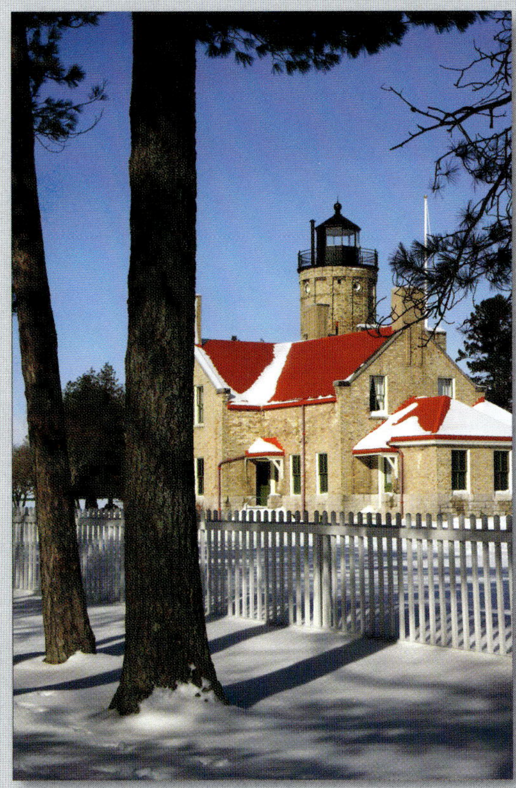

Mackinac 1
With picket fence running diagonal

Mackinac 2 *Framed by pine trees, south side*

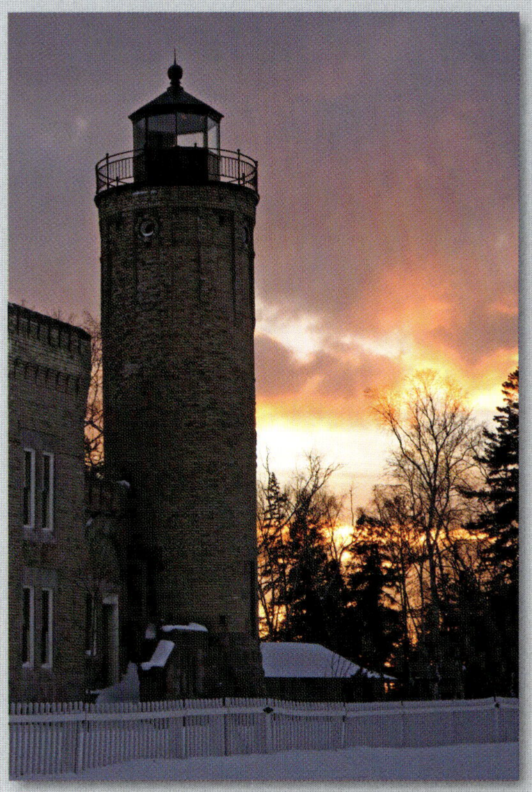

Mackinac 5 *Sunset, north side*

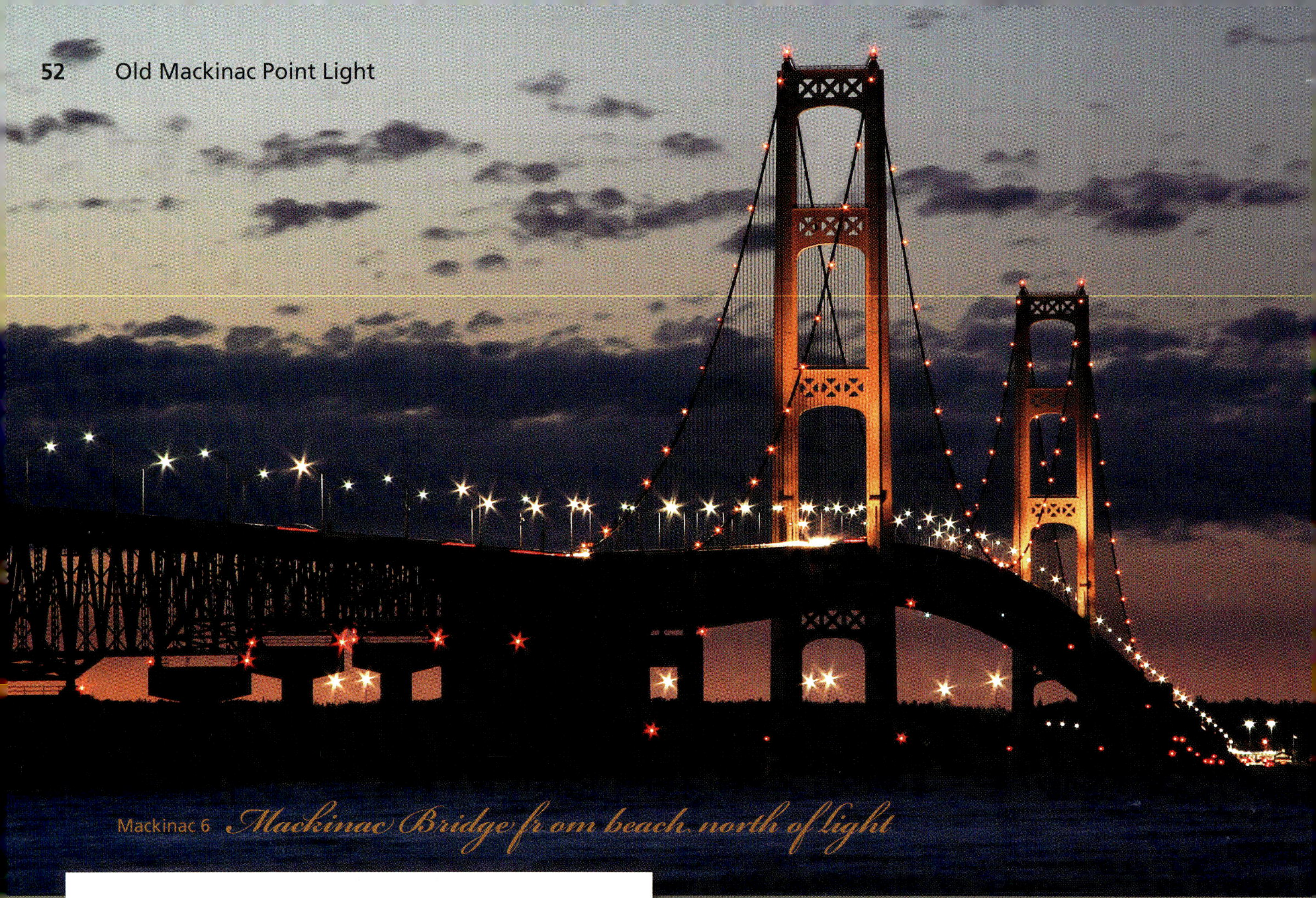

Mackinac 6 *Mackinac Bridge from beach, north of light*

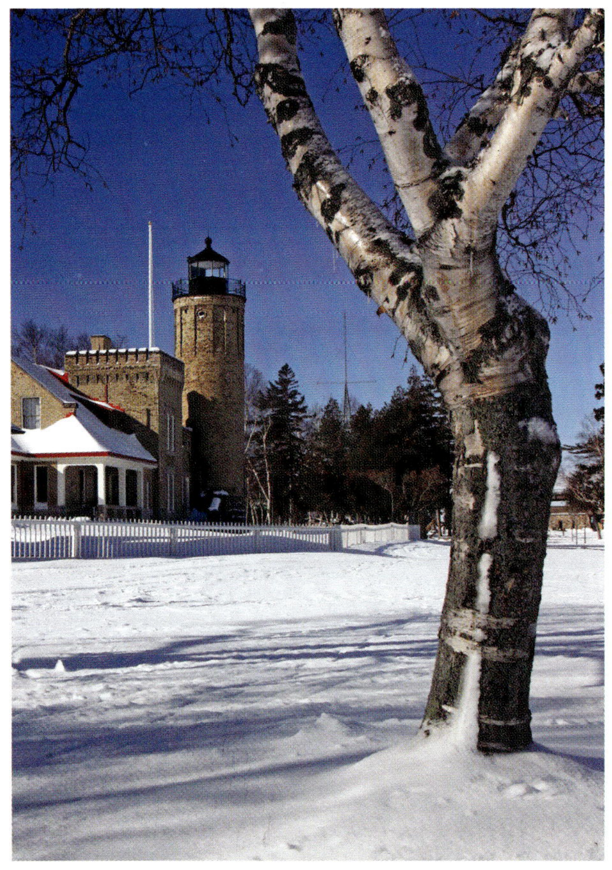

Mackinac 3 *Framed by birch, north side*

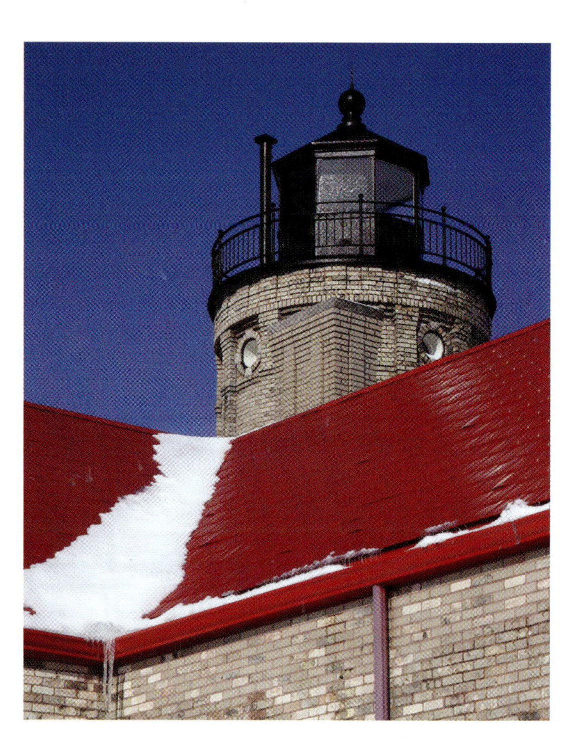

Mackinac 4 *Close up with long lens*

Cheboygan Crib Light

Cheboygan, Michigan

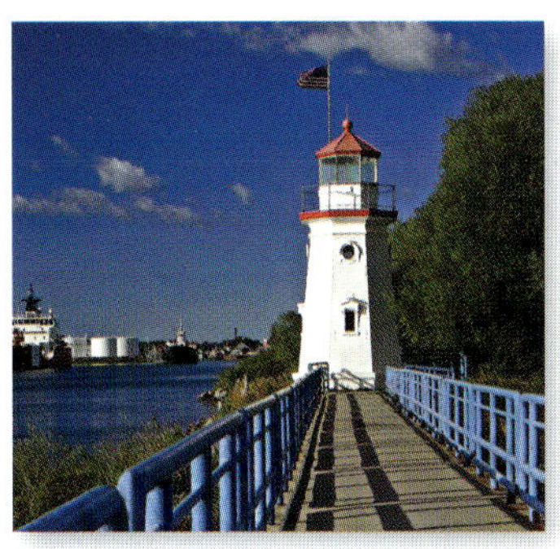

"Red, White and Blue"

DISTINGUISHING FEATURES

This picturesque short light has a patriotic look with white tower, red trim and blue railings. The long walkway with blue guardrails juts out to the lake, creating a colorful perspective when looking back to the light.

BEST TIME OF DAY

Morning hours are by far the best time, but afternoon will work for some shots.

SUGGESTED COMPOSITIONS

The blue railings on the narrow walkway northeast of the light make excellent leading lines and the shadows of the railings make an interesting pattern. In the morning, take several images fairly close with wide angle or normal lenses and further out with longer lenses for different perspectives **(1)**. In the afternoon, shoot from west of the light, and include the railing of the walkway and the shoreline **(2)**. Also, try close shots from the west and south to capture the nice detail of the lighthouse **(3)**. There are trees nearby that can be used for framing **(4)**. Since this is a short light, both horizontal and vertical formats work very well.

SUNSET/SUNRISE

A sunrise image is possible from the shoreline west of the light.

DIRECTIONS

From M 23, just west of the Cheboygan River in downtown Cheboygan, turn north on Huron St. and go about .7 miles to Gordon Turner Park. The lighthouse is a short distance east of the parking lot.

GPS coordinates: 45.656N, 84.465W.

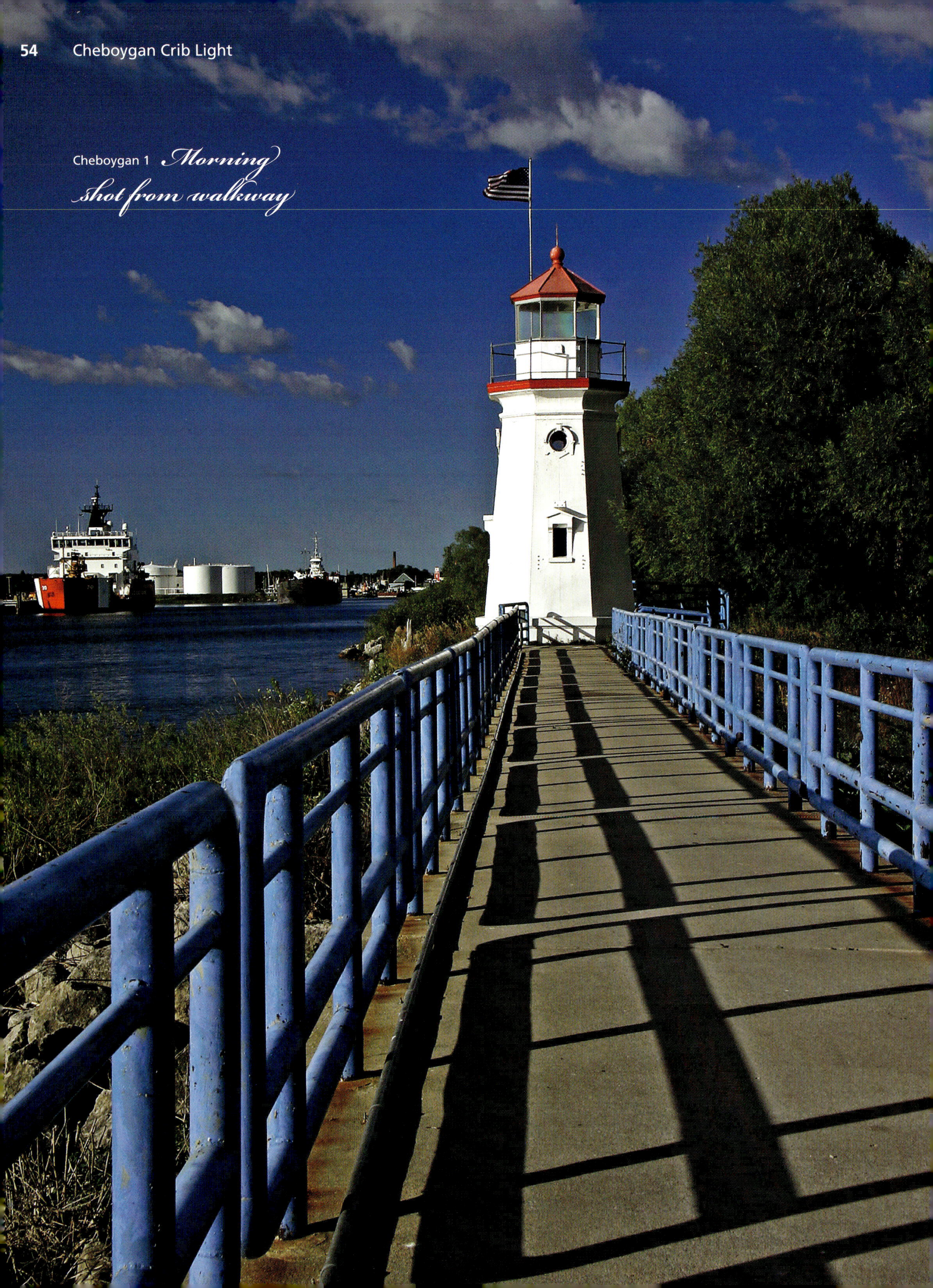
Cheboygan 1 *Morning shot from walkway*

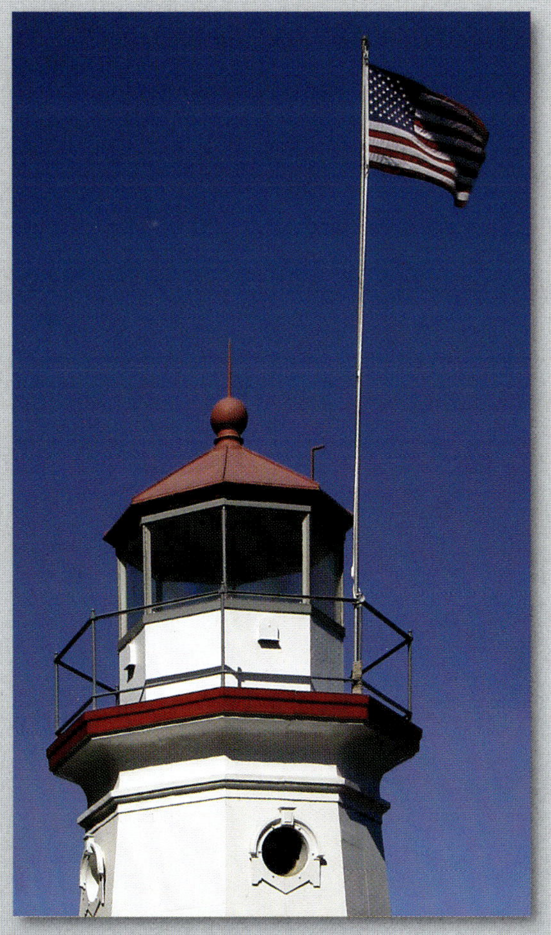

Cheboygan 3 *Close up, lantern room*

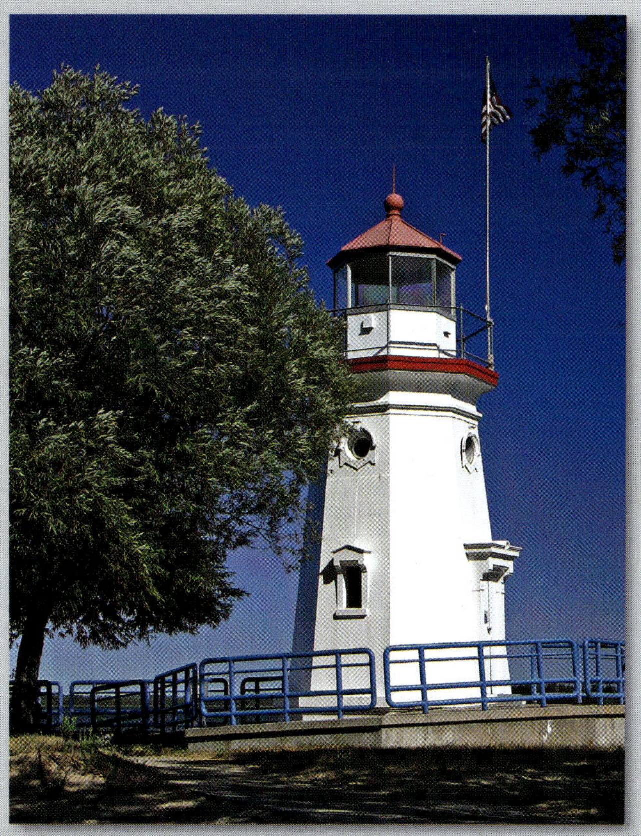

Cheboygan 4 *Close to light, south side*

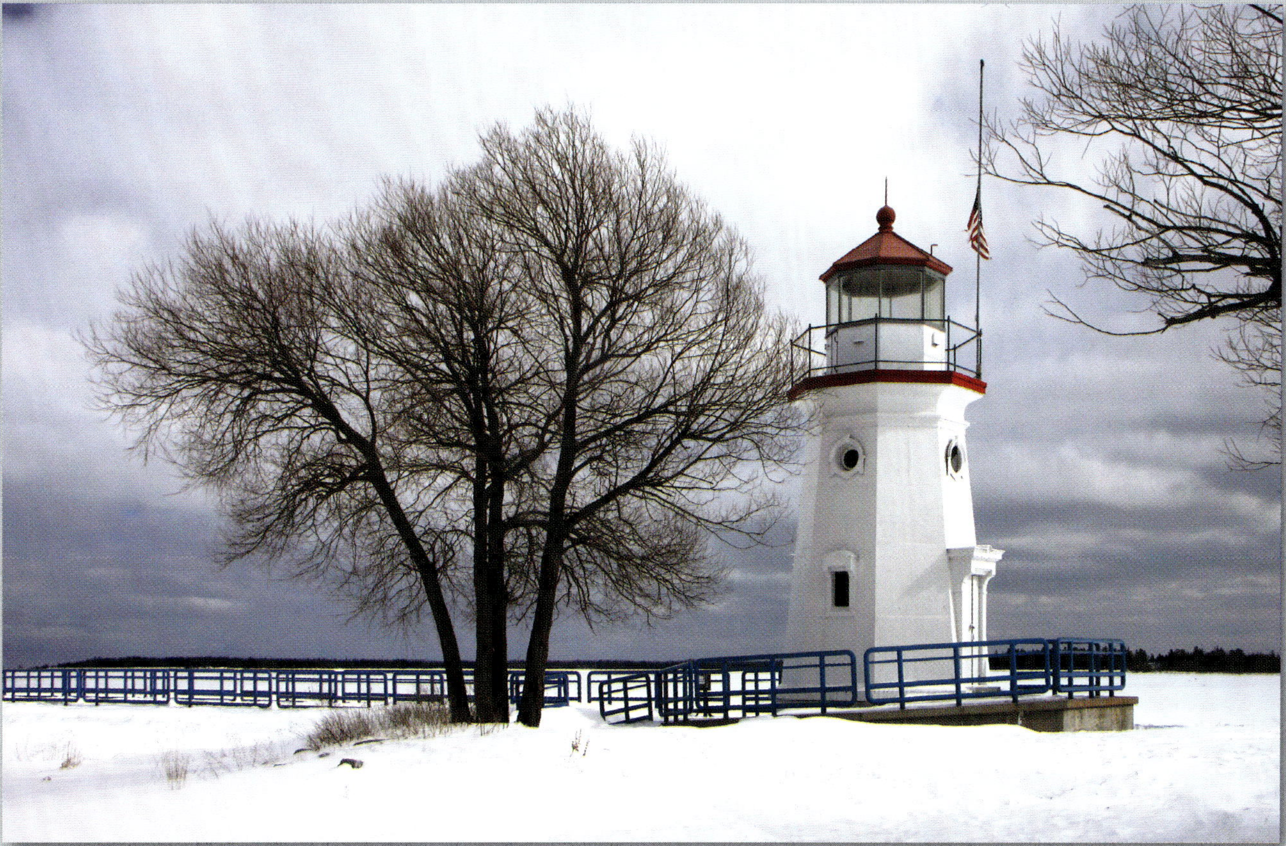

Cheboygan 2 *Afternoon shot, west of light*

Forty Mile Point Light

Near Rogers City, Michigan

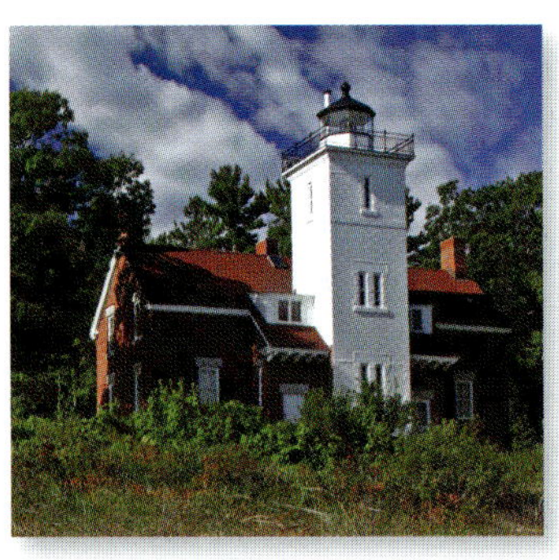

"A Square Deal"

DISTINGUISHING FEATURES

Forty Mile Point features a stark white square tower attached to a red brick keeper's house. This makes it a good black and white candidate **(5)** as well as color. A broad sand beach stretches out between the lighthouse and Lake Huron.

BEST TIME OF DAY

Morning light is definitely best when the lighthouse is illuminated from the eastern shore. Thick woods west of the light make shooting difficult from that direction in the afternoon.

SUGGESTED COMPOSITIONS

Southeast of the light is a small patch of sand and rocks which runs out toward the lake beyond the shoreline. This is a good spot to shoot back to the light while including the water **(2)**. Move up closer to the light to capture beach grasses in the foreground **(1)** & **(3)**. The lines and colors of the tower and peaked roofs contain elements for interesting close-ups **(4)**.

SUNSET/SUNRISE

Good sunrise or sunset shots will be very difficult here. The thick forest close to the light on the west prevents positioning for a sunrise and covers the house and most of the tower for a sunset.

DIRECTIONS

Drive about 6 miles north of Rogers City (or about 35 miles south of Cheboygan) on US 23 to a road to the east marked "Presque Isle County Lighthouse Park". It is a short distance to a parking lot near the lighthouse.

GPS coordinates: 45.486N, 83.913W.

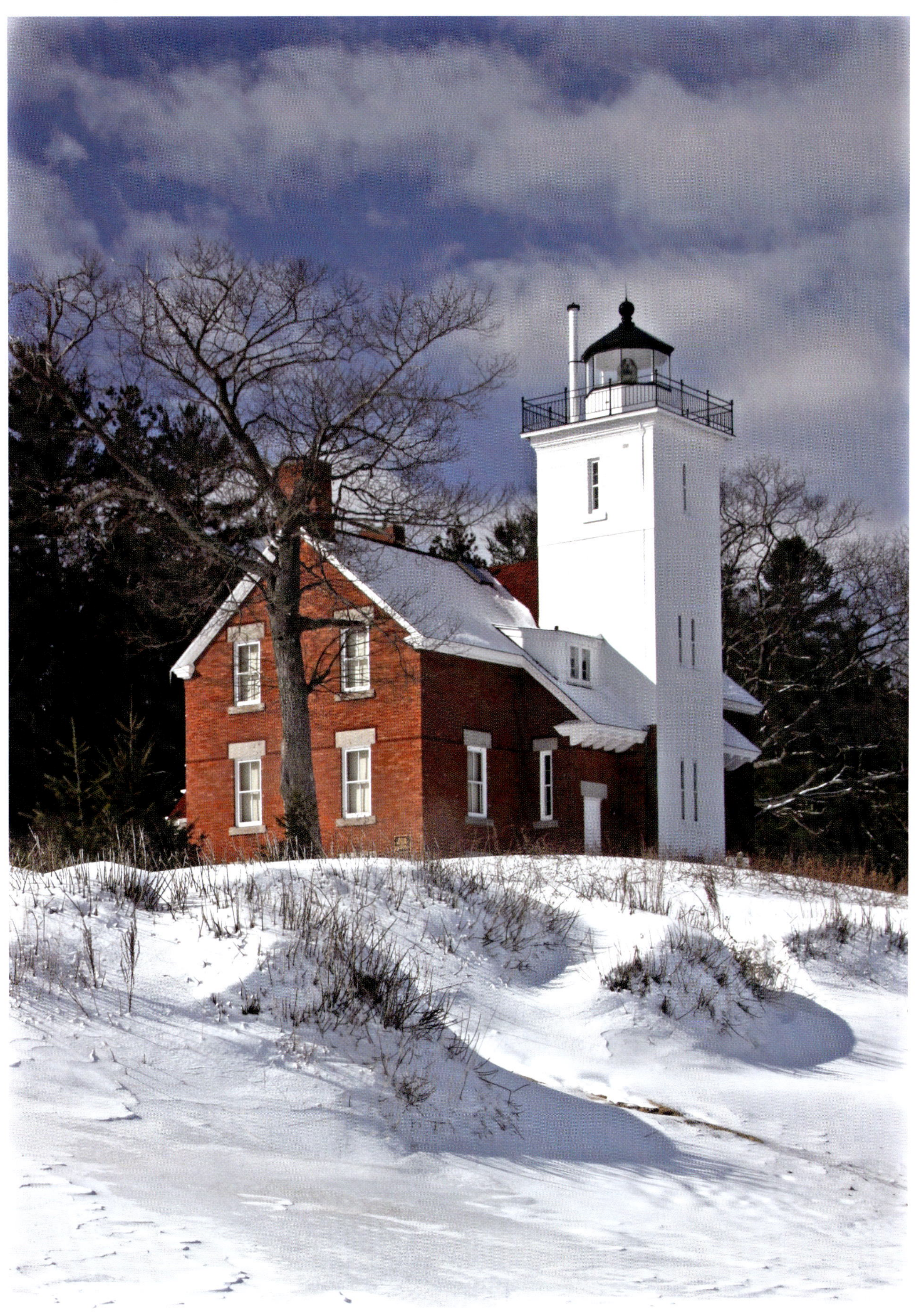

Forty Mile Pt 1 *With snow and protruding grass*

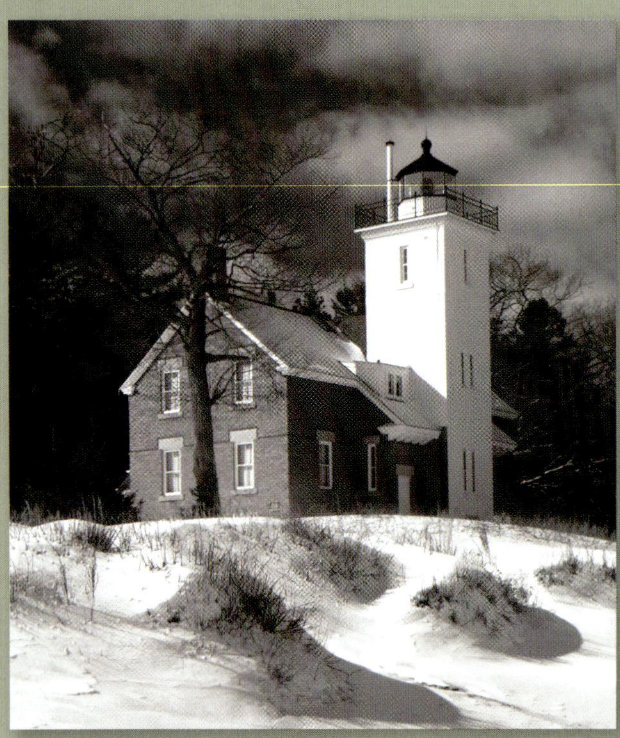

Forty Mile Pt 5 *Same as No. 1 in black & white*

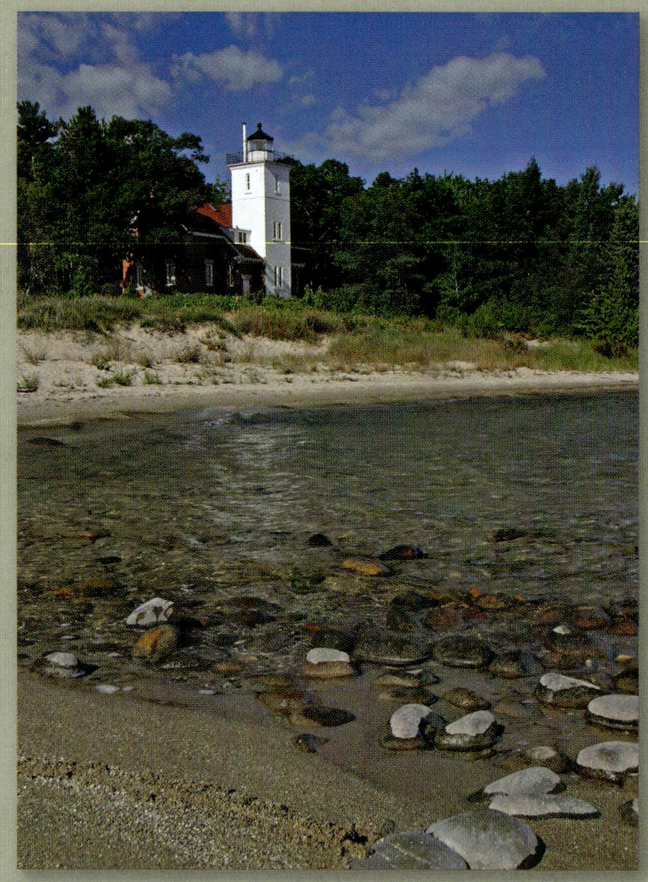

Forty Mile Pt 2 *From sand bar*

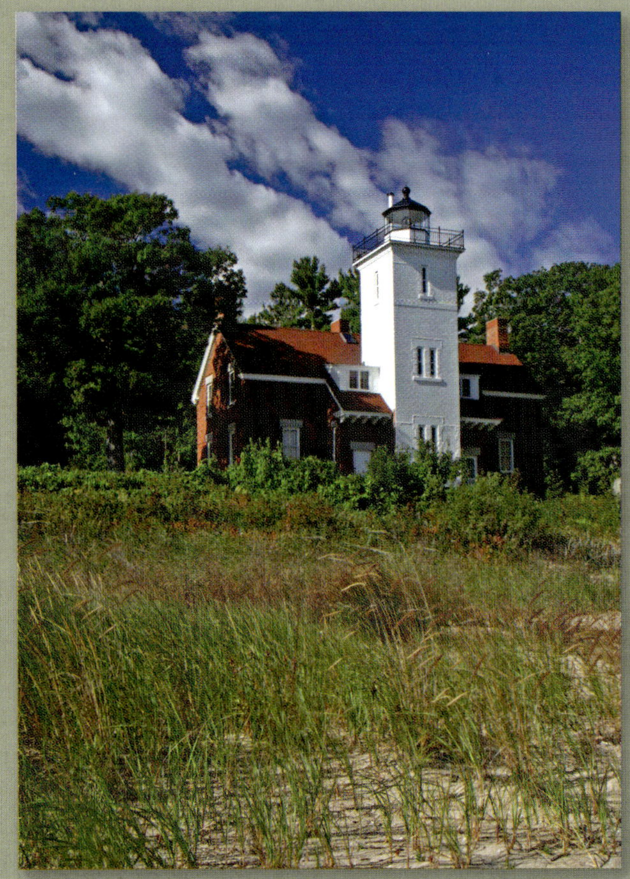

Forty Mile Pt 3 *With beach grass in foreground*

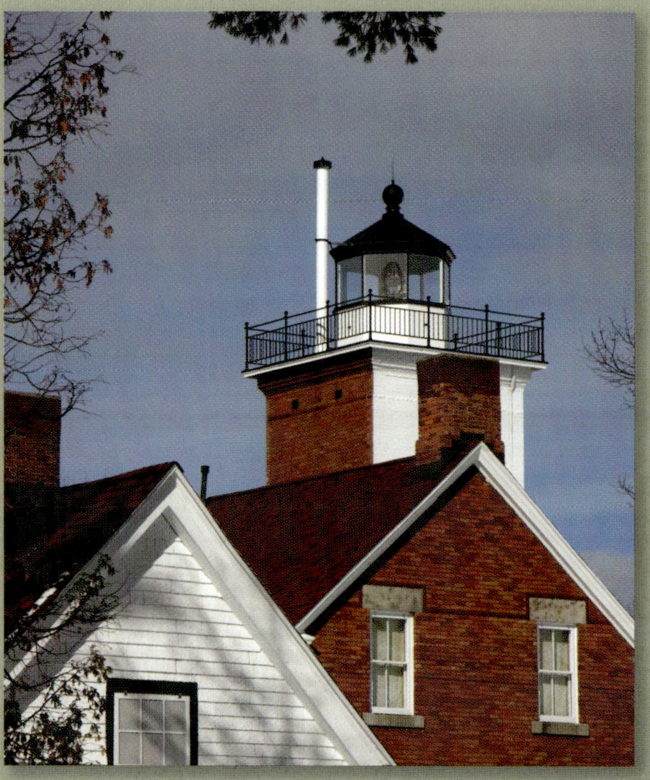

Forty Mile Pt 4 *Close up, tower and roof tops*

Old Presque Isle Light

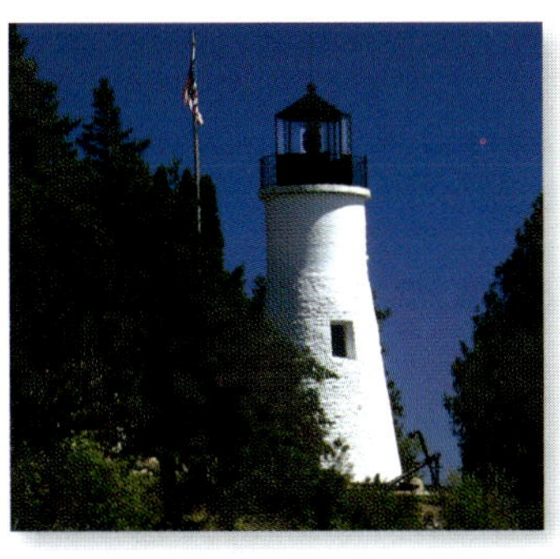

"Short and Sweet"

DISTINGUISHING FEATURES

The original (1840) lighthouse at Presque Isle is short in stature but long on charm. The stone tower has an unusual conical shape. The white keeper's cottage and the white lighthouse with black top also make ideal monochrome subjects **(5).**

BEST TIME OF DAY

The morning and afternoon light are both acceptable, but early morning is the best time.

SUGGESTED COMPOSITIONS

Because this is a short lighthouse, horizontal formats work well but take verticals also, close **(4)** and further out **(2).** Use the trees for framing where possible. From the shoreline, get down low with a wide angle lens to capture the rocks in the foreground **(1).** There is a bronze bell under a peaked canopy next to the lighthouse that can add interest to your image **(3).**

SUNSET/SUNRISE

Because of the limited height of the tower and the number of trees around it, a good sunrise image will be difficult to achieve, but it is possible from a small open area northwest of the keeper's cottage.

DIRECTIONS

From US 23 about 14 miles east of Rogers City (or about 21 miles north of Alpena), turn east on Highway 638 and go about 4 miles to a "T" at Grand Lake Rd. Turn left and drive about 1 mile to the sign for Old Presque Isle Light and turn right. It is a short distance to a parking area near the light.

In the winter, the short road to the light is closed. However, you can park by the side of Grand Lake Rd. and take the easy 5 minute walk to the lighthouse. Presque Isle Light is about 1 mile further north.

GPS coordinates: 45.342N, 83.478W.

Old Presque Isle 2 *South of light from beach.*

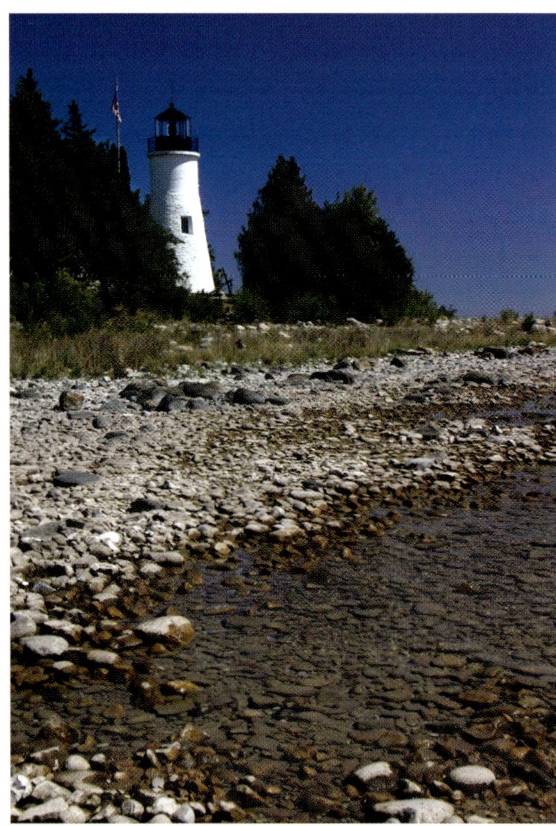

Old Presque Isle 1

From the Rocky Shore

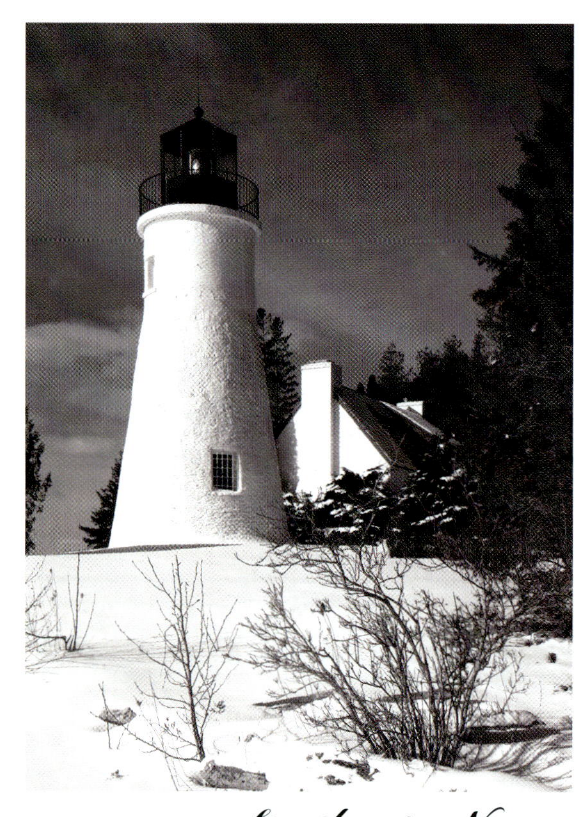

Old Presque Isle 5 *Similar to No. 4 in black & white*

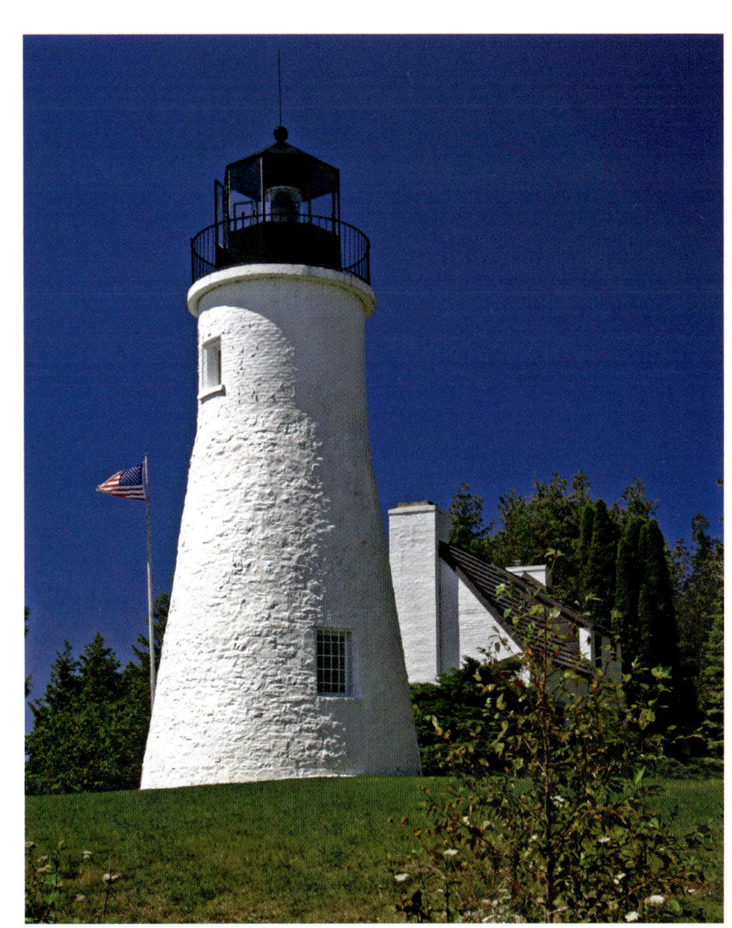

Old Presque Isle 4

Close to light, east side

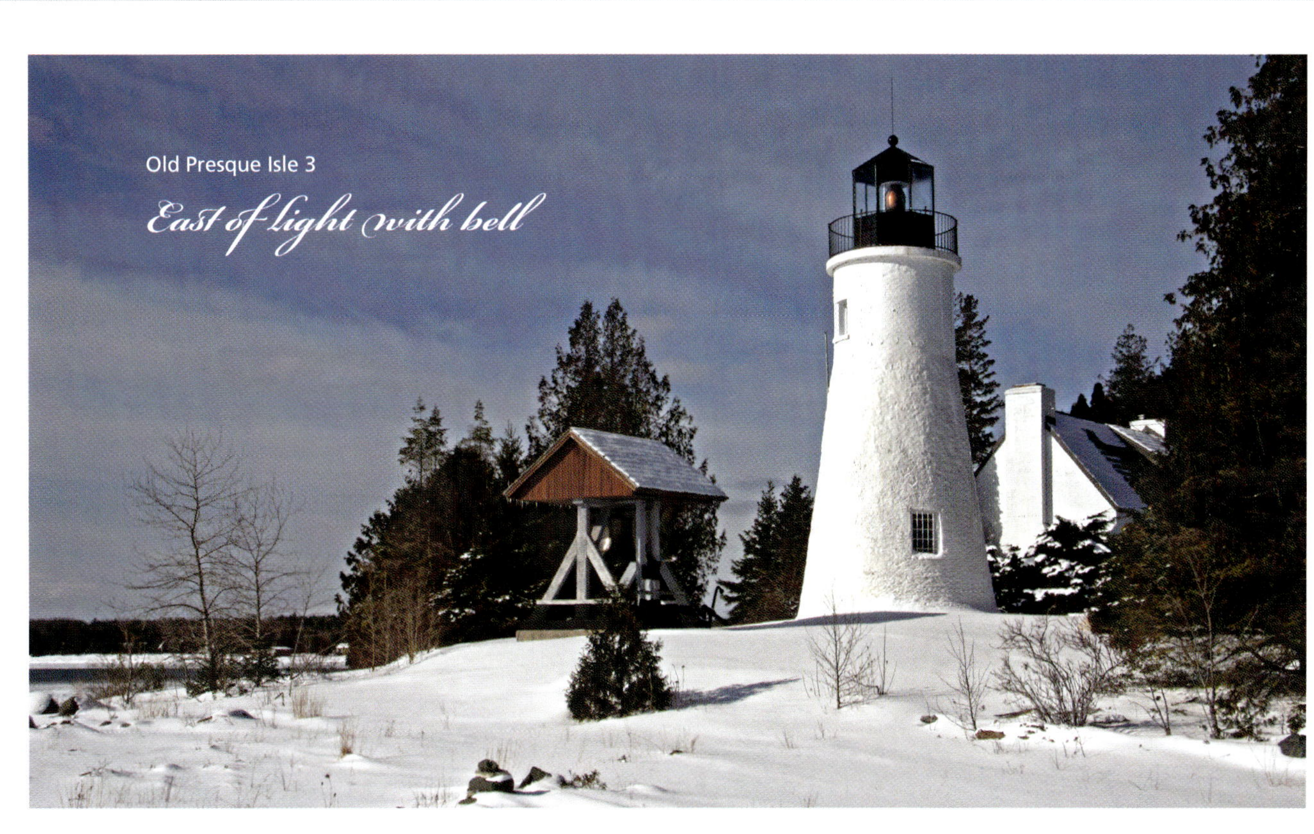

Old Presque Isle 3

East of light with bell

Presque Isle Light

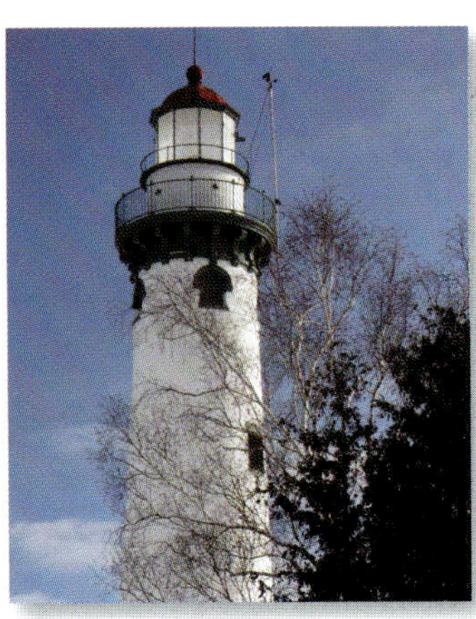

"Big and Tall"

DISTINGUISHING FEATURES

The "New" (1871) Presque Isle Light is an attractive tall lighthouse with an ornate parapet and red-capped lantern room. It sits in a park-like setting surrounded by a thick forest of cedars and pines.

BEST TIME OF DAY

Morning and afternoon hours are both good as the lighthouse is accessible on all sides.

SUGGESTED COMPOSITIONS

This very tall light is located well back from Lake Huron and is surrounded on all sides by thick woods with limited open spaces between it and the trees. Therefore, it is very challenging to find creative compositions. The practical format is vertical but some "keystoning" of the tower is likely. Walk around the edge of the tree line and look for interesting foregrounds. One possibility is the white chain link between posts on the entrance side **(1).** There are side roads leading to the water east and west of the lighthouse. Walk a short distance and shoot back to the light for images framed by the trees on each side **(2).** The detached keeper's house has unusual architecture and can be photographed with the lighthouse looming behind it **(3).** The top of the light tower has beautiful, colorful features, so close up shots with a long lens are recommended **(4).**

SUNSET/SUNRISE

Sunrise or sunset images are possible but due to the thick forest, only the top portion of the tower will be silhouetted against the sky.

DIRECTIONS

See the directions for "Old Presque Isle Light". Presque Isle Light is about one mile further north.

GPS coordinates: 45.356N, 83.491W.

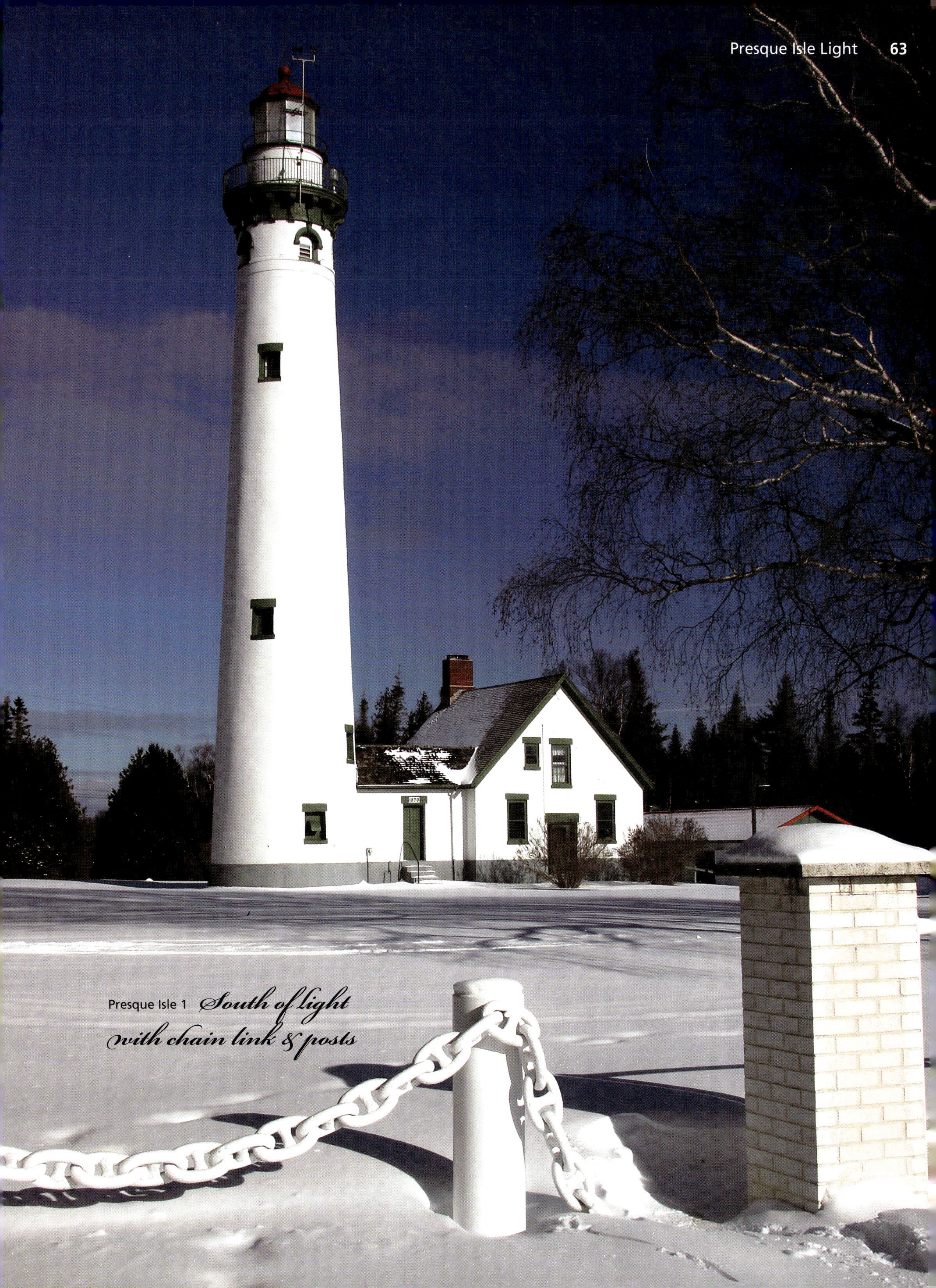
Presque Isle 1 South of light
with chain link & posts

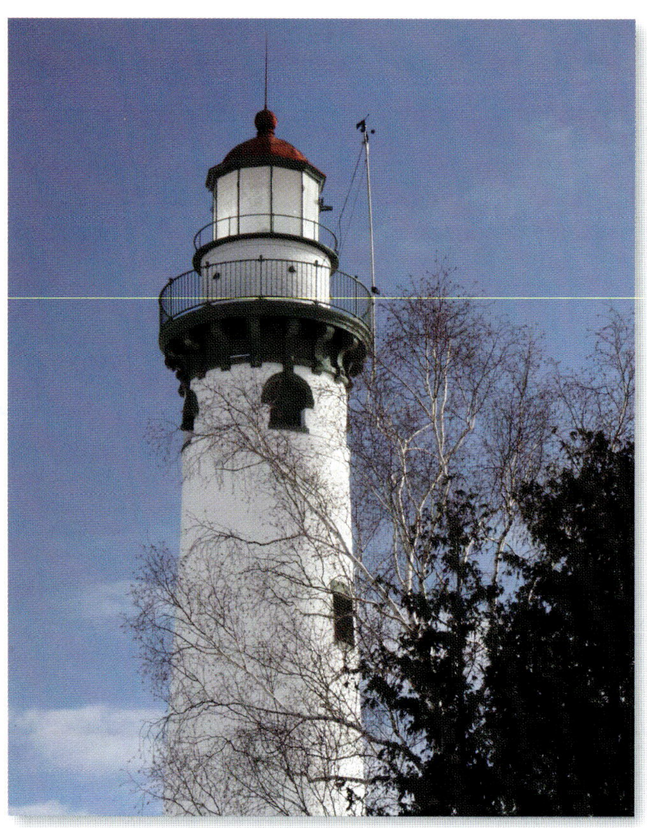

Presque Isle 4 *Close up with long lens*

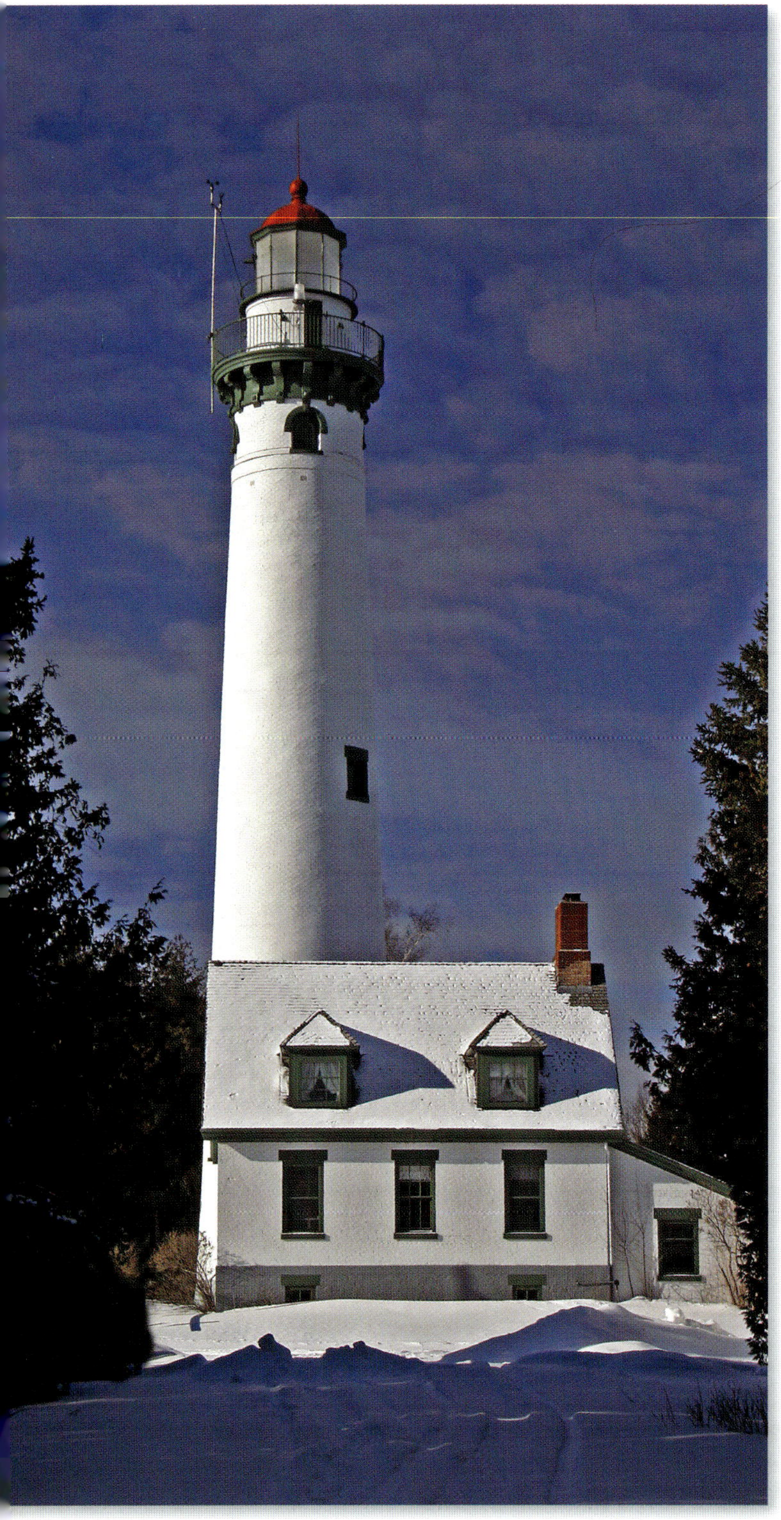

Presque Isle 2

From side road to the east

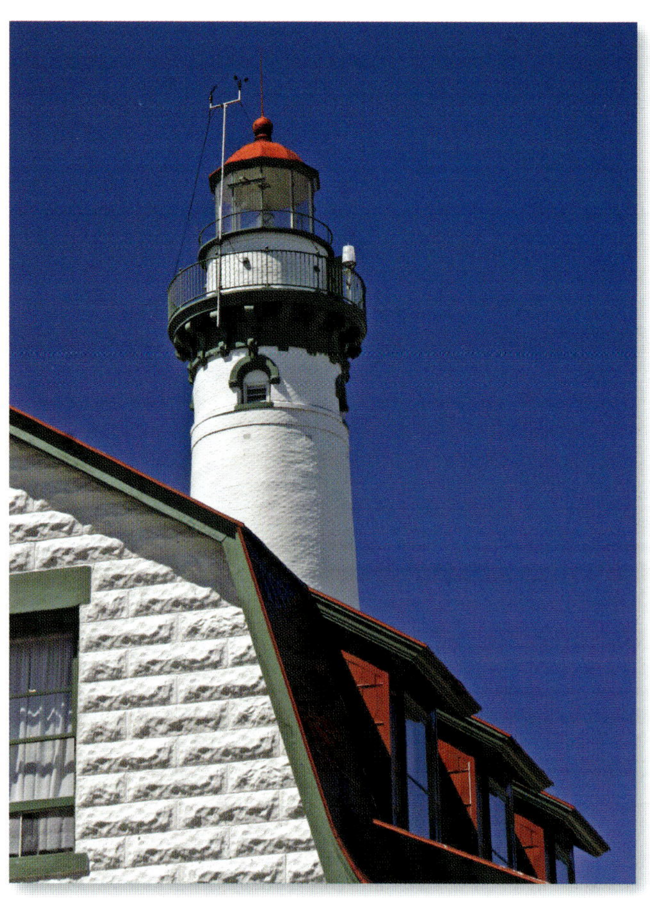

Presque Isle 3 *With roof line of keeper's house*

Sturgeon Point Light

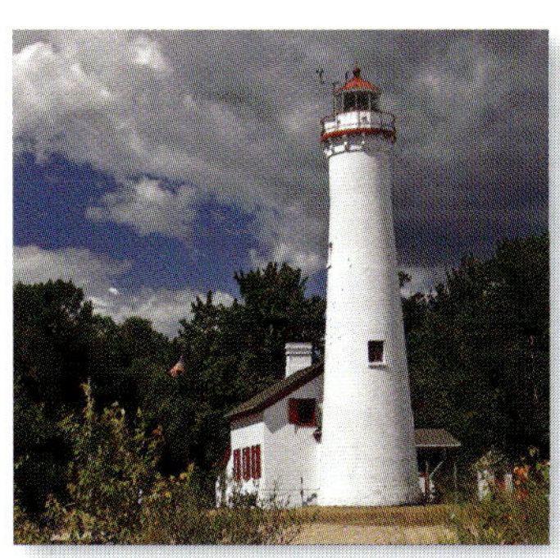

"Classic Light by the Lake"

DISTINGUISHING FEATURES

The bright red trim on the white tower and the matching red doors, windows and shutters on the keeper's quarters make Sturgeon Point a very impressive subject. The numerous trees around the lighthouse and the rocky shoreline provide many possibilities for creative compositions.

BEST TIME OF DAY

Morning hours are best looking west from the beach or from the south. Forest surrounds the lighthouse on the north and west, making it difficult to shoot from those sides. However, favorable light is available from the large open area to the south of the lighthouse, both in the morning and afternoon.

SUGGESTED COMPOSITIONS

South of the light, there are several large trees that can be used for framing **(1)**. Many fine compositions can be found along the beach, using beach grass for depth perception **(4)**. Look for paths or openings in the grasses as "lead-ins" **(2)**. There is a narrow peninsula stretching straight out to the lake where it is possible to include the shoreline and rocks in the foreground **(3)**. The red trim against the white brick house can yield interesting close-ups **(5)**. When the tower is open, climb the steps to the top and use a wide angle lens to catch the side of the lantern and view of the lake **(6)**.

SUNSET/SUNRISE

The thick forest just west of the lighthouse makes sunrise shots very difficult. However, the best chance is in the winter without leaves on the trees. Sunset images from the beach will only show the top half of the lighthouse against the sky due to the trees.

DIRECTIONS

From US 23 about 3 miles north of Harrisville, turn northeast on Lakeshore Dr. Go about 1 mile to Point Rd. and turn right. Drive about 1 mile further to the entrance to the lighthouse parking lot on the left.

GPS coordinates: 44.713N, 83.272W.

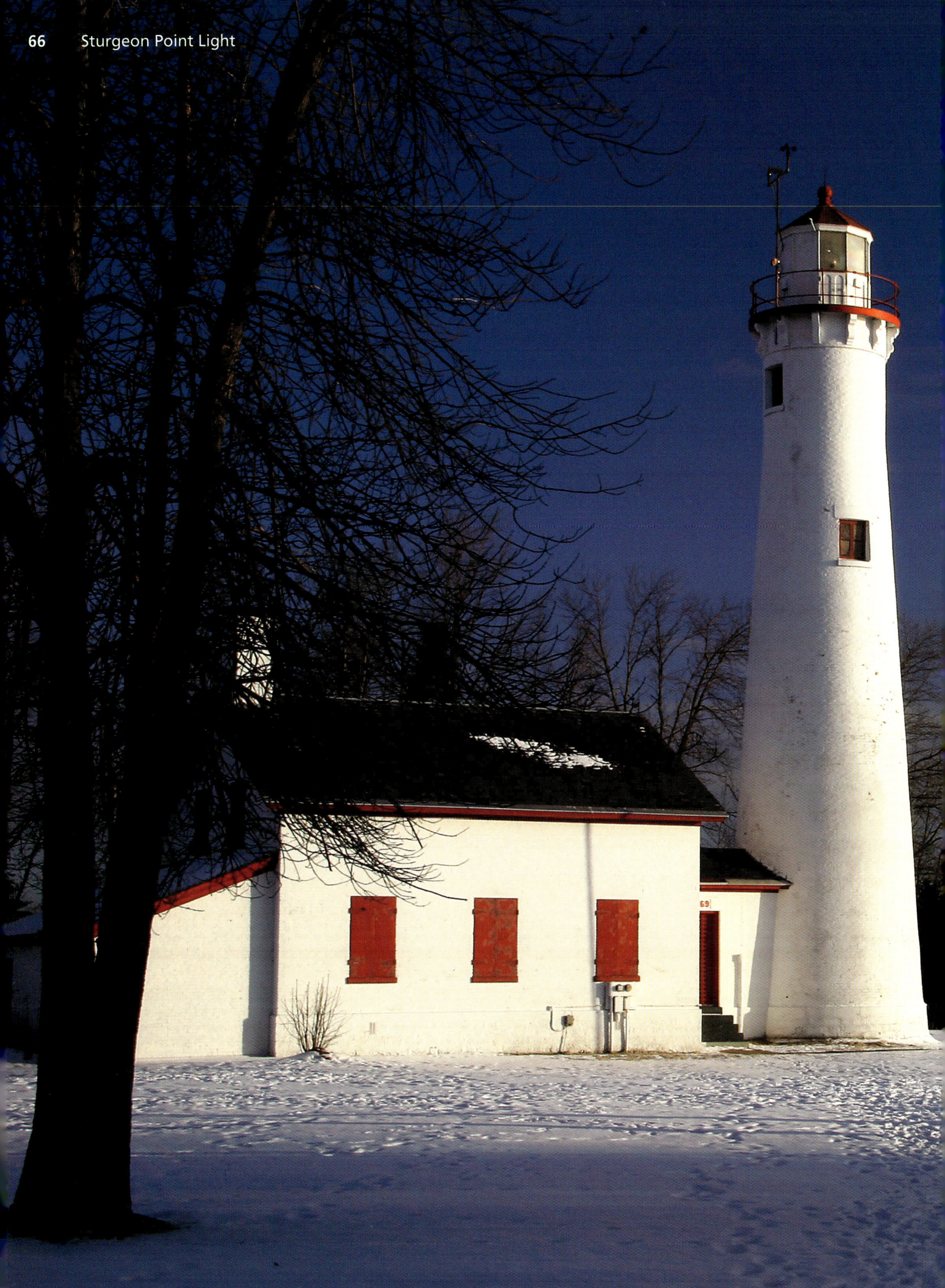

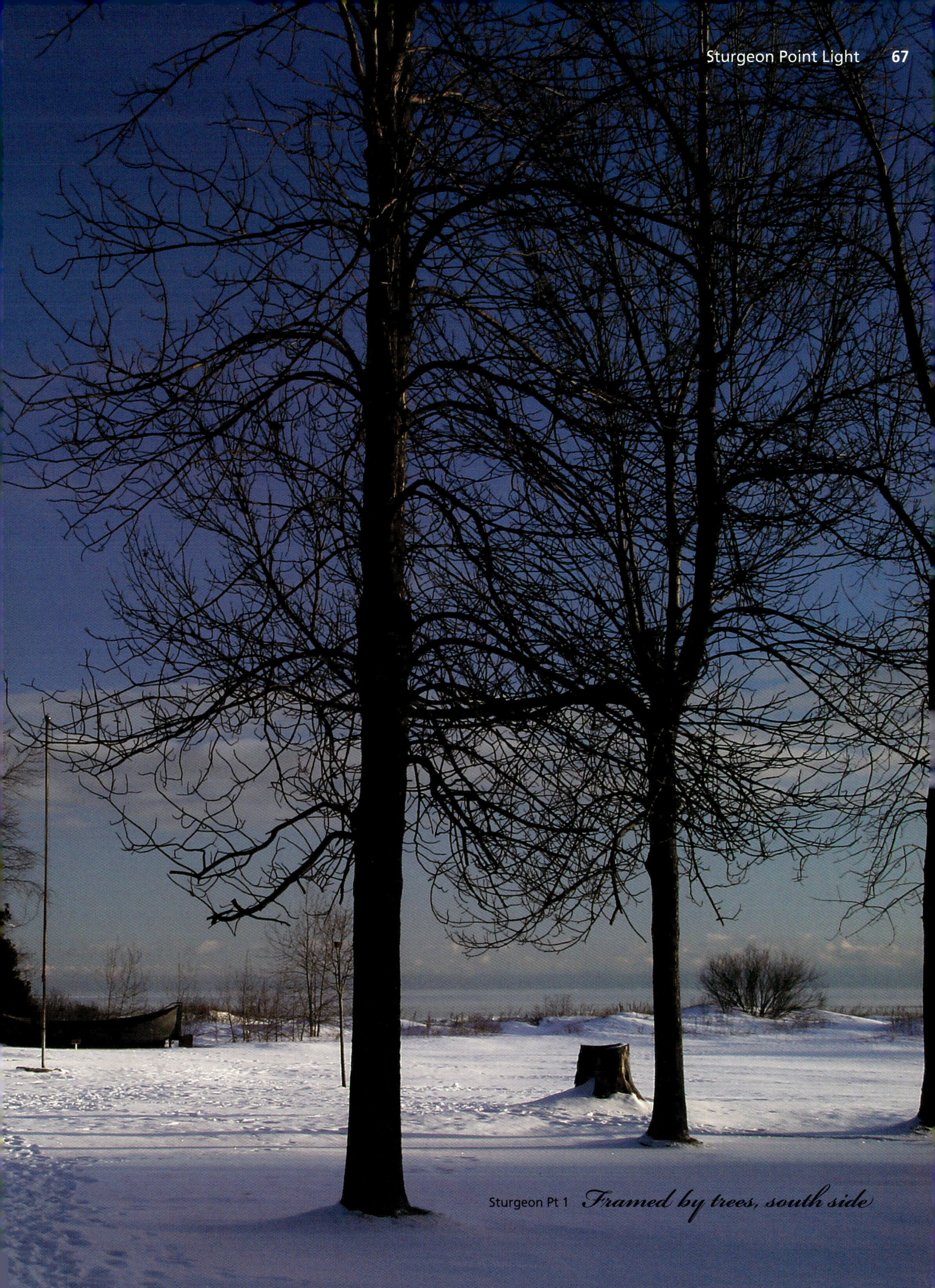

Sturgeon Pt 1 *Framed by trees, south side*

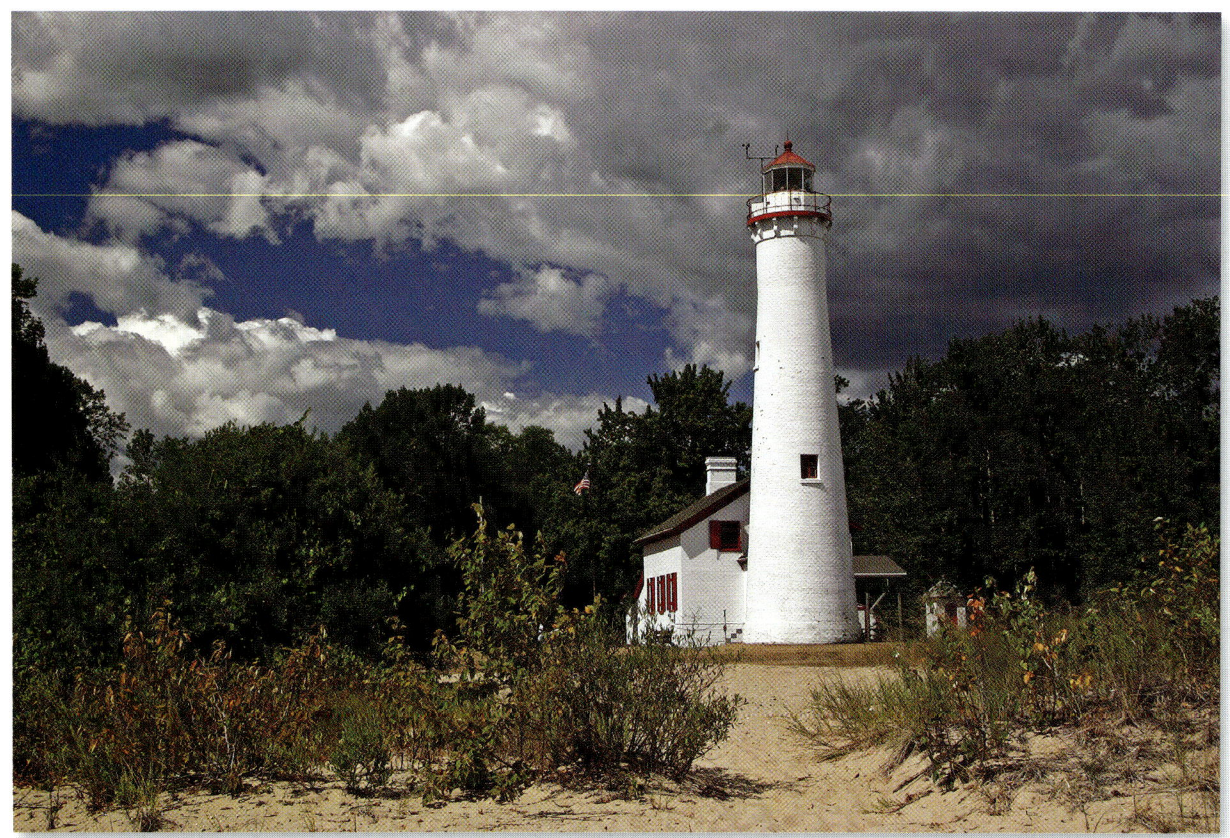

Sturgeon Pt 2 *From beach, east side*

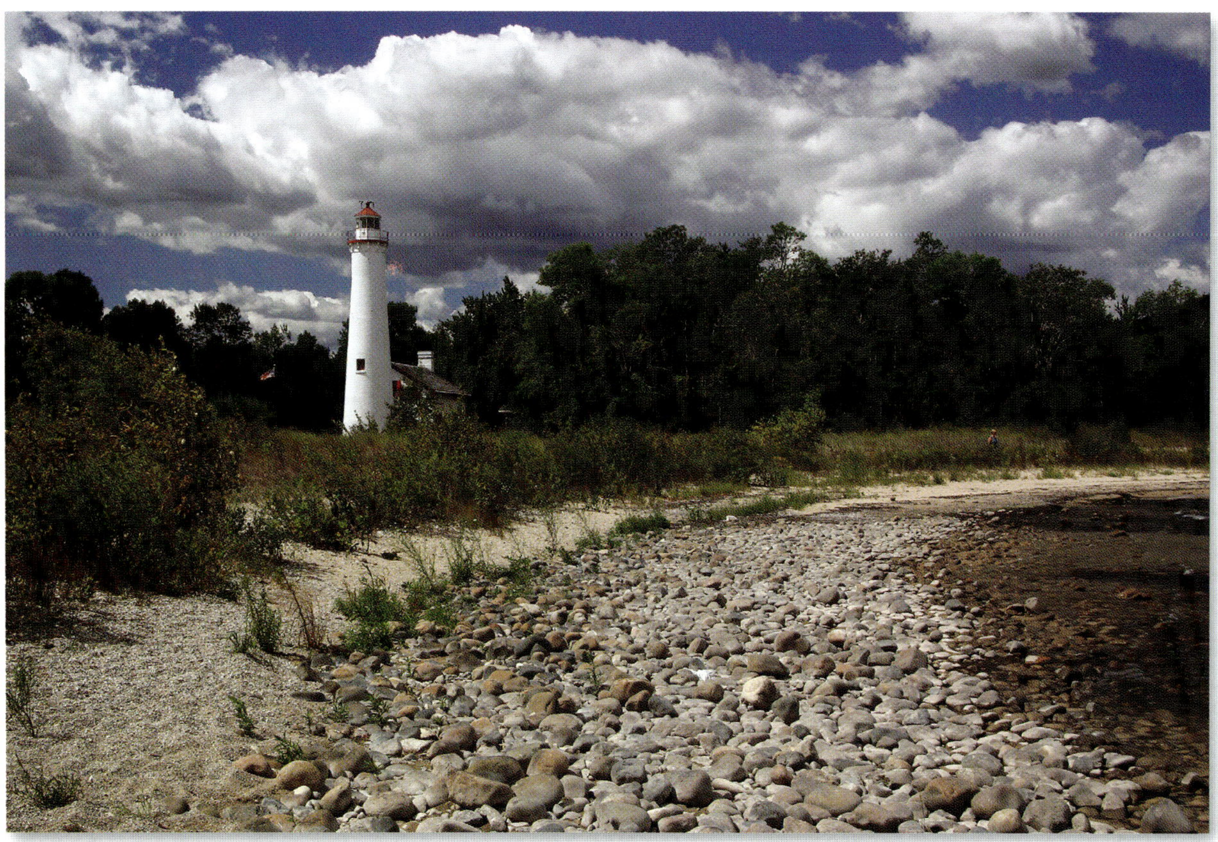

Sturgeon Pt 3 *From peninsula with rocky shoreline*

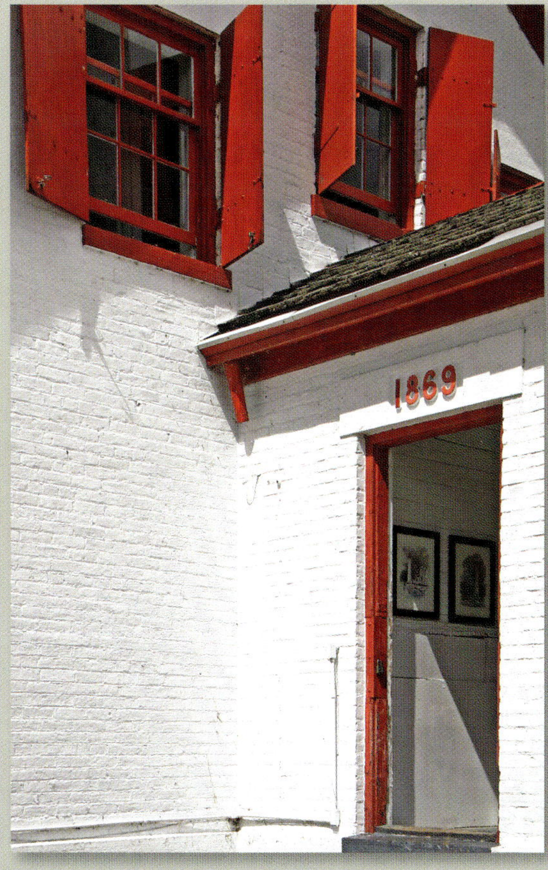

Sturgeon Pt 5 *Door & window detail*

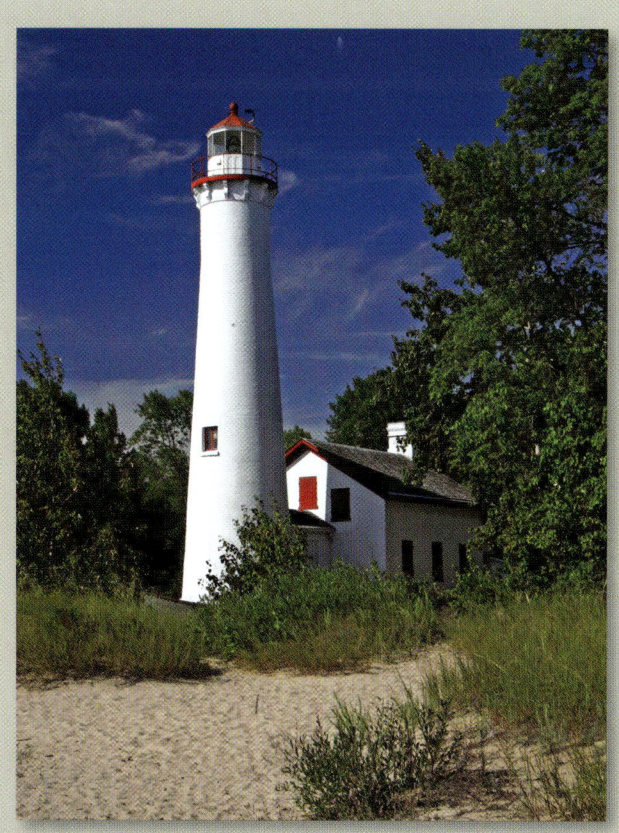

Sturgeon Pt 4 *Close to light, northeast*

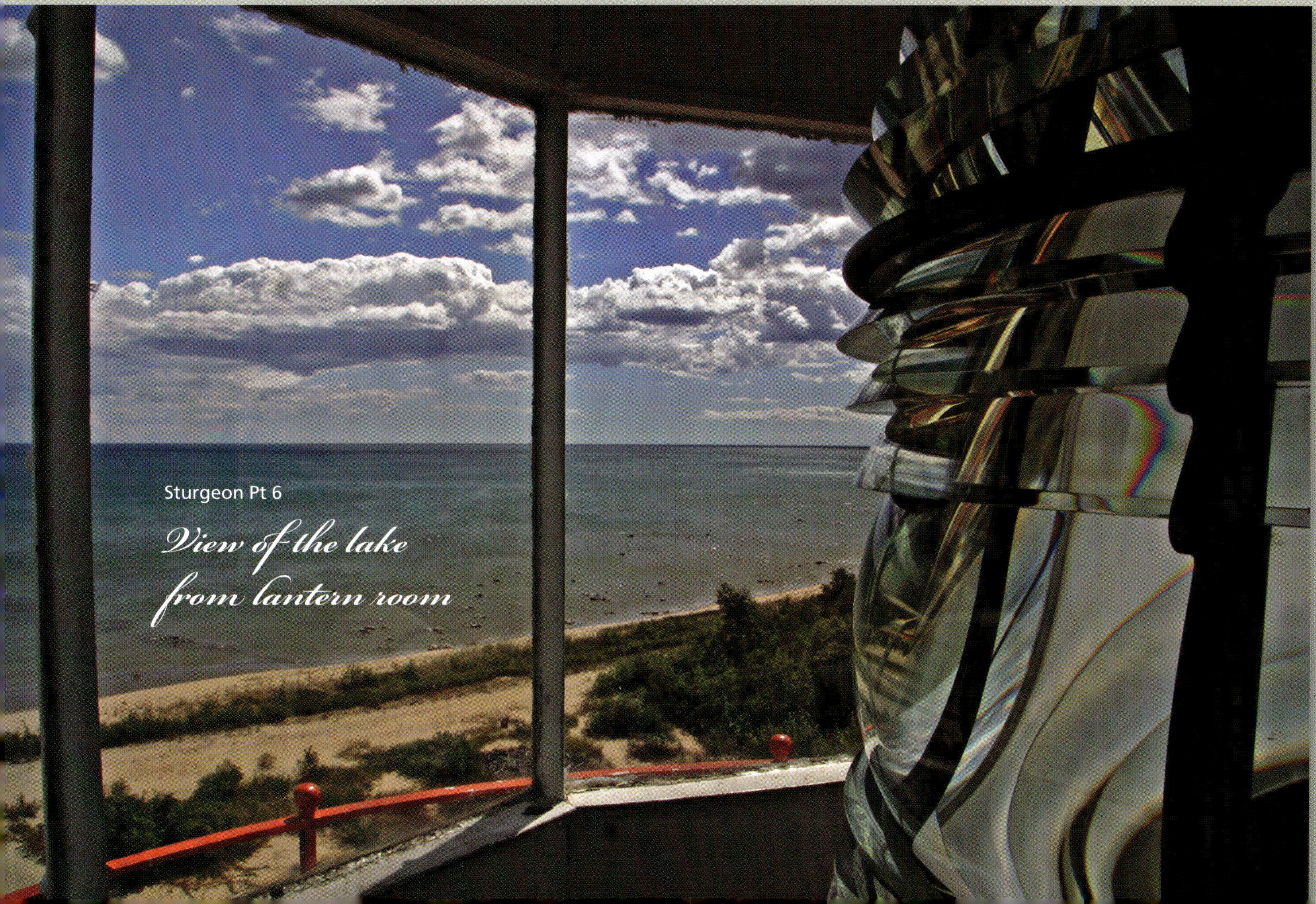

Sturgeon Pt 6
*View of the lake
from lantern room*

Tawas Point Light

East Tawas, Michigan

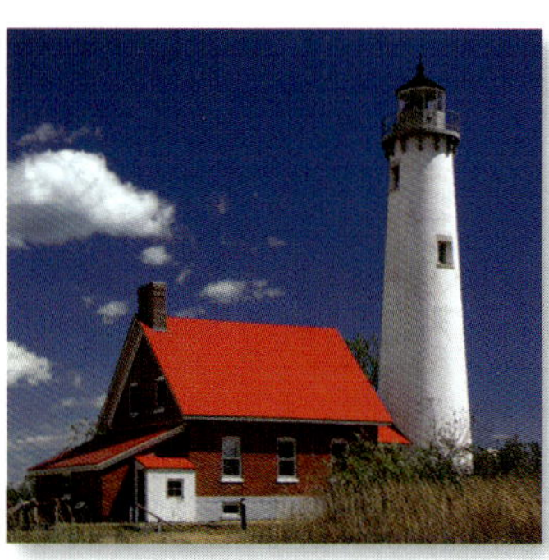

"Flaming Red Roof"

DISTINGUISHING FEATURES

This stunning light station sits near the end of a peninsula between Lake Huron and Tawas Bay. The vivid red metal roof on the red brick keeper's dwelling is very "eye-catching" in contrast to the white lighthouse tower. It also has the advantage of being accessible from all sides.

BEST TIME OF DAY

Good lighting is available in the morning or afternoon, but late afternoon is best due to the location of the surrounding trees and vegetation.

SUGGESTED COMPOSITIONS

From the parking lot, find trails that wind around the lighthouse. Use the small trees and vegetation at the edge of the clearing for various compositions **(1).** Look for openings between trees that can be used for framing **(2).** On the west and northwest side are opportunities with sand and beach grass in the foreground. One of the best ones is where a trail forms a leading line to the lighthouse **(3).** There are some red benches near the light which complement the red roof and add depth perception to an image **(4).**

SUNSET/SUNRISE

This is an unusual situation where both sunset **(5)** and sunrise images are possible from land.

DIRECTIONS

From US 23 in East Tawas, turn east at Tawas Beach Rd. and follow signs for about 3 miles to Tawas Point State Park. This is a Michigan State Park with entrance fee.

GPS coordinates: 44.254N, 83.449W.

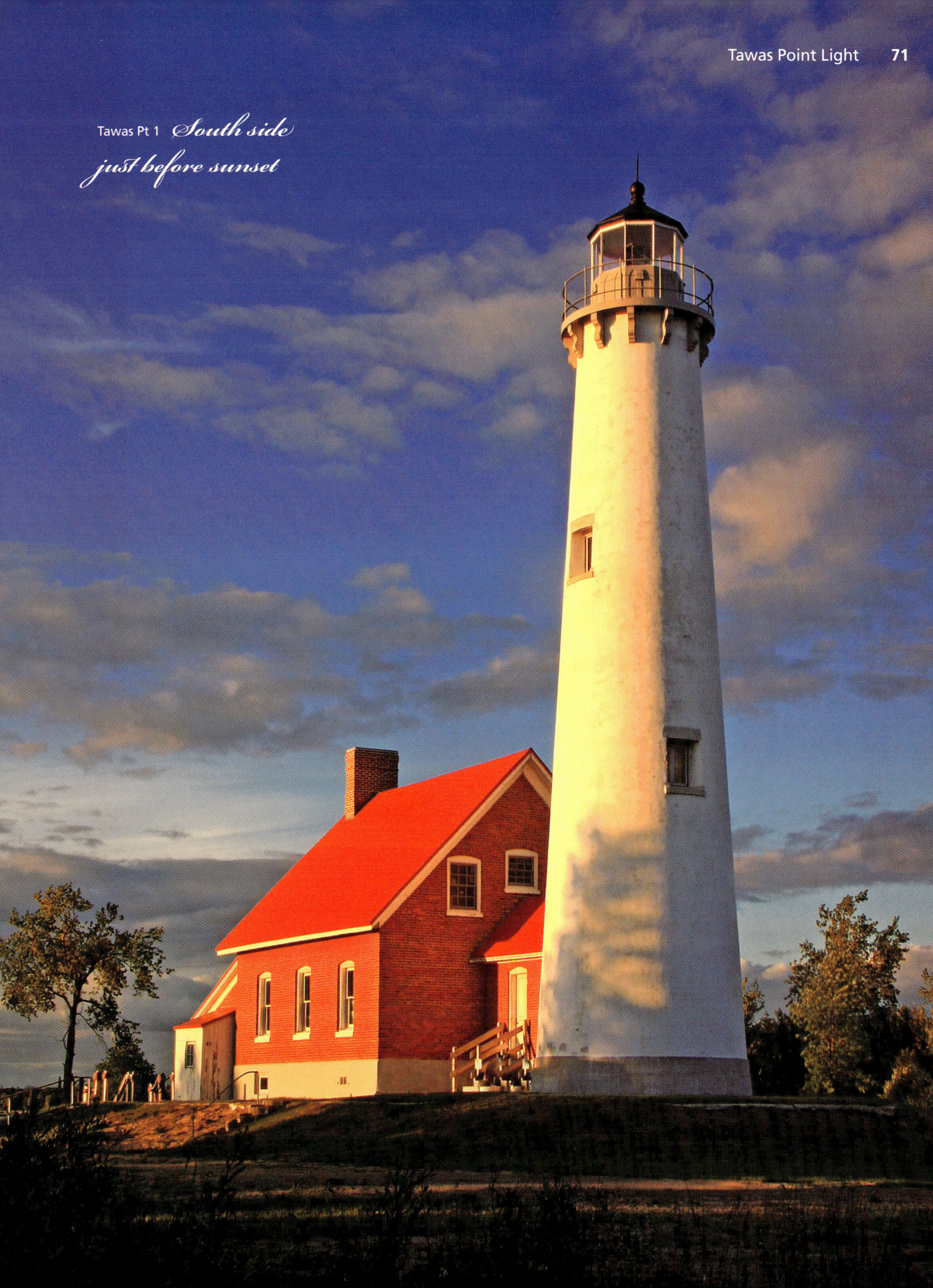
Tawas Pt 1 South side
just before sunset

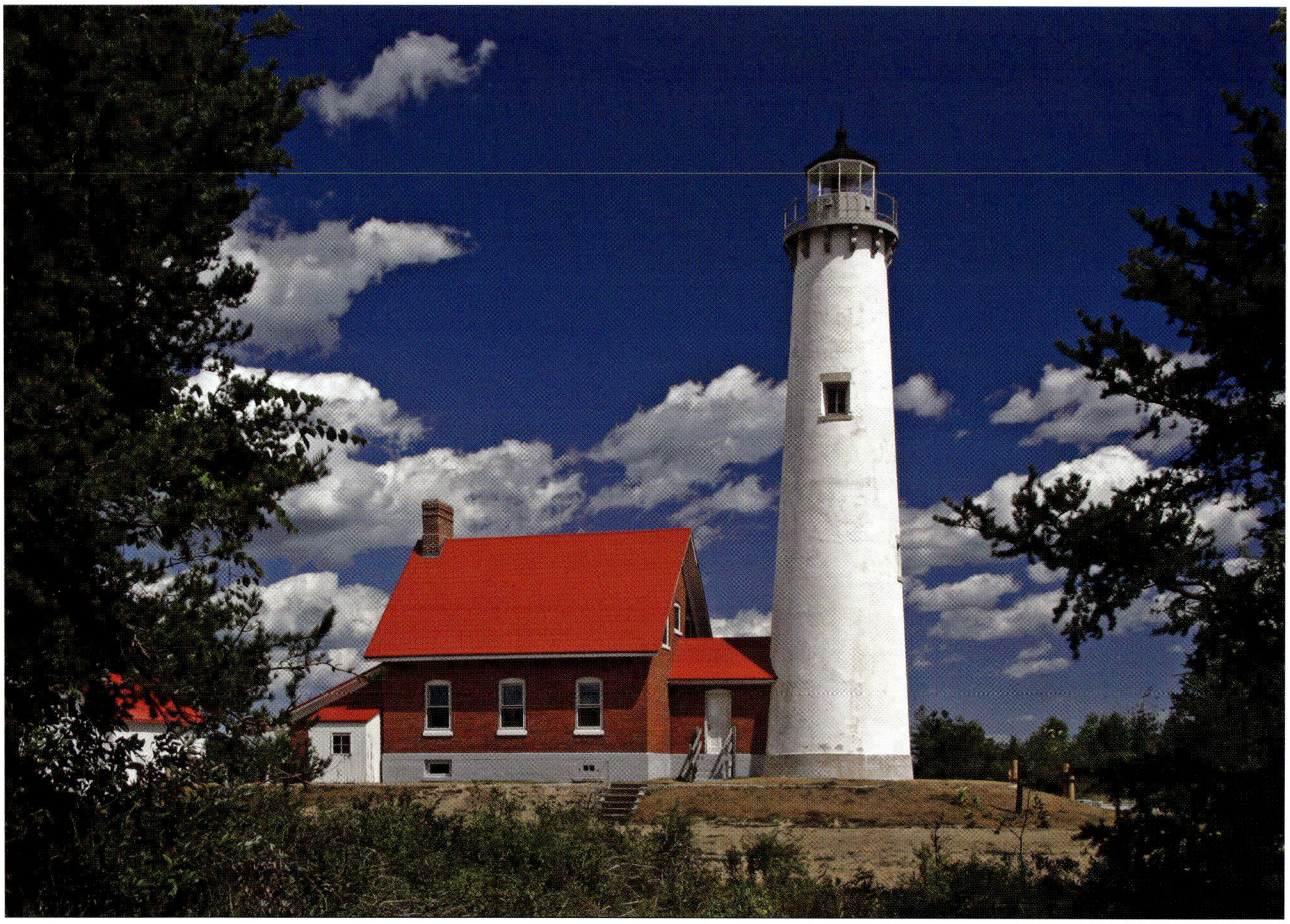

Tawas Pt 2   *West side framed by trees*

Tawas Pt 3

*From northwest with
trail as leading line*

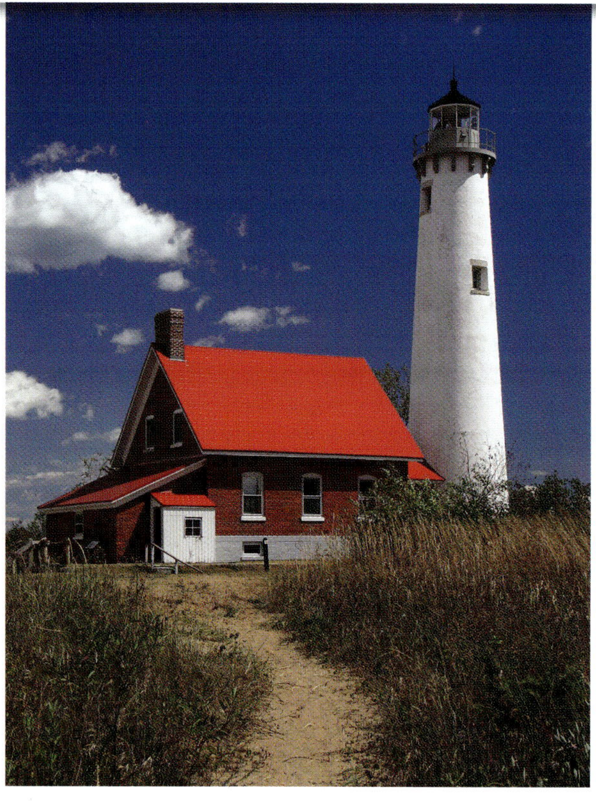

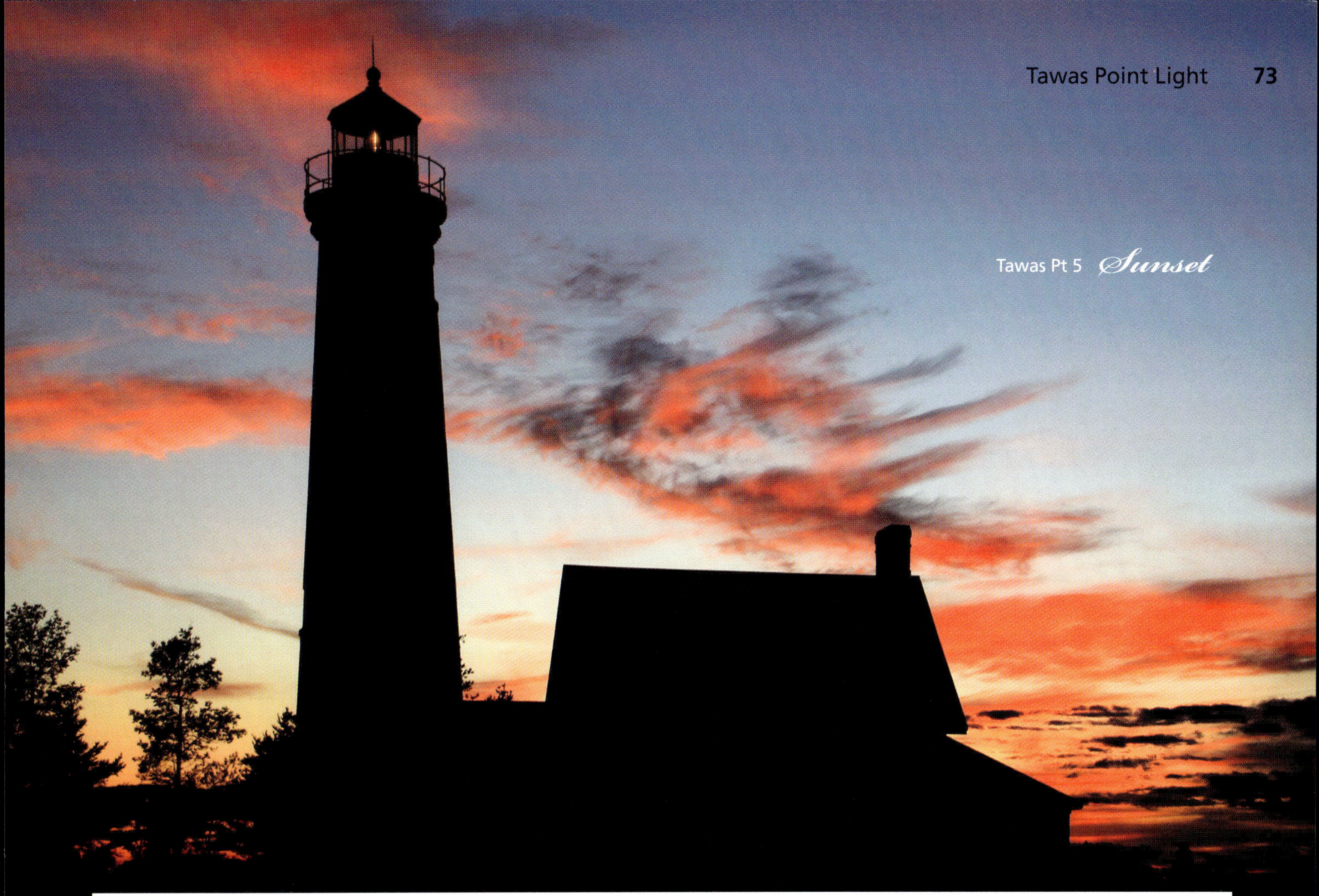

Tawas Pt 5 *Sunset*

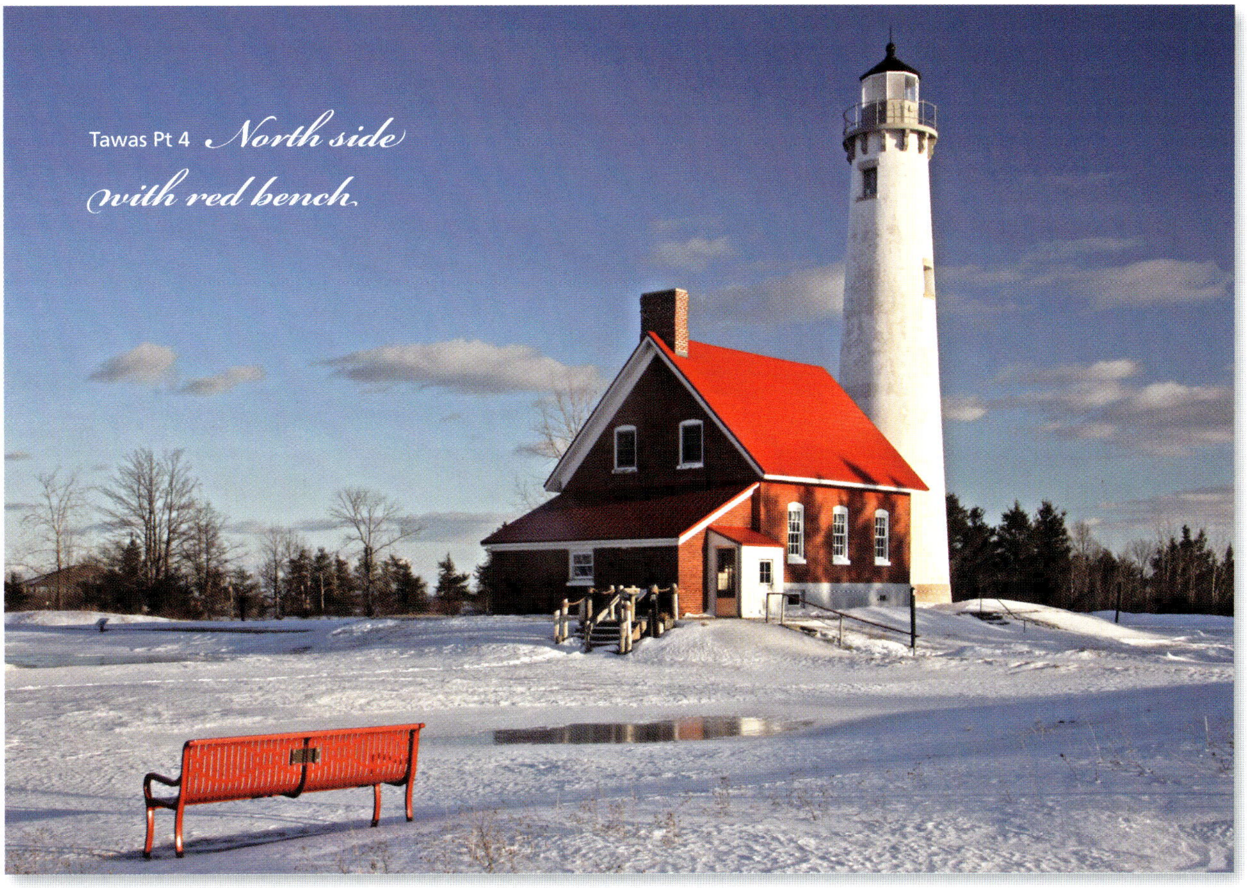

Tawas Pt 4 *North side with red bench*

Pointe Aux Barques Light

Near Port Hope, Michigan

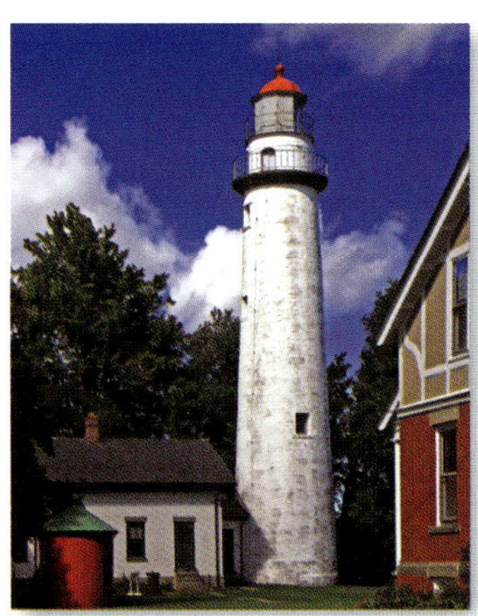

"Point of the Little Boats"

DISTINGUISHING FEATURES

Pointe Aux Barques is French for "Point of the Little Boats", a strategic spot at the tip of Michigan's "thumb" where Lake Huron meets Saginaw Bay. The white tower with red dome and green trim sits at the edge of a rocky shore.

BEST TIME OF DAY

Favorable lighting conditions are available morning and afternoon.

SUGGESTED COMPOSITIONS

South of the lighthouse and east of a storage building is a short concrete platform extending over the shoreline. Compositions from here can include the birch tree on the left **(1)** or the large rocks and the lake on the right **(2)**. The birch tree can also be used for framing **(3)**. Southwest of the light is a good vantage point that shows the red oil house on the left and the edge of the detached keeper's dwelling on the right **(4)**. The large trees to the west can provide framing possibilities for closer images **(5)**.

The maple trees north of the lighthouse produce nice autumn colors, with the peak season usually occurring in early to mid October.

SUNSET/SUNRISE

A sunrise image is possible here but will be difficult due to the number of large trees close to the light. You may only be able to see the top portion of the lighthouse over the treetops.

DIRECTIONS

About 6 miles north of Port Hope (or about 10 miles east of Port Austin) on M 25, turn north on Lighthouse Rd. It is about 1 mile to Lighthouse County Park where there is parking close to the lighthouse.

GPS coordinates: 44.023N, 82.793W.

Pt Aux Barques 5 (right)

West side framed by trees

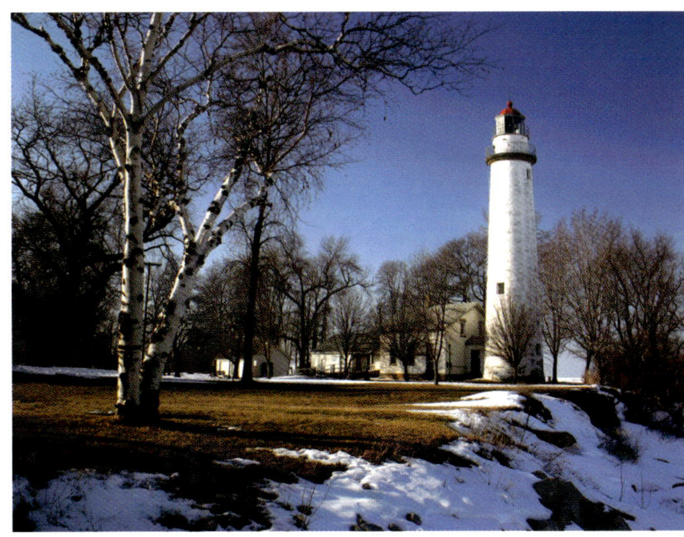

Pt Aux Barques 1

From platform with birch tree

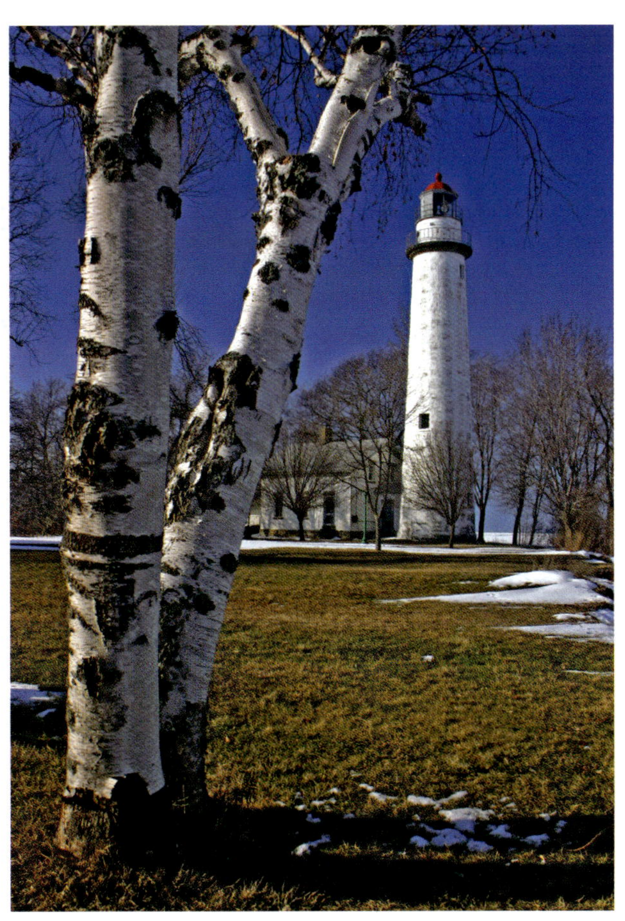

Pt Aux Barques 3   *Framed by birch tree*

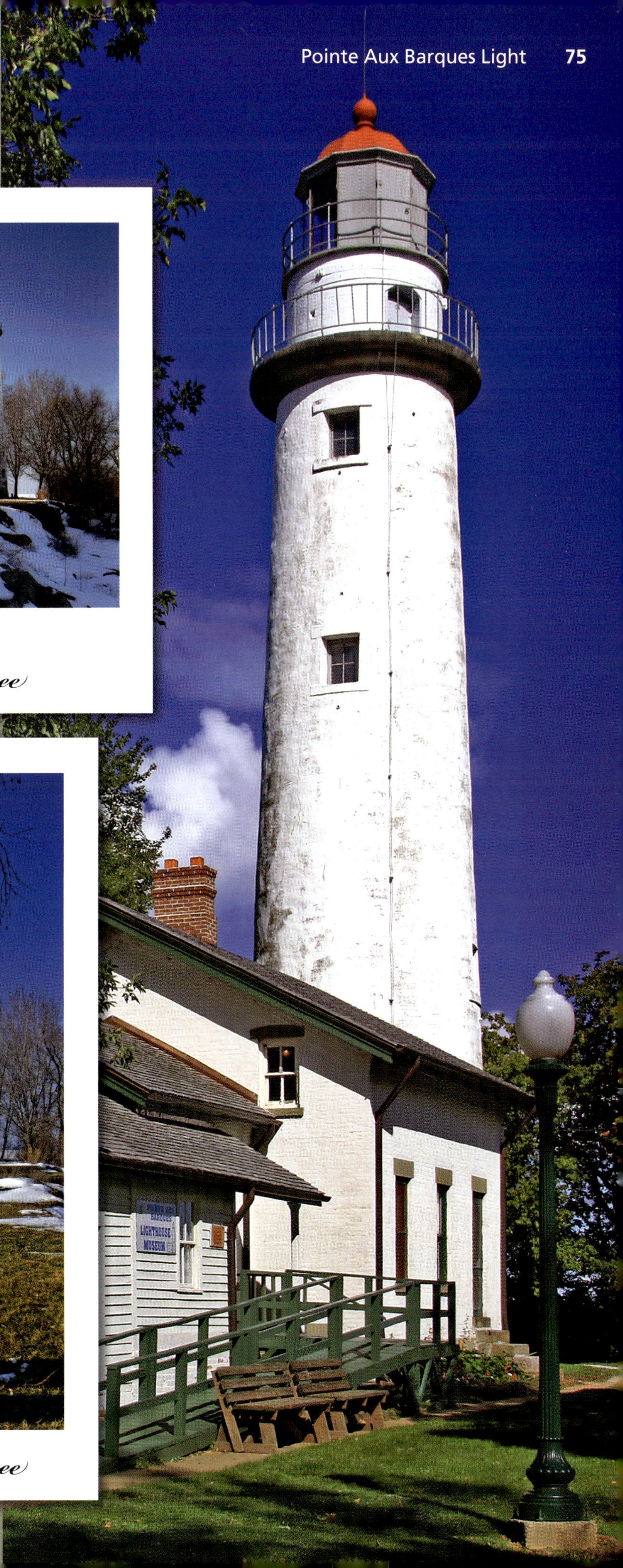

Pt Aux Barques 4 (right)

*With oil house &
keeper's dwelling*

Pt Aux Barques 2 (below)

*From platform
with lake*

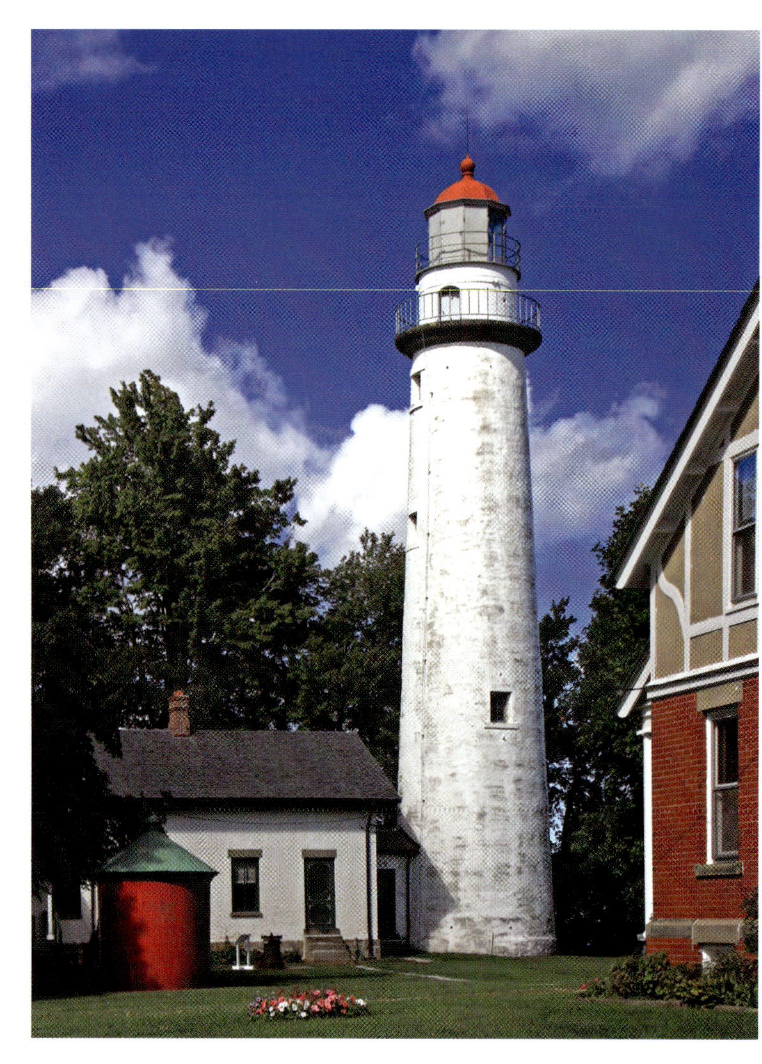

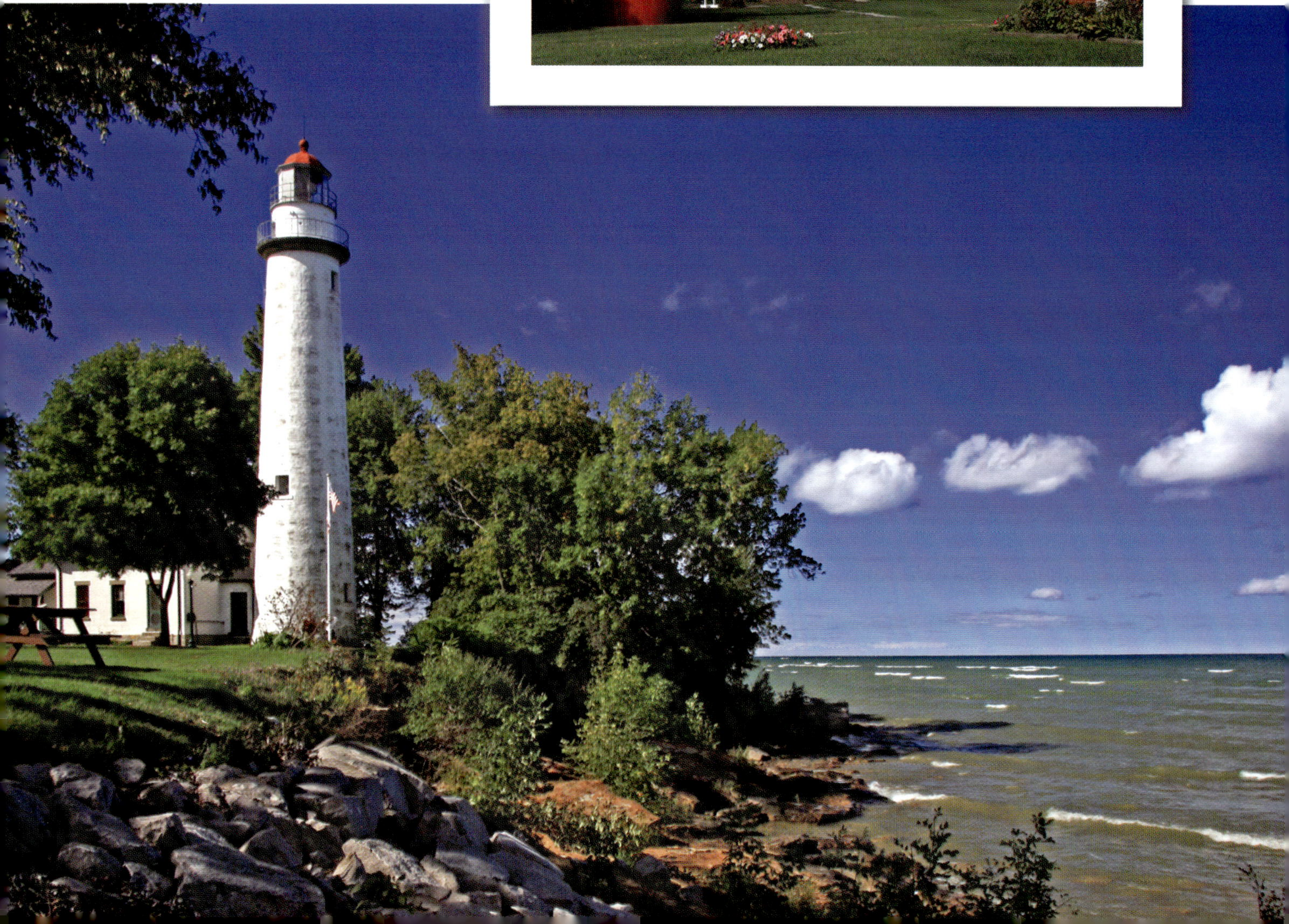

Port Sanilac Light

Port Sanilac, Michigan

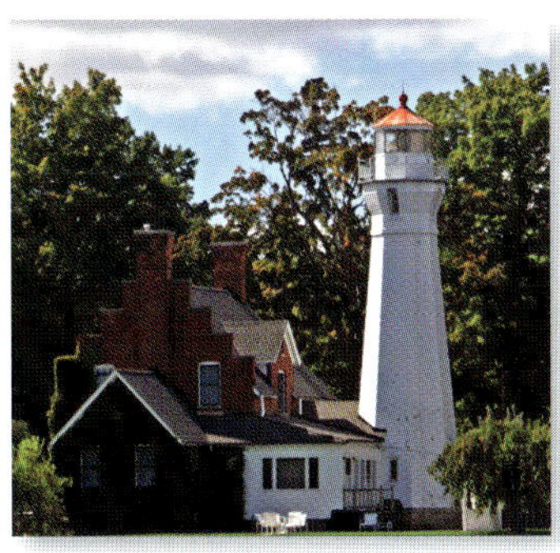

"Best Kept Secret"

DISTINGUISHING FEATURES

Port Sanilac is a hidden jewel on Michigan's "thumb". What you find is a lighthouse and attached keeper's cottage that is unusual and charming. The white octagonal tower narrows near the top and then widens to support the red-capped lantern room. The brick cottage has an interesting stair-step roofline.

BEST TIME OF DAY

Morning hours are best for unobstructed views from the east or lake side. The large trees on the west or street side make afternoon shots difficult except in winter when the trees are bare.

SUGGESTED COMPOSITIONS

Some of the best vantage points are from the extension of Cherry St. and beyond, south and east of the light. Start with compositions from the parking area looking northwest. There is a weathered picket fence for the foreground and trees for framing **(1).** Walk east on the breakwater that provides nice views back to the light **(2)**, some including the water **(3)**. Across the street, west of the light, compose images of the tower and the front of the keeper's cottage **(4).**

The first street north of the lighthouse leads to a boat dock from which there are other perspectives looking southwest **(5).**

Maple trees line the street next to the lighthouse and peak fall colors usually occur about mid October.

SUNSET/SUNRISE

With the number of large trees west of the lighthouse, a successful sunrise or sunset shot will be unlikely.

DIRECTIONS

From M 25 (also Ridge St.) near the center of town, turn east on Cherry St. and go two blocks to the end where there is a parking area in the extension of Cherry St. south of the lighthouse.

GPS coordinates: 43.429N, 82.540W.

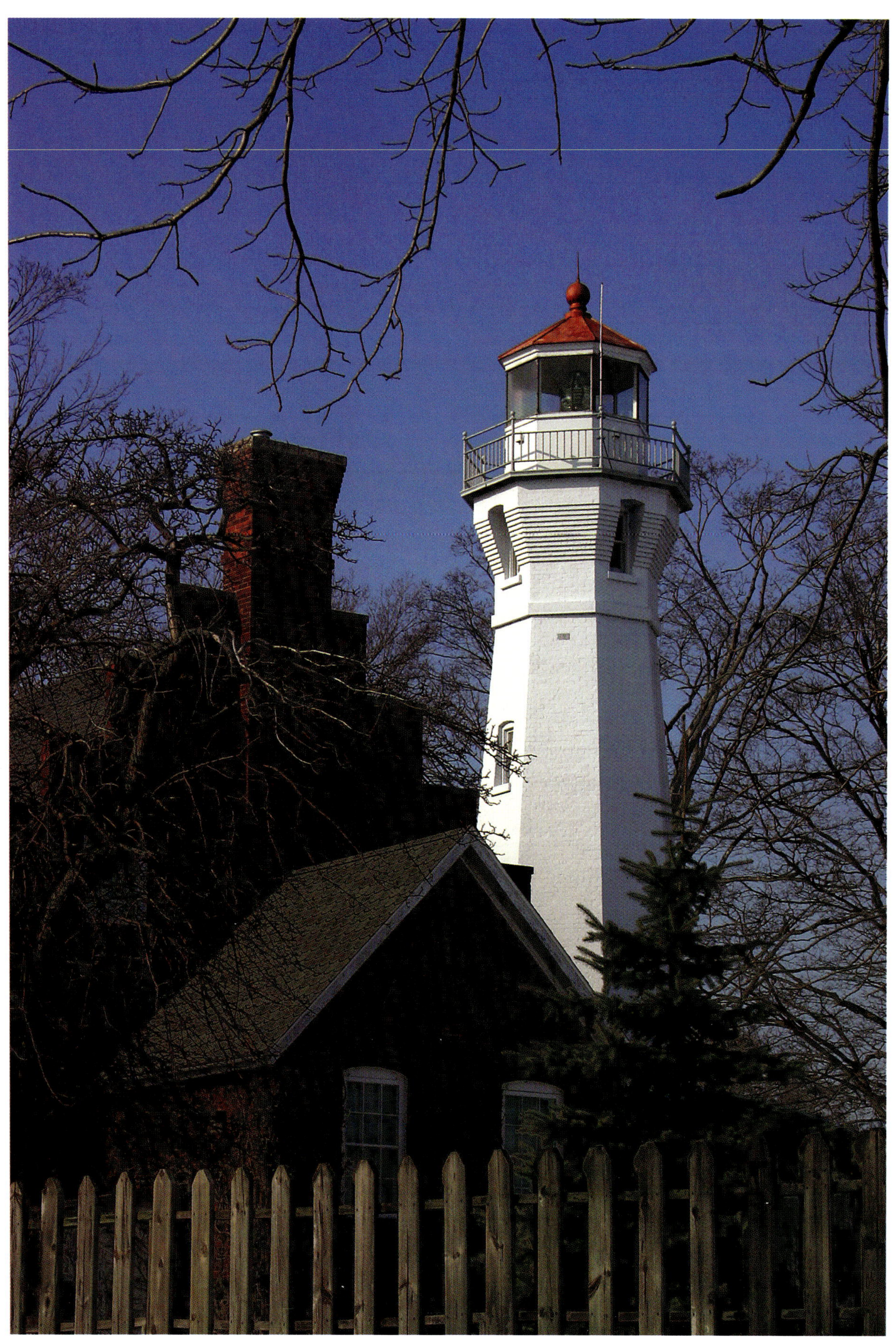

Port Sanilac 1   *South side with picket fence*

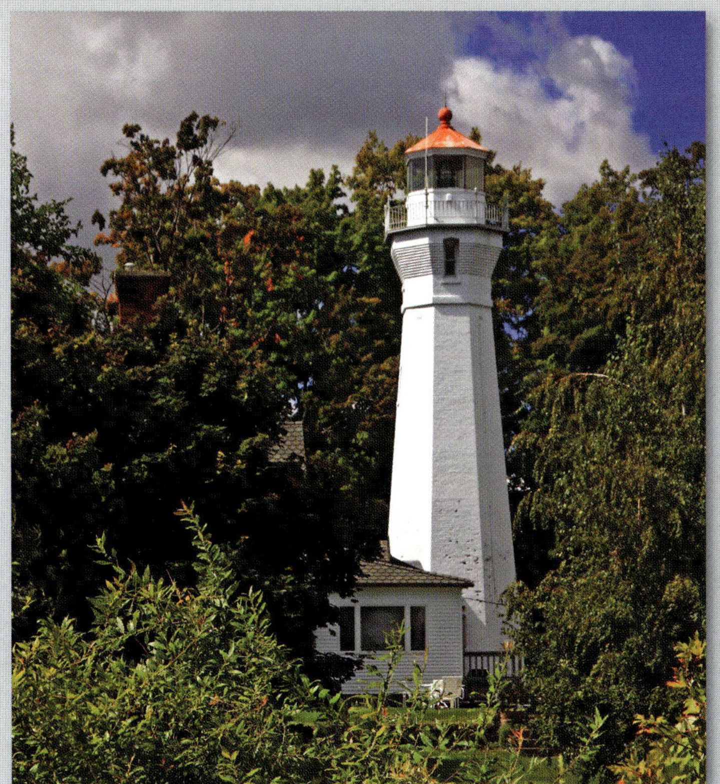

Port Sanilac 2 *From breakwater*

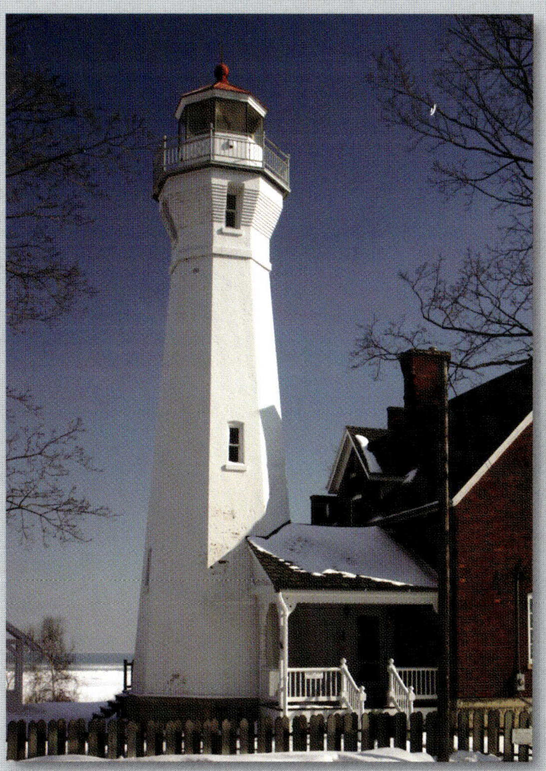

Port Sanilac 4 *With keeper's house*

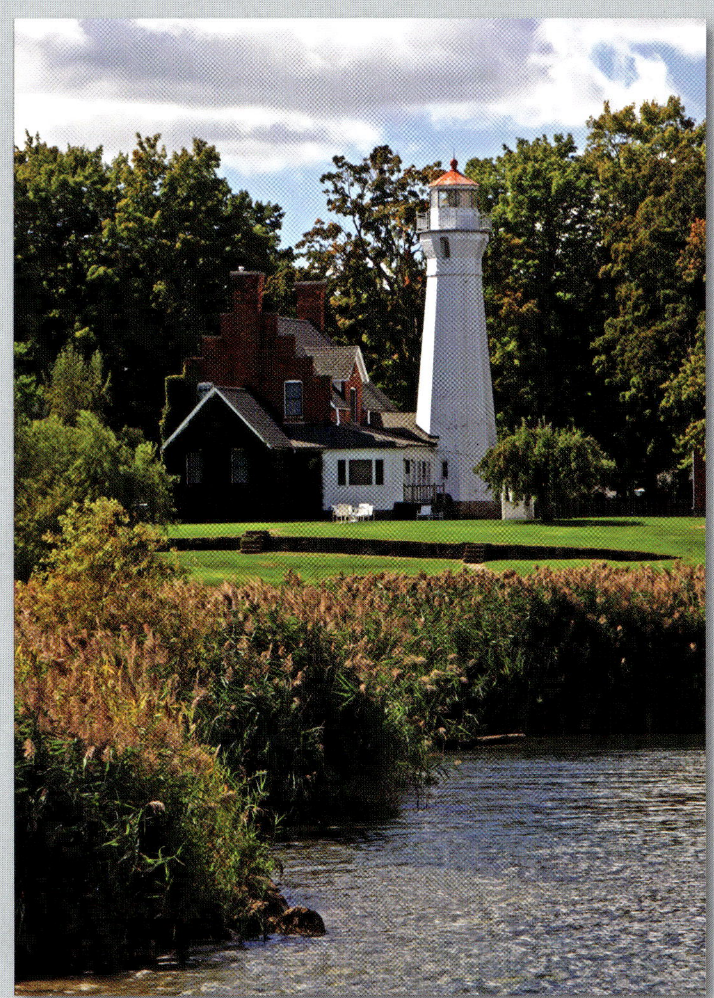

Port Sanilac 3 *From breakwater with shoreline*

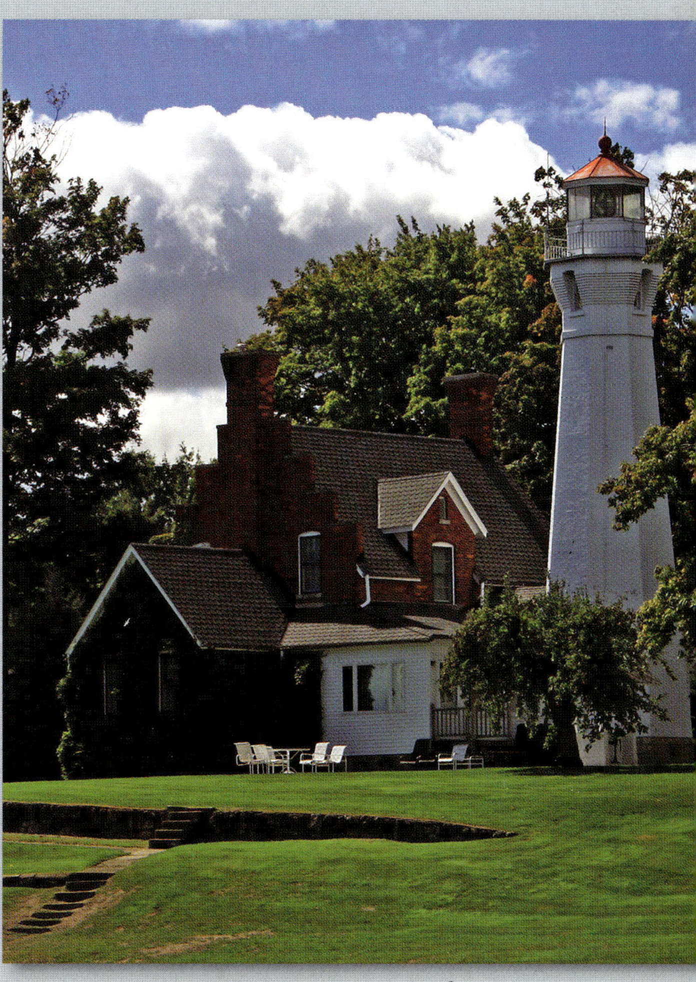

Port Sanilac 5 *From boat dock*

Fort Gratiot Light

Port Huron, Michigan

"Michigan's First"

DISTINGUISHING FEATURES

Michigan's oldest lighthouse (1829) is still standing where the St. Clair River meets Lake Huron. The white tower with red dome sits well away from the large brick keeper's quarters. Good vantage points are available from the park north of the light or across the river on the Canadian side.

BEST TIME OF DAY

Morning light is best for most compositions but afternoon light will work for shots close to the lighthouse. Morning hours are definitely best from across the river.

SUGGESTED COMPOSITIONS

From the parking lot north of the lighthouse, walk the short distance to the beach and shoot over the fence with sand and grasses in the foreground **(1)**. The beach directly in front of the lighthouse is closed to the public. From the lighthouse entrance on Omar St., walk around the light for closer shots **(2)**. From the west, another view of the light station is possible over the fence **(3)**.

Cross the bridge to the Canadian side (see Directions) for nice views across the river **(4)**. A long lens is needed (minimum of 300MM recommended) for both vertical and horizontal formats.

SUNSET/SUNRISE

Due to the large number of tall trees west of the lighthouse and the restricted area where the dwellings are located, a sunrise image would be very difficult. A sunset image from across the river would only silhouette the top section of the lighthouse due to the tall trees.

DIRECTIONS

From I 94, go north on M 25 (Pine Grove St.) a few blocks to Garfield St. and turn east. Follow it to the end at Omar St. Turn left to Lighthouse Park and a parking lot. You can also turn right on Omar St. and park on the street by the fenced lighthouse entrance. For information on the hours when this area is open, call 810 982-0891 ext. 19.

To reach the Canadian side, follow I 94 East across the toll bridge (be sure to have your passport). From Exit 1, go left (north) on Front St. to where it ends and turn left on Victoria St. Go several blocks to Fort St. and turn right to a parking area. There is a long walkway along the river.

GPS coordinates: 43.006N, 82.422W.

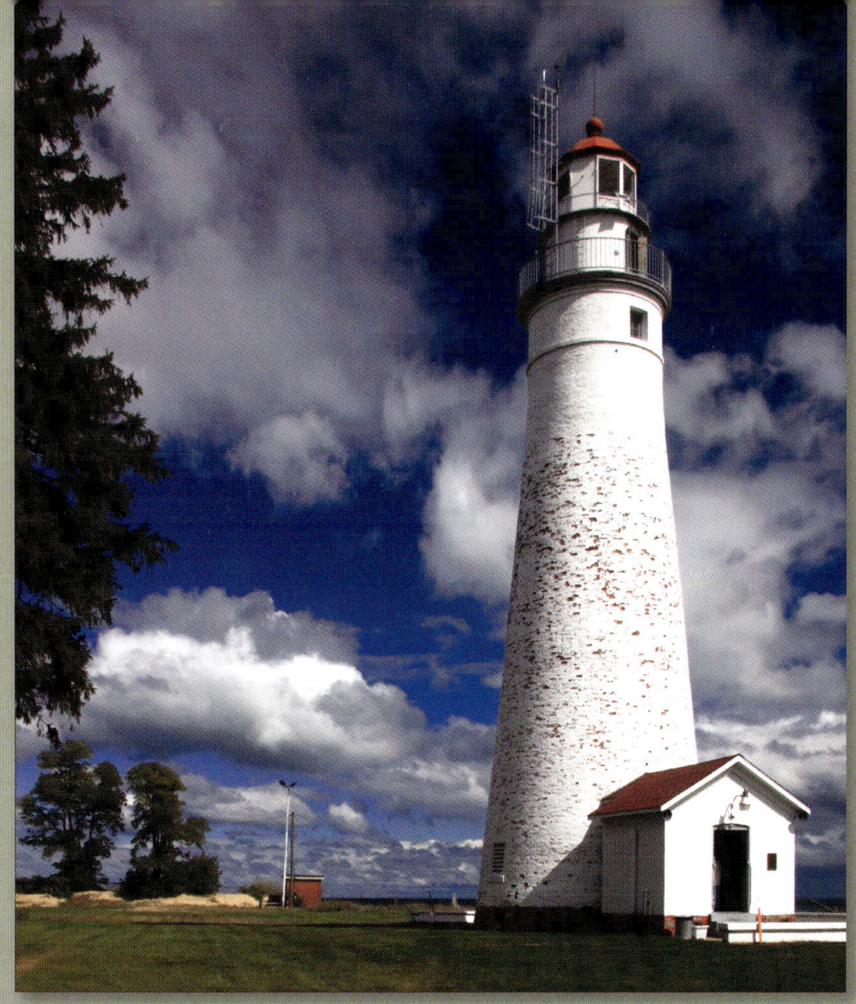

Fort Gratiot 2 (left)

Inside fenced area, close to light

Fort Gratiot 1 (below)

From beach, north of light

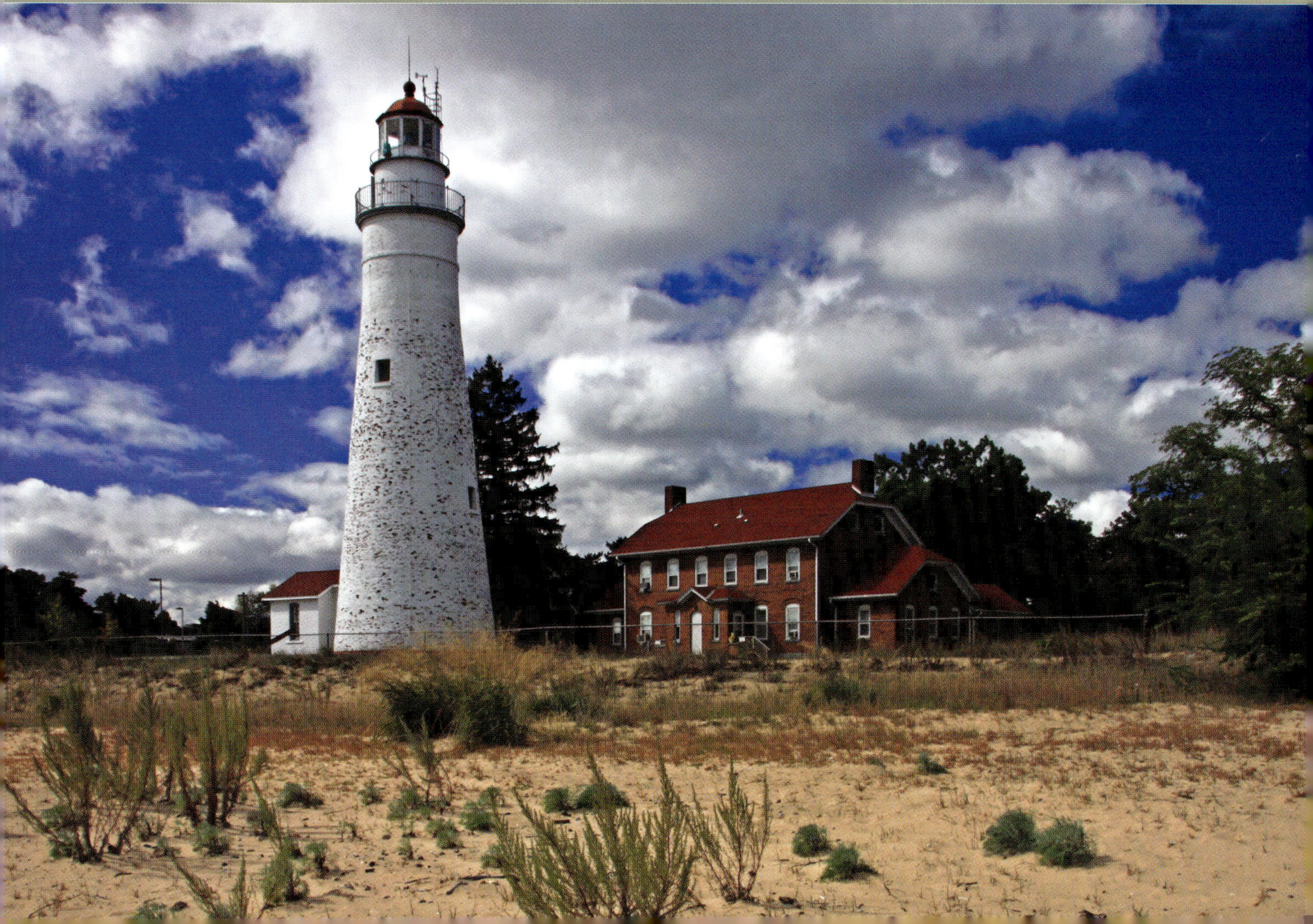

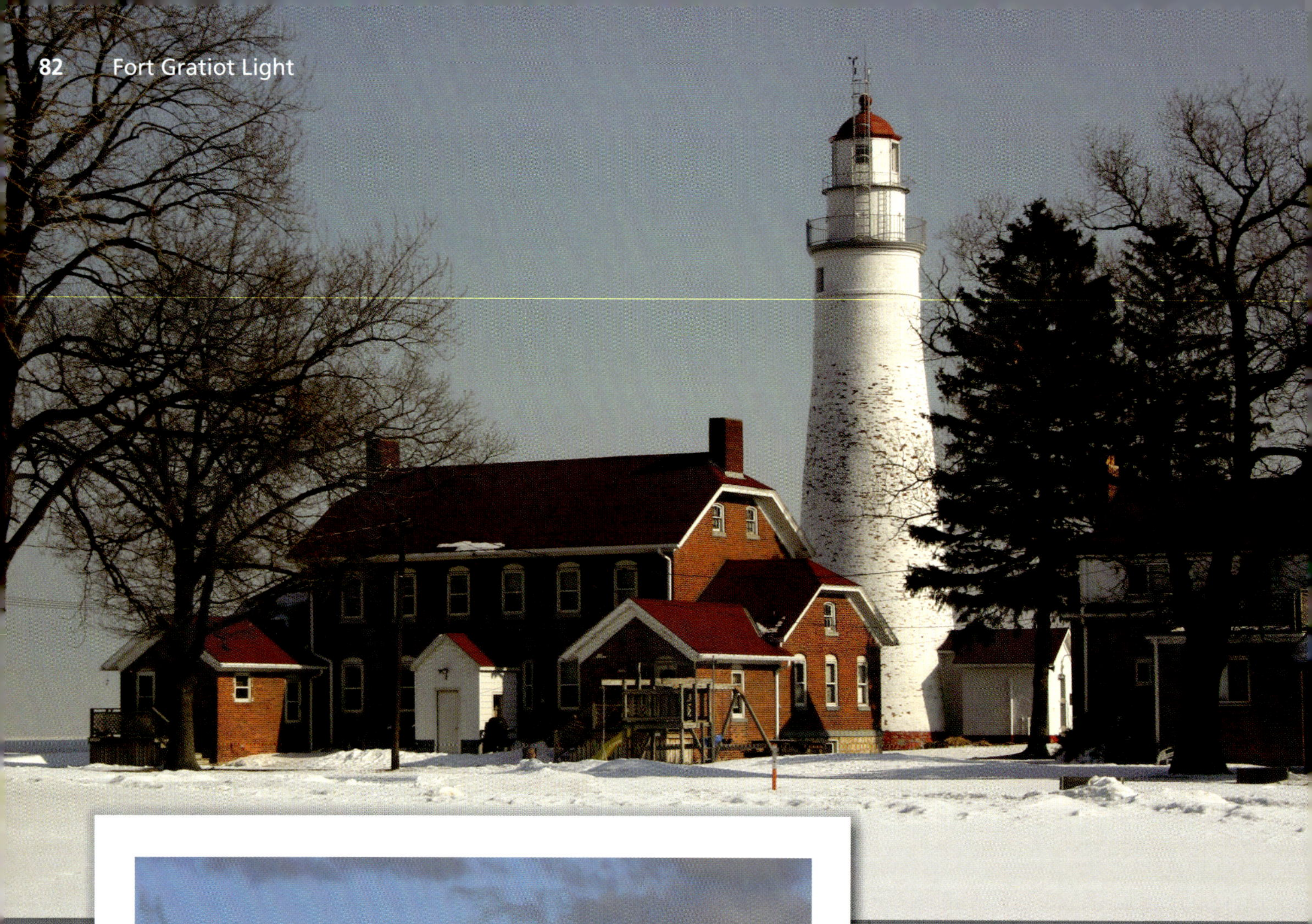

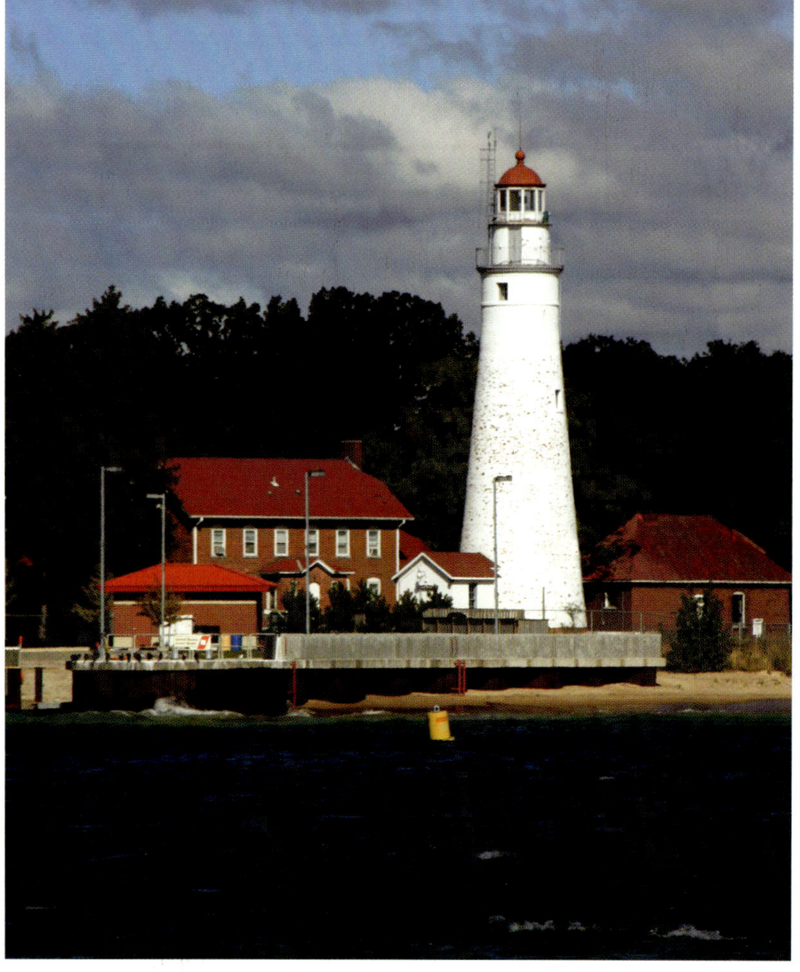

Fort Gratiot 3 (above)

West side

Fort Gratiot 4 (left)

Across river from Canadian side

Marblehead Light

Marblehead, Ohio

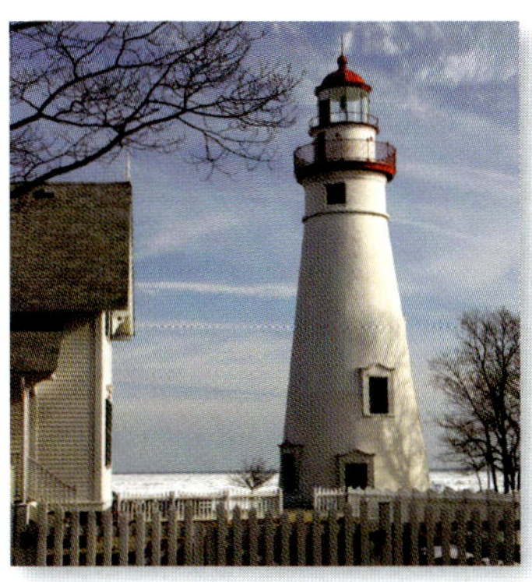

"Gem of Lake Erie"

DISTINGUISHING FEATURES

Besides being the oldest active lighthouse on the Great Lakes (flashing green light), Marblehead is one of the most beautiful. The classic white tower with bright red parapet and dome has made it a favorite of photographers for many years. Instead of the usual sand beach, it sits on a promontory point and is surrounded by large flat stones that provide easy access and interesting shorelines.

BEST TIME OF DAY

There is favorable light on the lighthouse in the morning and in the afternoon.

SUGGESTED COMPOSITIONS

Make the row of large rocks just west of the lighthouse a strong leading line **(1).**

A position on the flat stones along the west shoreline is one of the best spots to include more of the lake **(2).** From the shoreline southeast of the light, use the trees for framing **(3).** Place the picket fence surrounding the keeper's house in the foreground and frame the lighthouse with the overhanging branches **(4).** East of the house the picket fence can also be used as a leading line.

SUNSET/SUNRISE

Successful sunrise images are possible from the west shoreline, especially in the winter when the trees around the lighthouse are barren.

DIRECTIONS

From Highway 2, exit at Highway 269 N (between Port Clinton and Sandusky) and turn east on Highway 163. Follow it about 9 miles to the lighthouse that is in a small state park (no entrance fee).

GPS coordinates: 41.536N, 82.712W.

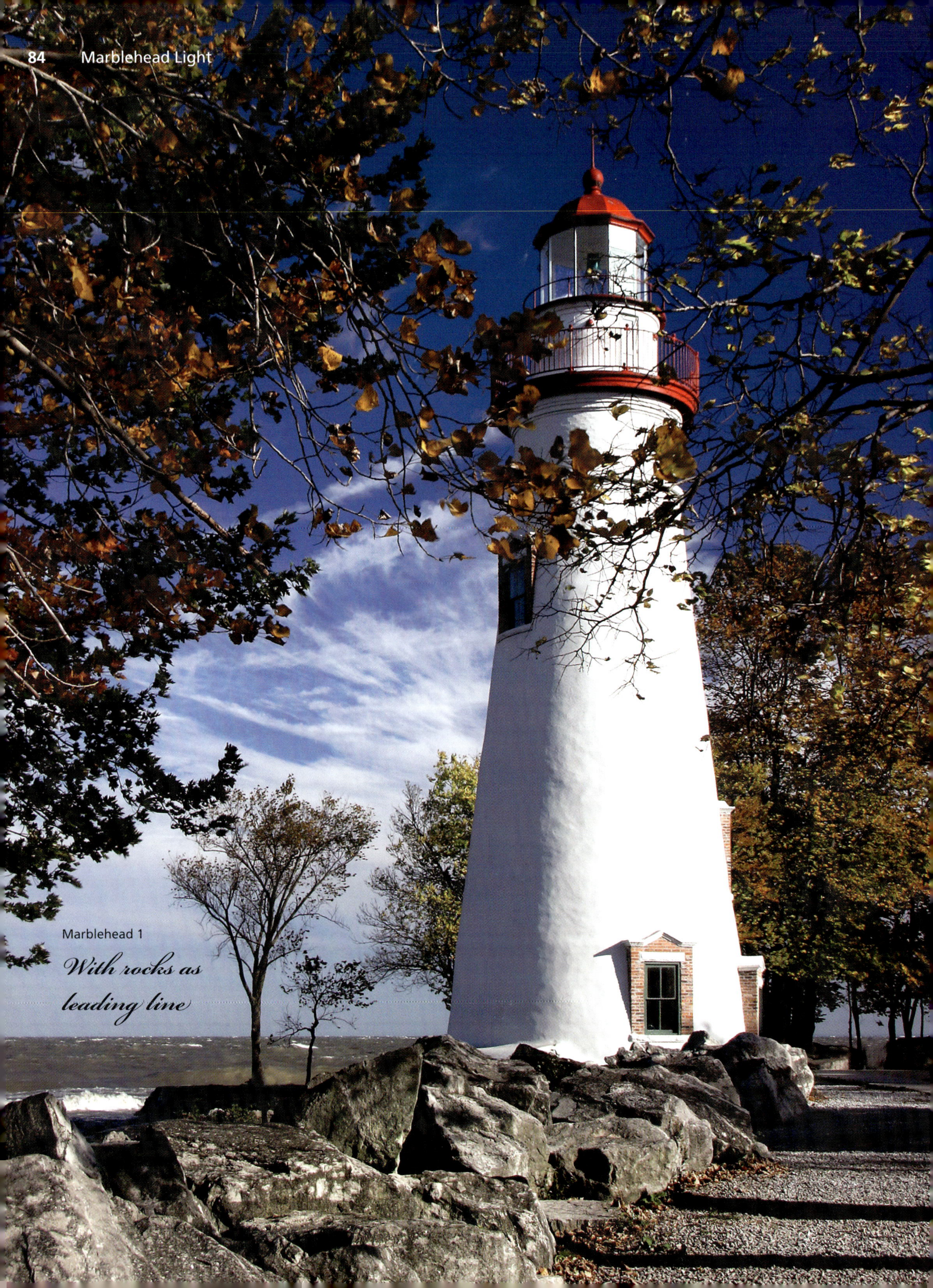
Marblehead 1
With rocks as
leading line

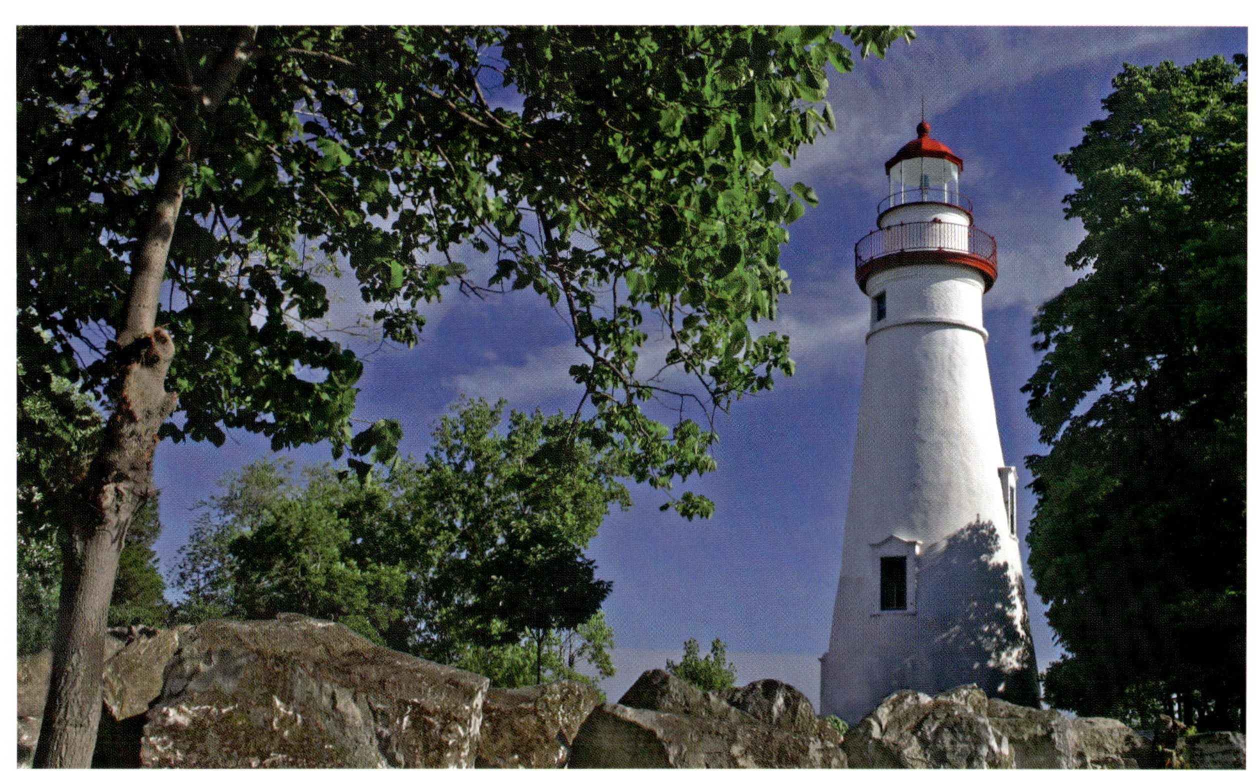

Marblehead 3 *Framed by trees, southeast side*

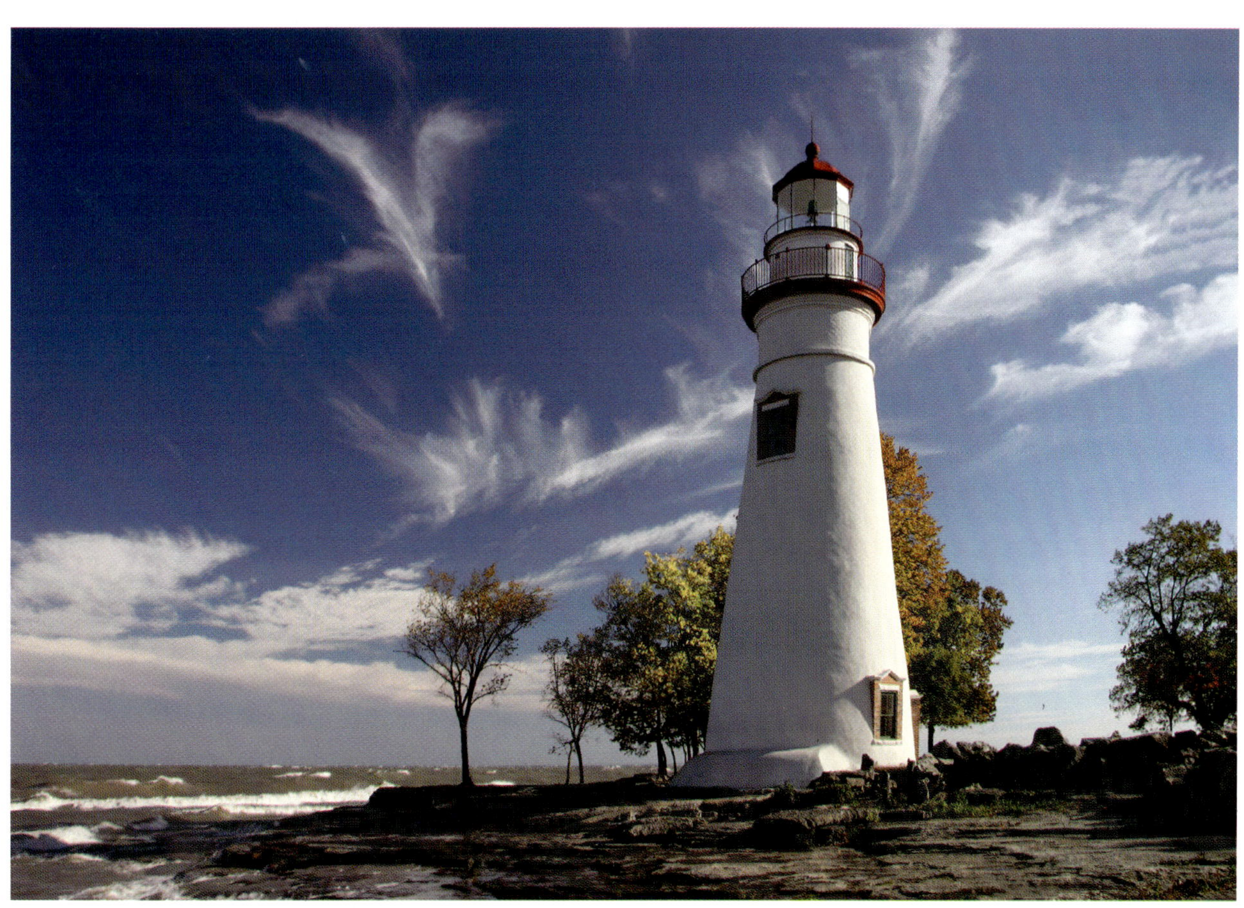

Marblehead 2 *From west shoreline*

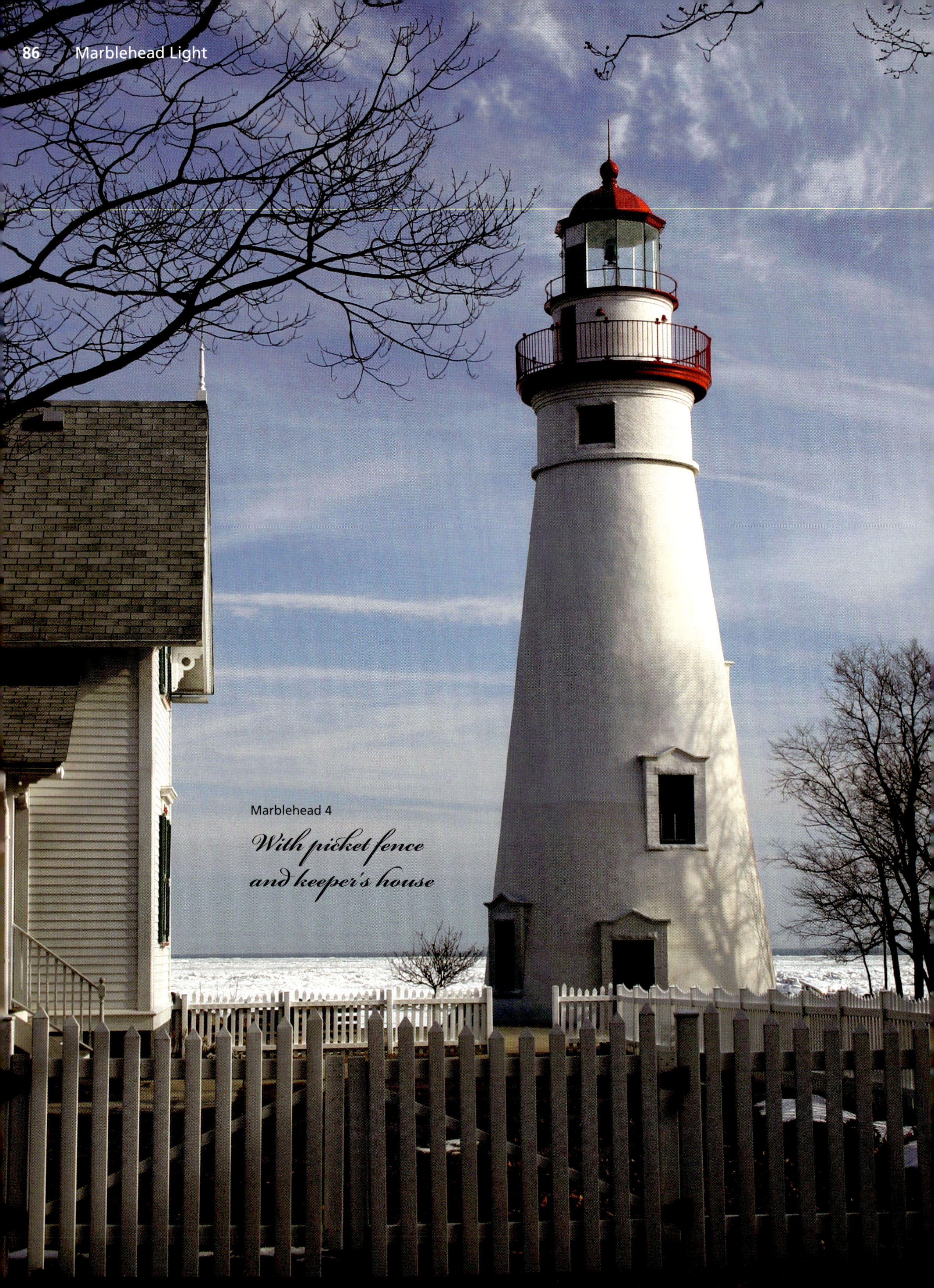

Marblehead 4

*With picket fence
and keeper's house*

Lorain West Breakwater Light

Lorain, Ohio

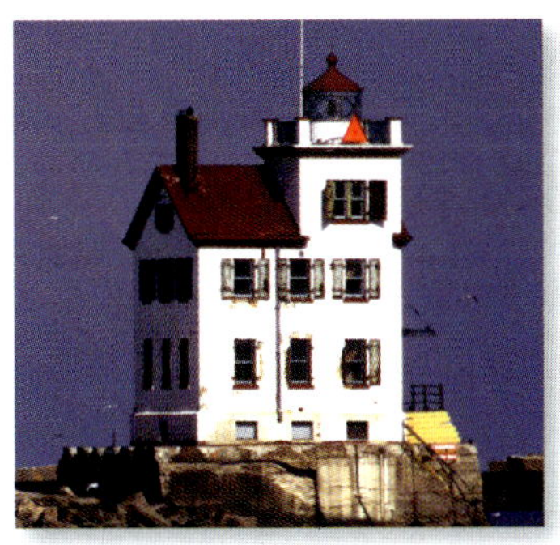

"Home of the Gulls"

DISTINGUISHING FEATURES

Located at the end of a long rocky breakwater, this lovely lighthouse is in the shape of a two and a half story house with many shuttered windows. The white building with red roof and trim make it a striking subject. There are always large numbers of sea gulls in the area that can add a maritime touch to photographs.

BEST TIME OF DAY

Good light is possible in the morning and in the afternoon.

SUGGESTED COMPOSITIONS

Since the stone breakwater leading to the lighthouse is not accessible to the public, all images from land must be captured using long lenses (minimum of 300MM recommended) from various piers or docks along the shore **(1)**. Look for patches of vegetation, gulls, boats, dock materials, etc. to use in the foreground for interest and depth perception **(2)**. Using a long lens down low will compress the image and make the objects in the foreground appear closer to the lighthouse than they actually are. If present, include boats in the frame for added interest and scale.

"Water taxis" take small groups out to the lighthouse during the summer months. This will provide the opportunity to photograph the light much closer from the boat **(3)** as well as to take detail shots while there **(4)**. Call 440 245-2563 for more information.

SUNSET/SUNRISE

The best vantage point for sunset images is the end of a pier east of the lighthouse (See Directions). To view the sun setting in the general vicinity of the lighthouse, be here from about late April to late September **(5)**.

DIRECTIONS

There are several large dock areas with parking for boaters, fishermen, etc. that can be reached from US 6 (Erie St.) near the center of town. West of the river, turn north on Broadway to the docks. East of the river, turn north at Colorado St. to Lakeside St., then left a short distance to a driveway on the right. Drive to a parking area next to a marina. Walk to the end of the long pier, past boat docks and small red sheds; this is also the suggested spot for sunset images.

GPS coordinates: 41.477N, 82.190W.

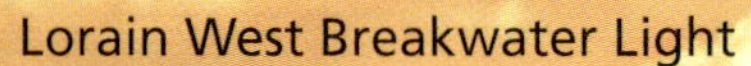

Lorain 5 *Sunset from end of pier*

Lorain 1 *With gulls in water and air*

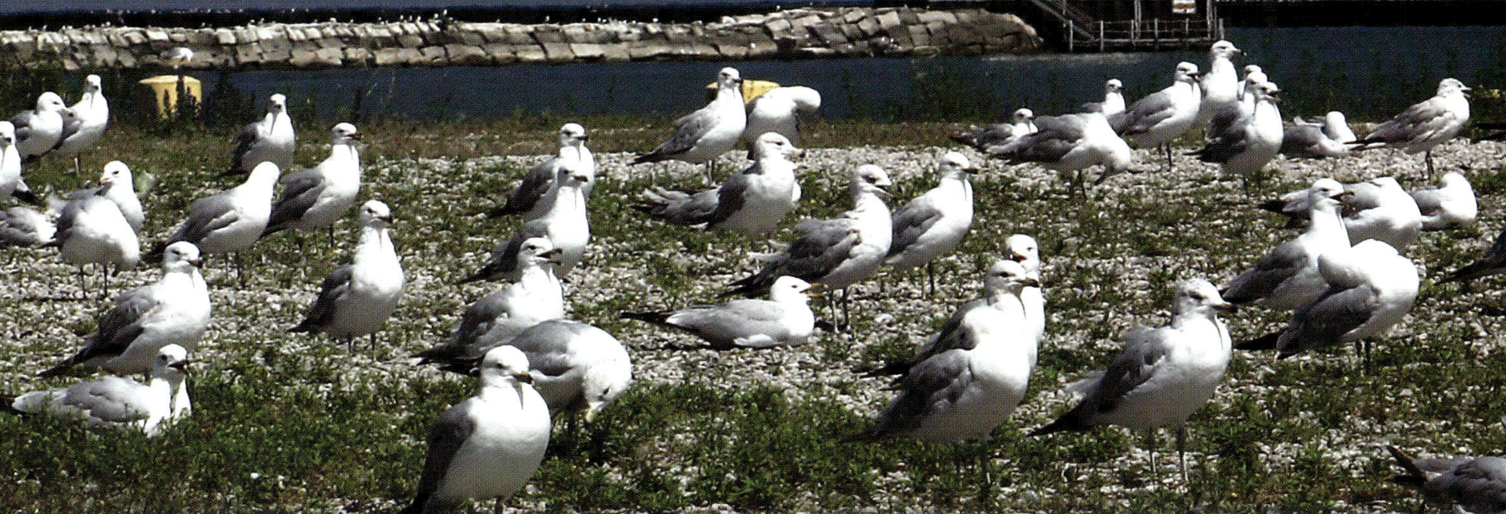

Lorain 2
With gulls on shore

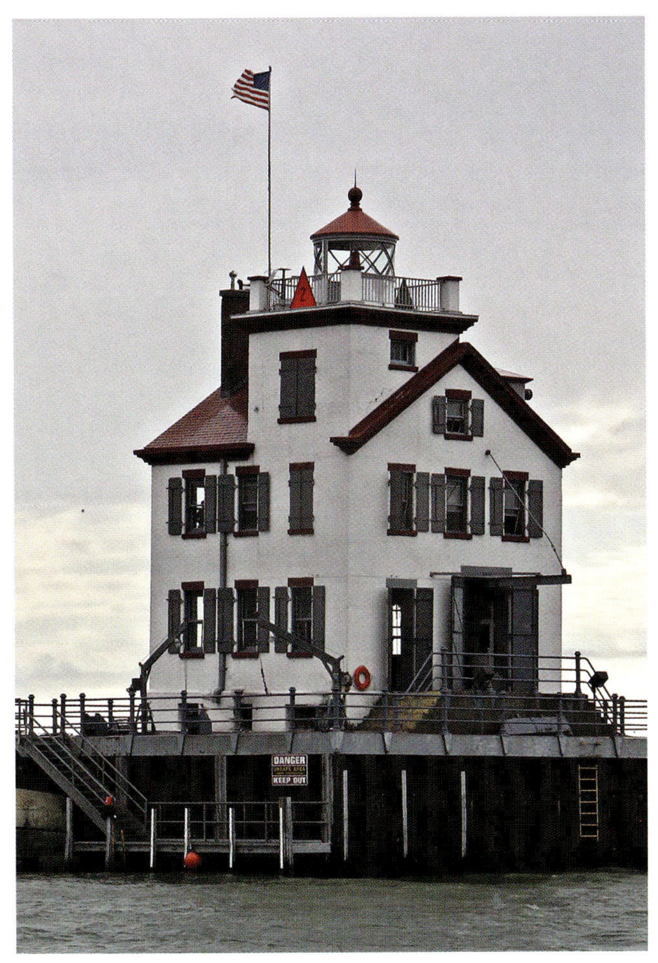

Lorain 3 *From "water taxi"*

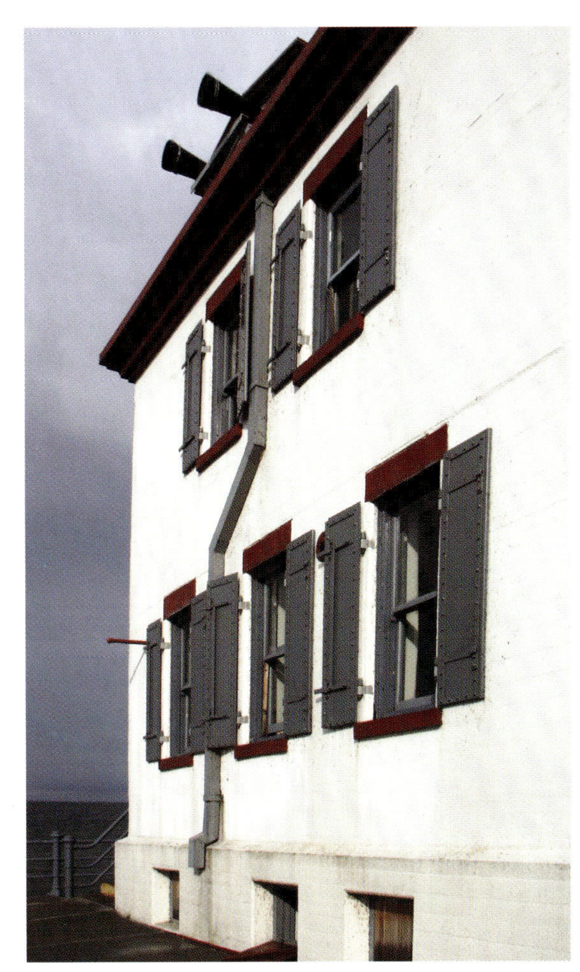

Lorain 4 *Window & shutter detail*

Fairport Harbor West Breakwater Light

Near Fairport Harbor, Ohio

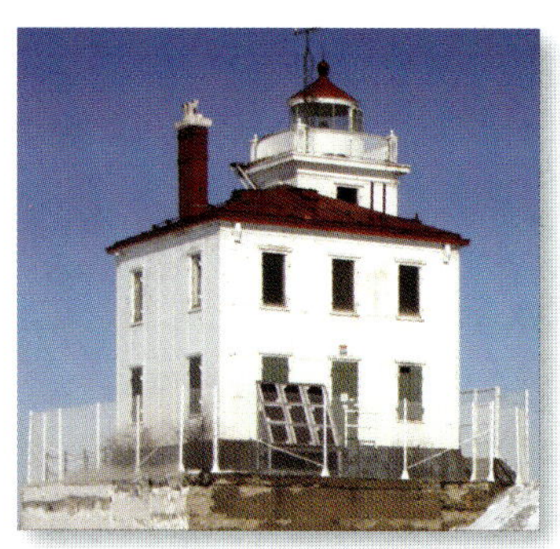

"Beauty on the Breakwater"

DISTINGUISHING FEATURES

This attractive lighthouse sits at the end of a long stone breakwater by a sprawling beach. It features a white square keeper's dwelling with a red roof and attached light tower with a red dome.

BEST TIME OF DAY

Morning and afternoon light are both good here.

SUGGESTED COMPOSITIONS

The rough stone breakwater makes an interesting leading line to the lighthouse. Start with shots from the beach **(1)** and include some of the numerous pieces of driftwood in the foreground **(2)**. Then move up next to the breakwater and compose images looking along the edge of the stones **(3)**. In the winter, take advantage of the snow and ice formations on the rocks **(4)**. Also go to the east side south of the bend in the breakwater for a different perspective.

SUNSET/SUNRISE

The best chance for a sunrise shot from the beach is mid summer when the sun is rising at its northernmost point on the horizon.

OTHER

The old (1871) sandstone lighthouse for this area still stands on a hill overlooking the harbor in the village of Fairport Harbor. The attached keeper's house is now a marine museum. This makes a very nice sunset or night shot as there are floodlights on the tower and house plus lights around the parapet **(5)**.

DIRECTIONS

From I 90, take Rt. 44 N (exit 200) for about 7 miles to Headlands Beach State Park (no entrance fee). Park in the east lot, P-1, and follow the trails to the beach and breakwater.

To reach the old lighthouse in Fairport Harbor, drive south on Rt. 44 from the state park and follow the "Lake Erie Coastal Ohio Trail" signs for about 4.5 miles.

GPS coordinates: Breakwater Light – 41.768N, 81.282W.
Old Lighthouse – 41.757N, 81.277W.

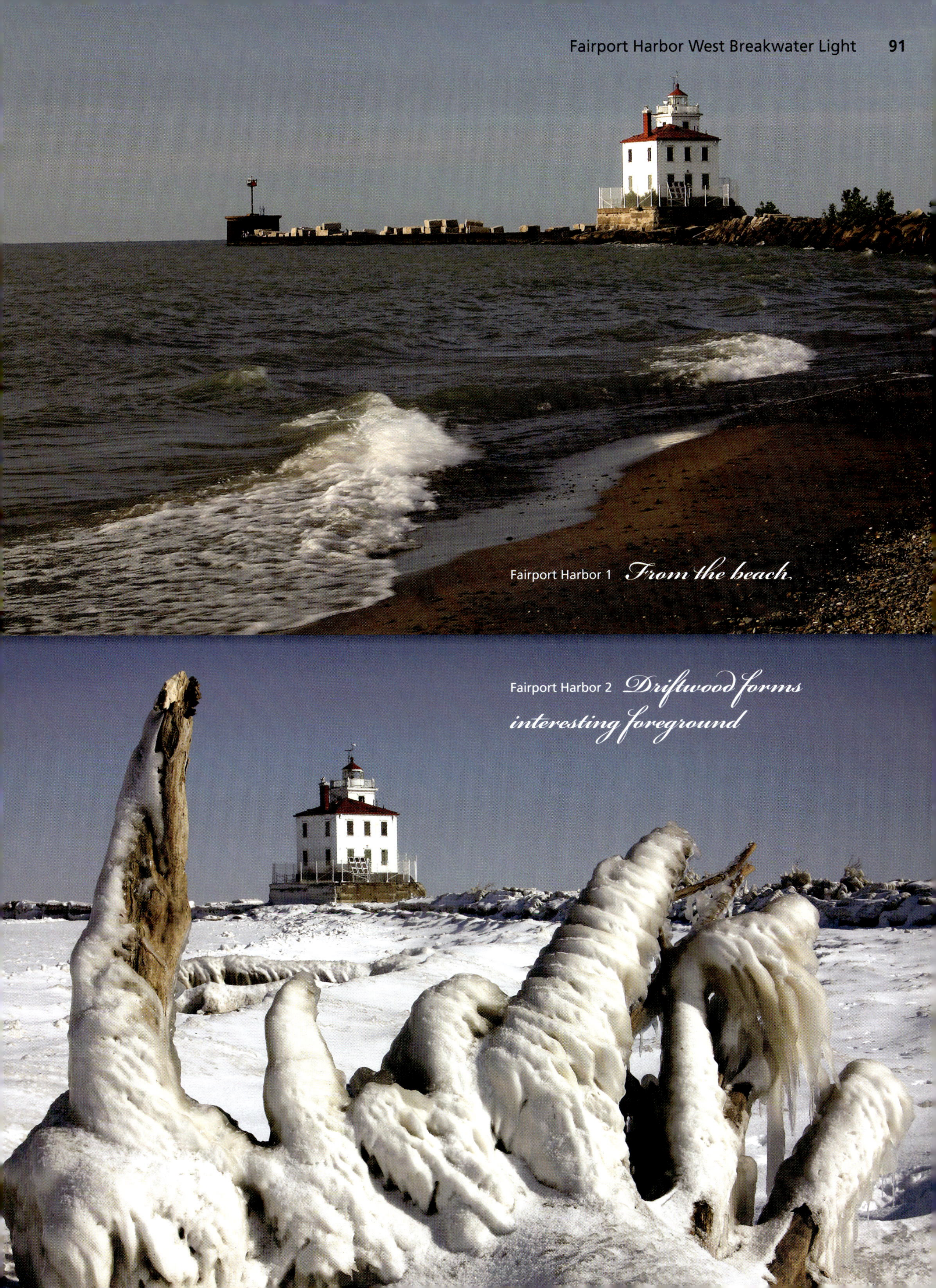

Fairport Harbor 1 *From the beach.*

Fairport Harbor 2 *Driftwood forms interesting foreground*

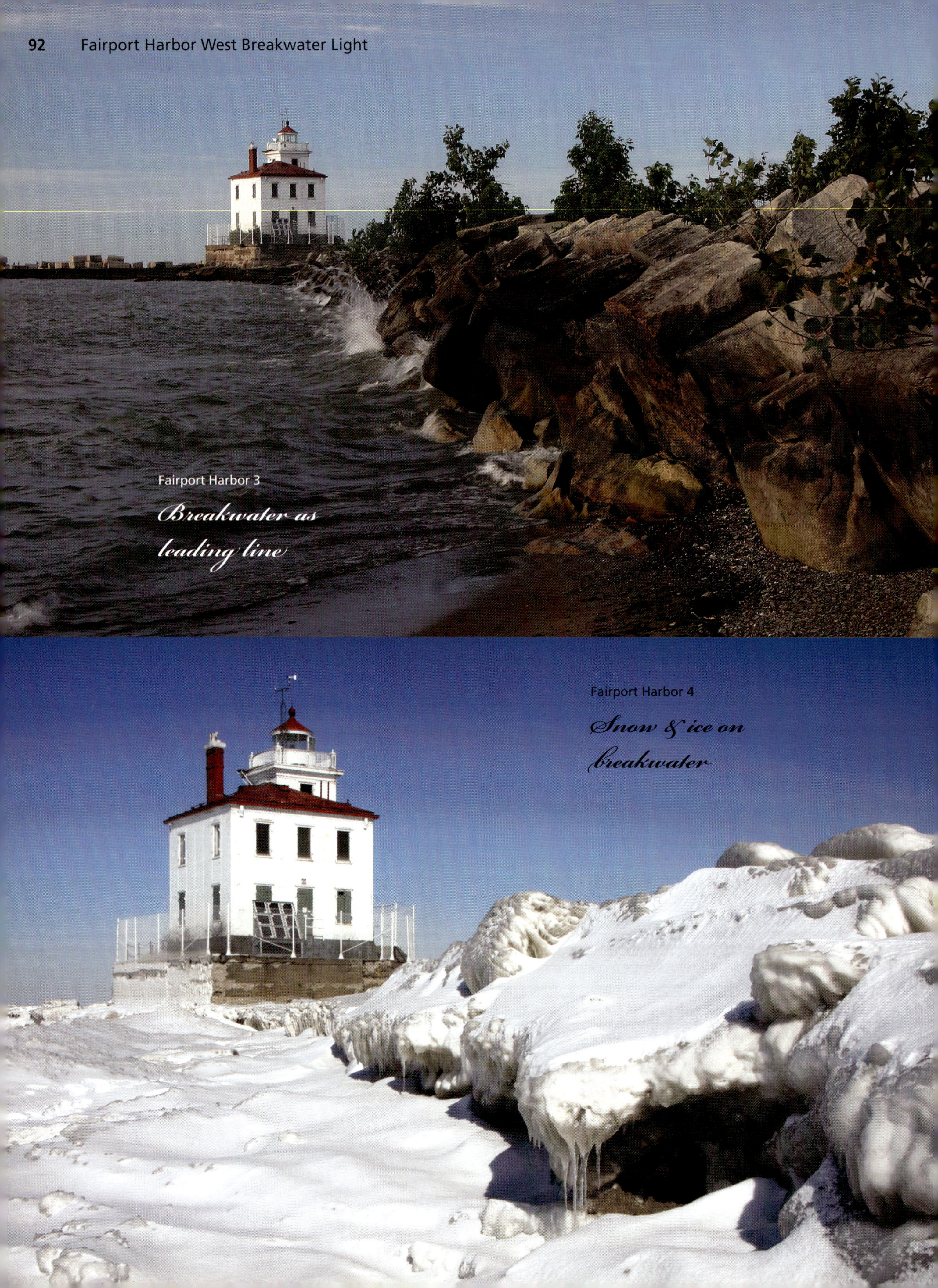
Fairport Harbor 3
Breakwater as
leading line
Fairport Harbor 4
Snow & ice on
breakwater

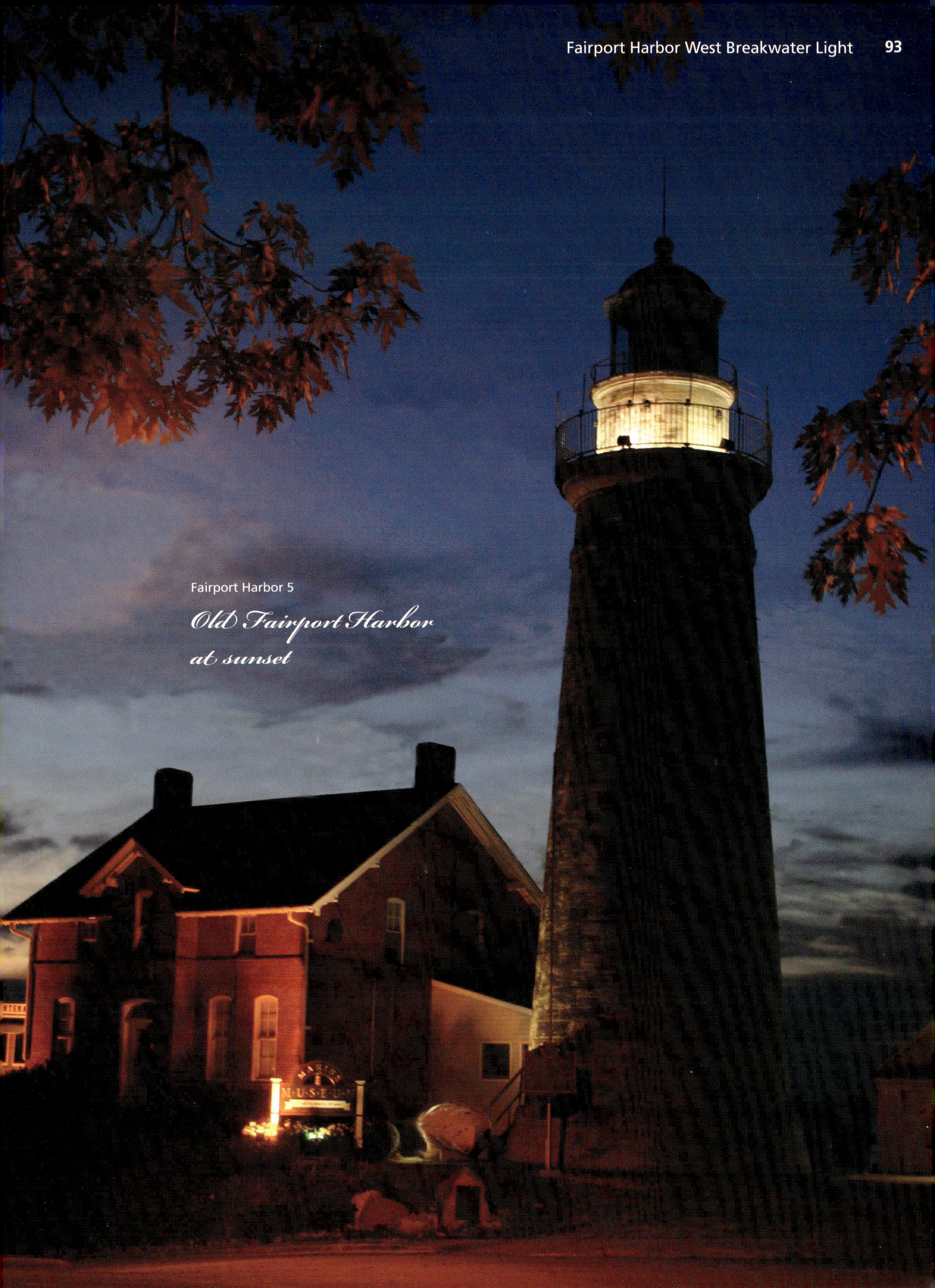

Fairport Harbor 5
Old Fairport Harbor
at sunset

About the Author and Photographer

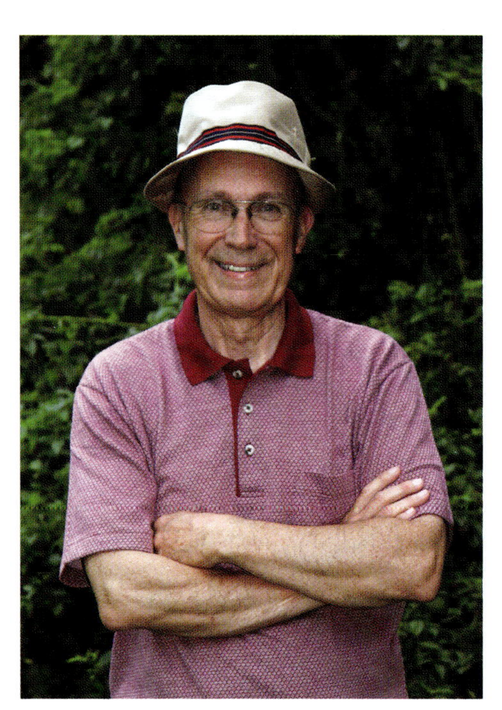

Richard (Dick) Edington

Richard (Dick) Edington has been a freelance photographer for over 25 years, specializing in landscapes and nature subjects. Having lived in Iowa, Illinois and Ohio, much of his work is of the Midwest. However, he has photographed many other areas, including both U.S. coasts, Canada and Europe.

Dick began his photographic interests in the darkroom, printing black and white images as well as color prints directly from transparencies. He has since moved to the digital world and has been using digital cameras and software for the past several years. All the images in this book were captured by Canon digital SLRs using various Canon lenses. The only filters used were a polarizer and split neutral density.

His credits include award-winning photos in numerous competitions and his images have appeared in several calendars and various publications. Exhibits in art centers and libraries have displayed his work. He has been a photo judge and instructor.

Dick and his wife, Pat, reside in Westfield Center, Ohio and have two adult children and two grandchildren.